In 1939, Wing Commander Yeo-Thomas was a director of Molyneux, the famous Parisian dressmaking firm. At the outbreak of the war he joined the RAF, and in 1942 was posted to the section of Special Operations Executive that was organizing the Resistance Movement in France.

He immediately became one of Britain's leading secret agents, dropping into France by parachute and establishing contacts amongst all the separate Resistance organisations across the country. One of his many cover names was 'The White Rabbit', and when the BBC broadcasts to France stated that the white rabbit had gone back to his hutch it meant that Yeo-Thomas had safely returned to England.

When one of his chief French colleagues was arrested by the Gestapo, Yeo-Thomas insisted on going to his rescue, and was himself arrested in Paris in 1944. What followed was an ordeal of incredible torture and suffering that only a man of indomitable spirit could have endured. He steadfastly refused to give the Germans the information they wanted, managed to manoeuvre his way out of a death sentence, and was one of the few British survivors of the camp at Buchenwald. He was later awarded the George Cross and appointed to the Legion of Honour.

THE WHITE RABBIT

BRUCE MARSHALL

CASSELL&CO

To the memory of the other brave

Cassell
Wellington House, 125 Strand
London WC2R 0BB

First published in Great Britain by Evans Bros Ltd in 1952
This paperback edition published in 2000

A CIP catalogue record for this book
is available from the British Library

ISBN 0-304-35697-2

Printed and bound in Great Britain by
Cox & Wyman Ltd., Reading, Berks.

CONTENTS

AUTHOR'S FOREWORD

I HAVE always thought that Wing Commander Yeo-Thomas's story ought to be given to the public, and I was glad when John Pudney persuaded him to allow it to be told, and flattered when Tommy asked me to do the telling. As a chronicler I have, however, only two qualifications: those of having been in 1943 and 1944 a reprehensibly chairborne Intelligence officer to 'R.F.' Section and of having lived in France for twenty years.

In order to tell the story tidily and without digression I have often been obliged to allow characters to disappear without stating their fate. It may, therefore, interest the reader if I say that Peulevé is now in England and Hessel in Paris; that the nine others who escaped with Yeo-Thomas from the death convoy are all alive; that Pister, Krautwurst, Schobert and Wolff were, largely on evidence given by Yeo-Thomas at the Buchenwald trials, condemned to death by the Allies and hanged; that Möller is now working on a farm in Germany; and that Hubble's chess set, also of the cast, is now in the possession of his family.

In order to avoid confusion only one name has been used for each agent, either his real name or his alias, according to convenience.

Although the opinions expressed in this book are not necessarily Yeo-Thomas's they are not those of one who has never been in action.

I have to thank Mr. W. Somerset Maugham and William Heinemann Ltd. for permission to quote from *Ashenden*; William Collins, Sons & Co. Ltd. for permission to quote from Mr. Arthur Bryant's *The Age of Elegance*; and Eyre & Spottiswoode Ltd. for permission to quote from Mr. Geoffrey Cotterell's *Strait and Narrow*.

Finally, my thanks are also due to Yeo-Thomas for the very considerable trouble which he has taken to set out his story for me.

BRUCE MARSHALL

"... il me faut dire dès maintenant, que personne, dans les rangs britanniques, ne fit plus pour nous aider que Yeo-Thomas."

Colonel Passy: 10 *Duke Street, Londres.*

CHAPTER I

NO ARMS AND THE MAN

'FACT', says Somerset Maugham in his preface to *Ashenden*, 'is a poor story-teller. It starts a story at haphazard, generally long before the beginning, rambles on inconsequently and tails off, leaving loose ends hanging about, without a conclusion.' His contention is generally true. In the case of *The White Rabbit*, however, which, like *Ashenden*, is the story of a British Agent, I shall hope to prove that there are occasionally exceptions to the rule.

At the beginning of the 1939–1945 war those who joined the colours most readily were the veterans of 1914–1918, who had sworn that they would have to be fetched if their country ever called upon them again. I don't know if Forest Frederick Edward Yeo-Thomas was among those who made this boast because I was not acquainted with him in the mean years, although his turbulent nature inclines me to believe that he may have shouted rebellion like the rest. At any rate, there was no question of the policeman being sent for him on 3rd September, 1939, and not only because he was then already thirty-eight years old.

Born of a family which had lived in France since 1855, Yeo-Thomas was a director of Molyneux, the famous Parisian dressmaker. I suppose that dressmakers get as bored with the sight of beautiful mannequins as sales girls in confectioners' shops are said to become tired of the taste of chocolates, although I should hesitate to ascribe both immunities to excessive consumption. Certainly it was not of mannequins that Tommy was thinking as he entered his office in the rue Royale on the morning of Monday, 4th September, 1939, and probably he didn't think of them even as they gave him their usual morning greeting. '*Bonjour, Monsieur Thomas,*' said the beautiful young women with the gravity of those whose profession is to serve the frivolous. Tommy returned their salutations and tried to settle down to work, because in war as in peace the variable and the changeable thing which Virgil called woman has to go on having variable and changeable clothes.

'Dresses are going to be slightly longer this year, Monsieur Thomas,' I like to think of a young woman in a black silk dress with a bottle-green sash saying to him. Perhaps the lovely Russian Countess Grabbe said something like this. If she didn't she ought to have, to give that twist to fact to make it as entertaining as fiction. But whether or not she said something significantly meaningless, when Tommy told her that he was going to enlist she gave him a small brown canvas sachet to wear round his neck for safety. And although Yeo-Thomas was not stupid enough to believe that his lack of faith in the Holy Ghost entitled him to believe in the sacramental potency of black cats, white heather, frothblowers' cuff links and the great Umkulukulu, he wore this charm all through the war in order to please the donor.

'Rhetoric has ruined religion,' Thornton Wilder once wrote with permissible alliteration and considerable accuracy. It may also be said to have almost annihilated patriotism, for among statesmen only Mr. Churchill takes the trouble to mint new phrases which inspire rather than tire. But in 1939 Mr. Churchill wasn't speaking very often and the politicians who were kept trotting out trite and dusty words about 'glory' and 'supreme sacrifice', and of this highfalutin' balderdash the French talked even more than the British. Tommy must have heard the big-mouthed belchings in two languages. It is to his credit that he managed to be patriotic in spite of them.

For it was burning patriotism which prompted Yeo-Thomas to exchange his comfortable job with Molyneux for the rough and tumble of life in the ranks. And burning patriotism was harder to find in 1939 than in 1914, because old soldiers had learned by experience, and their sons by hearsay, to distrust promises of fidelity made by politicians and principal boys in pantomimes. Perhaps it was because he didn't 'only England know' that Tommy, born in England, and educated for the most part in France, was patriotic. Or perhaps it was because he was a very honest decent pagan who paradoxically admired that approximation to Christian thought and action of which the British are almost certainly the world's most noteworthy practitioners. Or perhaps it may have been because he had two countries to love instead of one and liked doing something difficult.

Whatever the reason, Yeo-Thomas, like a great many other hard-boiled and disillusioned men, unhesitatingly chose to risk his life in defence of a morality which politicians by their practice, intellectuals by their scepticism and clergymen by their badly aimed predications, had done their best to destroy. It was, subconsciously perhaps, the conviction that cruelty, and not girls showing their knees in church, was the unforgivable sin which led Tommy immediately to volunteer to fight against the first swarm of barbarians which uncontrolled progress had raised up to threaten Europe.

It is not unlikely that his decision was strengthened by the fact that he was temperamentally ungovernable. Born in London, on 17th June, 1901, he had been educated at three schools in France and one in England, from two of which he had been expelled for unruly behaviour. Although under age he had served with the Allied armies in the latter part of the 1914–1918 war and, not satisfied with this introit to arms, had fought for the Poles against the Russians during 1919 and 1920. He was captured by the Bolsheviks at Zitomir and sentenced to death, but managed to escape the night before he was due to be shot. Since then he had worked in Paris, first as an apprentice mechanic with Rolls-Royce and later as an accountant with a firm of travel agents. After working with three banks he was engaged as a temporary audit clerk by an international firm of accountants. In 1932 he entered the firm of Molyneux.

But if Yeo-Thomas was ready for the Army, the Army was not ready for him, in spite of Lord Halifax's statement, broadcast earlier in the year from the Lord Mayor's Banquet, that all steps had been taken to resist aggression against Poland from whatever direction it might come. The Military Attaché at the British Embassy in Paris told Tommy that no further volunteers were being accepted for the moment, as the Army had more recruits than it required. This rejection was tempered by the information that if Yeo-Thomas were willing to travel to England at his own expense there was always the possibility that he might be accepted after a wait of several months. An attempt to join the French Foreign Legion also failed, because the authorities had instructions not to enlist Britons.

In desperation Yeo-Thomas accepted an invitation to place his services and car (without payment) at the disposal of the Air Attaché. A fortnight later this altruism was rewarded by permission to join the R.A.F. A man whose method of arguing with bank managers was to lay them out on the floor of the bank naturally wanted to fight; but Tommy's request to be employed as an air gunner was refused on account of his age. In spite of his protest that he did not wish an office or a base line job he was enlisted as an A.C.2 interpreter and, as no uniforms were available, was given a light blue armlet with the letters I.C. embroidered on it in green. After a few days he was promoted corporal.

Tommy's phoney war was like everybody else's: a mixture of enforced indolence and being pushed around *au ralenti*. He met the average sensual men, cads and potential saints who are to be found in all assemblies of human beings, but whose less pleasant attributes are accentuated when they are separated from their womenfolk. He reacted to the cads, and especially to those more highly placed than himself, with an uncompromising vehemence unlikely to accelerate his promotion. To a squadron leader who, referring to a pilot officer, asked him to 'send that sod out there in', Tommy replied that he would comply with the order when it was properly expressed. I don't know how he answered the monocled pipsqueak flying officer who said to him classily: 'Of course, you're not an officer and you can't expect the same respect as I can,' but I can imagine that Tommy's round, ruddy face was full of resentment and that his pale blue eyes held an insubordinate gleam. This same officer, when he learned that Yeo-Thomas was in the dressmaking business before the war, exclaimed: 'My God, what is the R.A.F. coming to!' Tommy subsequently became interpreter to the Forward Air Ammunition Park at Nogent l'Abbesse. By this time he had been promoted to acting sergeant (unpaid).

Towards the end of the year he was ordered to report to H.Q. Fighter Command at Stanmore in England, but when he arrived there he found that the authorities had no knowledge of him. As there were no spare sleeping quarters available he was given seven days' leave, which he spent in hotels in the West End of London, where he was received with suspicion because he was wearing a sergeant's uniform. It was during this period that Yeo-Thomas first discovered the discrepancy between public acclaim of the defenders of the realm and private practice towards them. In his own words 'our gallant soldiers for whom nothing could be too good were expected to pay for their room in advance when they had only a haver-sack for luggage'. This baseness of innkeepers and potboys and of civilians generally ought not to have astonished anyone with suf-ficient history to remember the aftermaths of Waterloo and of the 1914–1918 war.

In the end they found room for Yeo-Thomas at Stanmore, with the Bomber Liaison Section in the filter room. Having been in the Army myself, I don't know what they do in filter rooms, but I find it easy to believe that Tommy's perfect knowledge of French was as wasted there as the fluent Arabic of the soldier who was sent to Ice-land. Once again an application to become an air gunner was refused.

But what is important about Tommy's stay at Stanmore is that it was here that he first met Barbara, who was then a young W.A.A.F. of twenty-four. I don't know quite what to say about Barbara ex-cept that she was, and still is, slim and beautiful. Except in fiction, when one can transmute one's own early miseries into imaginary characters' happiness, it is impossible to write about other people's love affairs. Tommy refers to her, not very originally, as having been his 'inspiration'. Now that romance has mellowed into domes-ticity I have heard him tell her that she was other things as well, but such frankness is common to couples who have the daily ir-relevancies of holes in socks and gas bills to cope with. What I do know about Barbara can be said in a single sentence: she is one of the few exceedingly pretty women I have known who are also sweet and humble and charitable. It was one of Barbara's friends who nicknamed Tommy 'the white rabbit'.

On 6th April, 1940, Yeo-Thomas returned to France, in time to assist at the disaster which ought to have surprised nobody who was familiar with the internecine quarrels of contemporary French poli-ticians.

As soon as the attack began the rot set in, and Yeo-Thomas saw a great deal of it. Stationed with a Bomber Liaison Section at Le Bourget, he tried to forget the moaning of a defeatist French air-craftman in his pity for the refugees streaming down the roads. The bombing of the aerodrome on 3rd June again aroused his desire to fight. But there was to be no fighting in France for Yeo-Thomas, or, indeed, for many others for a long time. On 11th June, when all lines of communication had been broken, the O.C. of the Section, Flight Lieutenant James, and Tommy reported to the Air Attaché's office for instructions and found that the whole British Embassy staff had left. They decided to fall back to Tours.

Yeo-Thomas, who had been sleeping at his father's flat, went to Passy to pack his things. The sky above the city was covered with a huge black cloud of smoke which came swirling down into the streets and darkened them. This smoke came from the burning oil factories at Port Jerome near Rouen, and even the summer sun was powerless to pierce it. Like a gigantic pall it lay over the whole town, seeming to symbolize the extinction of hope.

There were few people on the pavements, and those who were looked sullen and cast angry looks at Tommy in his R.A.F. uniform. '*Tiens, un Anglais,*' one of them said. '*Je croyais qu'ils avaient tous foutu le camp depuis longtemps.*' '*Aussitôt que les Anglais entendent parler de la guerre ils font dans leur culotte,*' was his friend's attempt to explain the French reverses. Although resenting the reproach, Yeo-Thomas realized its partial justice. The British, owing to the folly of their own politicians, had sent too few troops and too few planes. Tommy was bitter, feeling that he had two sets of buffoons to be ashamed of.

Because he loved Paris and was afraid that he might never see it again, Yeo-Thomas walked slowly through the familiar streets. The Champs-Elysées were deserted, invisible almost in the fog of rolling smoke. He walked slowly along the Avenue Kléber, took a last look at the Trocadéro and the Eiffel Tower, and dropped into a small café at the corner of the rue Franklin for a drink. He was the only customer. He drank in silence because the patron was too numbed and shattered to talk. After dining in an empty restaurant he went home and wrote a farewell note to his father, who was in the country.

Next day the small unit left Paris in three cars. Miserable and angry, Tommy was further distressed by the terrible scene. The roads were jammed with refugees. There were limousines filled with the glossy rich. There were young women riding in hearses. Lorries, buses, carts and wagons crept slowly away from the city in a never-ending stream. The cyclists moved as quickly as the cars and the pedestrians moved as quickly as the cyclists. Children pushed babies in perambulators or barrows. Old men and women shuffled along with tears in their eyes and fear or fury on their faces. There were soldiers too in the crowd, soldiers who had thrown away their arms and officers hurrying from the battle. Every now and then German aeroplanes flew overhead and dived to bomb the rag-taggle procession, and the wretches rushed in terror to the ditches.

The section carried on with its duties for a few days at Tours, until the rapid German advance compelled them to retreat to Limoges. The announcement of Pétain's request for an armistice forced them to move on from there by night to Bordeaux, and in the darkness they lost a car with two of their men in it. In Bordeaux they caught a glimpse of that grand old man General Gouraud, Military Governor of Paris, erect and dignified even in defeat. For Yeo-Thomas this was the last sight of the honour of France.

At Bordeaux they were ordered to drive with all speed to Pointe-de-Grave, about sixty miles distant, whence two cargo-boats were on the point of sailing with the last British troops. Flight Lieutenant James and Yeo-Thomas sent the others on ahead while they remained behind to have a last look round for the two missing men. Failing to find them, they warned the local military authorities to keep a look-out for them and themselves set out for Pointe-de-Grave. On their way they ran out of petrol and had to threaten the driver of a chance-encountered tanker in order to obtain a couple of gallons.

There were about forty assorted military personnel still to be ferried out to the cargo-boats when they reached the harbour. While they were waiting their turn Tommy made a brief pilgrimage to the monument on the Pointe which commemorates the landing of the American troops in 1917. Here, at a stall, he bought a postcard which he sent to a lifelong school-teacher friend, Mademoiselle José Dupuis. 'Dear José,' he wrote, 'I know how you're feeling at present, but don't get discouraged. We will return and liberate France.' This postcard reached its destination.

Gazing at the sun shining on the bright blue sea, he was saddened again by the mockery of the fine weather. The irony of flight on such a day from a country he loved was almost unbearable. For a moment he was tempted to stay behind and help the French to prepare for the invasion which he was sure would take place when

Britain had had time to build up her strength. But he knew that if he did so he would have no means of communicating with England and that he would be branded as a deserter. So quite untheatrically the obstinate, cantankerous, insubordinate but utterly loyal little Briton swore his oath; as soon as he reached England he would offer to come back to France and raise volunteers to help the British on the happy day on which they should land again. Then he went back to the harbour and lined up with the other airmen and the soldiers and the F.A.N.Y.s.

It took them three days to reach Milford Haven. When they arrived a highly polished R.A.F. warrant officer crusader was waiting to greet them. 'Make it slippy, you f—ing lot of slovenly bastards,' he barked at them.

It was a happy homecoming.

CHAPTER II

MARKING ETERNITY

CARRYING out his resolution to return to France was not as easy as Yeo-Thomas had imagined it would be as he stood in front of the American monument at Pointe-de-Grave, and it took a long time; so perhaps the title of this short chapter is not too far-fetched.

After a brief but happy reunion with Barbara he was posted to the Personnel Dispatch Centre at Uxbridge, where he was given the job of conducting parties of airmen to the Burroughs Wellcome Institute near Euston Station for inoculation against yellow fever. His talents were not as wasted as might be imagined, for he used this unpromising task to develop the ingenuity which was later to stand him in good stead when he became an agent. It was difficult to get a pass out of the camp, but no questions were asked when, two or three times a week, Tommy showed the guard an O.H.M.S. envelope addressed to 'The Medical Officer, Burroughs Wellcome Institute, London'. He procured two similar envelopes, stuffed them full of blank paper, addressed one to the Medical Officer at the Burroughs Wellcome Institute and the other to 'The Commanding Officer, No. 1 P.D.C., Uxbridge'. He was thus able, without a pass, to get in and out of Uxbridge as often as he liked.

At Odiham in Hampshire, where the Free French Air Force officers and men were being trained, he served as an interpreter, and in October was recommended for a commission. His fellow candidates, in his own words, were 'wingless wonders determined, if chosen, to do all they could to save the Administration Branch'. When his turn to be interviewed came, Yeo-Thomas, with shining buttons and neatly pressed uniform, marched smartly in and saluted the selection board. Critically, coldly, searchingly, superciliously, the beribboned inquisitors stared at him.

'You are Sergeant Yeo-Thomas?' an air commodore with a face as wrinkled as a walnut asked him.

'Yes, Sir.'

'How long have you been in the Air Force?'

'Since 27th September, 1939, Sir.'

'Where did you live before the war?'

'In France, Sir.'

'Why did you live in France?'

'Because my father and my mother and my family lived in France, Sir.'

'Why did they live there?'

'Because my grandfather and my great-grandfather lived there, Sir.'

'Why did *they* live in France?'

'Because they had business interests there, Sir.'

'Where were you educated?'

'At the Collège de Dieppe and the Lycée Condorcet, Sir.'

'Collège de Dieppe? Never heard of it. What sort of college was it?'

'It is a college belonging to the Académie de Caen, Sir.'

'What was the Lycée Condorcet?'

'A Lycée belonging to the Université de Paris, Sir.'

'What is that equivalent to?'

'I imagine, Sir, that it is approximately the same as Oxford or Cambridge, Sir.'

'You speak French fluently then?'

'Yes, Sir.'

'*Ays-ke parlay-voo fronsay?*' a squadron leader asked.

'*Oui, mon commandant.*'

'His French is good, Sir,' the squadron leader said.

'What have you been doing since your incorporation in the R.A.F.?' the air commodore asked.

'A bit of everything, Sir.'

'In other words, you don't know much about anything?'

'So far I have managed to do everything that has been asked of me, Sir,' Yeo-Thomas replied, restraining his anger because of his respect for Group Captain Flower, who had recommended him for a commission.

Military psychology was then in its infancy and Yeo-Thomas was not asked what colour of dress Queen Elizabeth had worn at her wedding or at what age he had left off wetting his bed. Perhaps because of this omission his candidature was accepted. But the Medical Board, although it passed him A1-4B, disappointed him by the decision that he was too old for flying duties and must remain chairborne. Still anxious not to let down Group Captain Flower by expressing his natural tendency towards revolt, Pilot Officer F. F. E. Yeo-Thomas reported to Baginton, near Coventry, for duty as an intelligence officer with 308 Polish Fighter Squadron.

It was not until 3rd February, 1942, and then only after threatening the Air Ministry to have the matter of his mis-employment brought up in Parliament, that the right man found his way into the right place, in the 'R.F.' Section of Special Operations Executive.

CHAPTER III

THE OLD FIRM, OR EXPLOSIONS ARRANGED

PRIOR to the 1914-1918 war Christian nations had required only armies and navies to protect them from the dastardly deeds of other Christian nations. (This is not a sneer at religion, but at our manner of practising it.) By the end of that war, however, science had so far outstripped morality as to make an Air Force an essential item in a nation's armoury; and in 1940 a fourth and not very easily classified form of warfare had been added: subversive activities or hitting the enemy behind his lines, but not necessarily below the belt.

The British organization for prodding the Germans in unexpected places had its headquarters, unsuitably perhaps from a security point of view, in Baker Street, where the ghost of Sherlock Holmes driving past in a phantom hansom with Watson, might notice the variegated uniforms disappearing into the main entrance and murmur deductions in the doltish doctor's ear. Outside the door of Norgeby House a black *plaque* with INTER-SERVICES RESEARCH BUREAU engraved upon it in gold letters attempted to explain to a possibly curious public the number of Naval, Army and Air Force officers, British, American and French, constantly entering and leaving the building. Michael House, on the upper floors of which the high brass sat, pitched between heaven and Marks and Spencer, was slightly more discreet, because the admirals, the generals and the air commodores entered from a lane at the back. Into both buildings, morning and evening, there also poured a stream of pretty secretaries. Some of them, to judge by their literacy, might have been employed as a cover. There the pleasantry ends: in Special Operations Executive, known to its members as the Old Firm, even the sedentary were much too busy to have any time for dalliance.

For the purpose of S.O.E. was deadly serious, and men's lives depended upon its efficiency. The organization operated under the direct control of the Ministry of Economic Warfare, with tentacles reaching out to the Admiralty, the War Office, the Air Ministry, the Foreign Office and the algebraic M.I.s. Its activities, as Yeo-Thomas says, were 'multiple, secret and complicated', and their purpose to harass by all means possible the enemy in his own country and in those which he had occupied. This was achieved, for the most part, by the infiltration of agents who alone, or with other agents recruited locally, disrupted the enemy's communications by blowing up railway tracks or hindered his war production by destroying pylons, electricity generating plants and machinery in factories. This form of warfare was both more accurate and benign than aerial bombardment. An agent insinuated into a factory could sabotage effectively and without loss of human life a piece of essential machinery which a squadron of bombers would be lucky to hit by chance. *Pace* Air Chief Marshal Harris, cruelty at a remove is, as the late George Bernard Shaw pointed out, still cruelty, even if the flight lieutenant who lets the phosphorus bomb drop doesn't see the baby catch fire.

For practical purposes and to maintain secrecy, S.O.E. was divided up into a number of water-tight compartments. Yeo-Thomas was sent to work in the Western Europe Directorate, commanded by Lieutenant-Colonel Keswick. Under this Directorate there were two French Sections, 'F.' Section and 'R.F.' Section. 'F.' Section, commanded by Major (afterwards Colonel) Maurice Buckmaster, was a purely British-operated section employing agents, French or French-speaking British, recruited by the British and not connected officially with any of the French Resistance Movements. 'R.F.' Section, commanded when Tommy joined it by Captain Piquet-Wicks, was a British-staffed section which worked in close liaison with General de Gaulle's Bureau Central de Renseignements et d'Action; it arranged the supply and parachuting of arms and equipment to the French Resistance Movements and the transport to and from France of agents recruited and employed by the Free French.

Colonel Passy, the head of the French B.C.R.A., deplores, in his *10 Duke Street, Londres*, the existence of 'F.' Section, and, in conversation, Yeo-Thomas does not always refer to it cordially. The attitude of both is comprehensible. Passy, a loyal and very courageous Frenchman, did not like to see the British meddling in what he considered to be a purely French province; he forgot that if it had not been for Britain's example there would almost certainly have been no large-scale French Resistance Movements to encourage and arm. Yeo-Thomas, impulsive by nature but certainly understanding the French much better than many of his masters, was perhaps actuated by healthy rivalry; experience has shown that the competitive spirit, if carried only slightly too far, can make an Argyll and Sutherland Highlander hate a Cameronian in the same brigade much more thoroughly than the German whose misdeeds he only reads about in the newspapers.

There were, however, many good reasons for the existence of 'F.' Section. The British wanted to be sure of having at their sole disposal and under their sole control on 'D' day a number of small groups in French territory on whom they could rely to destroy military installations. The fact that these groups were small and had no communication with one another or with the larger French Resistance Movements increased their security, never a very strong quality of the French. There was also the uncertain French internal political situation to be taken into consideration and the primadonna-ish vapours of de-Gaulle, who would temporarily cut off all dealings with the British when he imagined that he had been snubbed by Churchill. In any case, the value of the work done by 'F.' Section has been widely proved, and one of its heroic agents, Odette Sansom, has made its excellence known to the public.

This, however, is a polemic upon which I would not insist, and I mention it only because others have done so.

'R.F.' Section, in those days, 'lived out' at No. 1 Dorset Square, in a house in which, suitably enough according to the Section's critics in Baker Street, they had succeeded as tenants the directorate of the Bertram Mills Circus. It was here that Yeo-Thomas, running through reams of mostly supererogatory courier from the field, had to learn to separate the essential from the useless and the possibly informative from the certainly nonsensical. It was here that he memorized the symbols of his colleagues so that he was able to act immediately when AD/E ordered him to contact D/R about the communication which MA2 had received from L/IF.

Yeo-Thomas had by now been promoted to flight lieutenant to enable him to cope with his new responsibilities.

In between reading superfluous intelligence about German divisions on the Eastern Front which had been issued with women's knickers and brassières in mistake for Balaclava helmets, he had to equip and prepare the section's current operations. His work soon brought him in contact with his colleagues of the French B.C.R.A., with some of whom he was to work later in the field. He came to know and like the cool, steely-eyed and efficient Commandant (later Colonel) Passy and his hard-working second-in-command Capitaine Manuel. He made friends with their assistants and agents, with Pichard, a slim young man with wavy chestnut hair, and with Ayral, and with other agents with whom he was afterwards to be intimately associated in the field.

1942 was a building-up period for the Free French and 'R.F.' Section, and the B.C.R.A. worked without respite. In spite of the protests of their commanding officers the best men available were selected from the French troops to be trained as agents. When they had been screened by the B.C.R.A. and M.I. they were sent to schools specializing in the functions for which they had been chosen. Radio operators and saboteurs and men to train agents recruited in France had to be instructed. Others had to be taught the difficult art of finding new landing and parachuting grounds in France and organizing reception committees to man them. These last were picked with special care, as many of them would ultimately be required to supervise all air operations in a large area.

By the autumn the section had grown to such importance that a lieutenant-colonel was appointed to command it. Colonel J. R. H. Hutchison was a dapper little cavalry officer with a passion for tabbing documents with pink slips inscribed with the order: 'PLEASE SPEAK'. Under his instructions French was exclusively spoken at No. 1 Dorset Square and, as not all the staff was bilingual, liberties were taken with the language of Racine. An agent was once referred to as *un vrai fil vivant*, and such literal translations as *chanson de cygne* and *moi, mon vieux, si j'étais dans vos souliers* enlivened the rooms where Bertram Mills had once contracted their clowns. 'Hutch', as he was inevitably called, was an enthusiastic and courageous soldier: in 1944, when he was more than fifty years old, he was dropped into France, where he valiantly conducted himself as a 'Jedburgh'.

Yeo-Thomas was now in charge of Planning, and Johnson had been recalled from Inchmery to supervise Operations. But, although he no longer needed to waste time reading administrative irrelevancies about Polish and Czechoslovak officers being required to pay for the maintenance of their trusses, Tommy was not happy in his job. Perhaps the memory of a signal received from France in July helped to unsettle him: ALLEZ VOUS ENVAHIR AVANT LE QUINZE AOUT? REPONDEZ OUI OU NON. He felt guilty briefing men for dangerous missions when he himself had never been in the field, and he remembered the vow which he had made at the American Monument at Pointe-de-Grave. He made repeated requests to be sent to France, but all were refused on the grounds that his presence at Headquarters was essential. At last, however, it was agreed that if a mission important enough to require his special knowledge could be found he would be sent to France. Yeo-Thomas quickly found himself this mission.

At that time the Navy was short of small craft for coastal operations. Tommy remembered that Captain Molyneux, his peacetime employer, owned a fast motor-yacht which was moored in Monte Carlo harbour. Thinking that the vessel might interest the Navy, he proposed that he should be entrusted with the mission of seizing her and making a dash for Gibraltar. This suggestion was finally approved and Yeo-Thomas was authorized to approach Captain Molyneux, who agreed to hand over his yacht without compensation. An agent called Charvet, recently sent to unoccupied France, was to provide a crew of three. Four hundred and fifty gallons of petrol, fifty of oil, food and two light machine-guns would be provided by felucca operation. Yeo-Thomas himself would be infiltrated in by the felucca or by parachute or Lysander operation. For this operation he was given the not very opaque name of 'Seahorse'.

To Tommy's disappointment the whole situation in the Mediterranean suddenly changed and the project was abandoned. He was, however, allowed to hold himself in readiness for another mission and on 29th November, 1942, set off for the parachute school at Wilmslow.

CHAPTER IV

TOMMY WOULD A-JUMPING GO...

WHEN Yeo-Thomas returned to Dorset Square he found that the situation in France had become critical. The Free French agents working for the B.C.R.A. were in constant and grave danger. They were tracked and harassed not only by the Gestapo but also by the Vichy Police, the Group Mobile and Darnand's Milice. The weakness of the various Resistance Movements was accentuated by the fact that, largely because of their political differences, they were all working independently. In order to increase their efficiency it was necessary both to finance and to co-ordinate them. And if they were to aid the Allies when they invaded France, the paramilitary organizations of all groups must be welded into a unified Secret Army, working under a single Commander with an efficient staff. In particular, the activities of the Communist Party must be ascertained and their leaders persuaded to allow their combat units to join the united paramilitary branches.

It was therefore decided to send Colonel Passy and Commandant Brossolette to France to effect the co-ordination of the Resistance Movements in the Occupied Zone.

Passy, the head of the B.C.R.A., who had taken his *nom de guerre* from the métro station, was then thirty years old. Fearless, cultivated and intelligent, his real name was André Dewavrin. He had been educated in Paris at the Collège Stanislas, the Lycée Louis le Grand and the Ecole Polytechnique. In 1938 he had been assistant professor of fortifications at St. Cyr and in 1940 had fought in Norway. He had left France to join General de Gaulle on 18th June, 1940. At the end of the war he was to hold the British D.S.O. and M.C. as well as French and Norwegian decorations.

Pierre Brossolette, still under forty, was small and thin. He had thick black hair with a bright white lock in front. Passy says of him: '*Brossolette fut, sans conteste, l'homme qui, parmi tous ceux que j'ai été amené à rencontrer dans ma vie, fit sur moi la plus forte im-*

pression.' [1] Educated at the Ecole Normale, where he had taken his degree in history, he had, before the war, been a regular contributor to the Socialist daily *Le Populaire*. The Popular Front Government had appointed him an official foreign news commentator on the national radio, from which post he had been dismissed in 1938 because of his violently expressed disapproval of the Munich Agreement. After the Armistice in 1940, refusing to write for the collaborationist Press, he had purchased a small bookshop in the rue de la Pompe near the Lycée Janson de Sailly, whose pupils were his principal customers. He had arrived in England in April, 1942, and had already been on a mission in France.

Passy felt, rightly or wrongly, that British agents making use of Frenchmen living in France often left them under the impression that they were working for de Gaulle, whereas in reality they were working only for the British. Suspecting, too, that British agents had caused trouble by contacting groups already linked with the B.C.R.A., he wanted to find out the truth for himself. This he proposed to do during his mission of co-ordination. But in order to avoid his report being regarded as biased he requested that a British officer should be sent with Brossolette and himself to make an independent report, both on this subject and on the co-ordination of the Resistance Movements. Because of his knowledge of France and of his perfect command of the language Yeo-Thomas was chosen. Security was increased by his retaining the code name of Seahorse. He was sent immediately to Beaulieu, where he learned the difficult art of sending messages in cypher.

On his return to London, Yeo-Thomas was given false papers in the name of François Thierry, whose story he had to learn by heart and make his own. He had been born on 17th June, 1901, at Arras, and was a bachelor. Before the war he had lived at 41 rue St. Ferdinand, Paris, and had worked as a clerk. During the war he had served with the 34th Bataillon de l'Air and had been demobilized at Marignane on 27th August, 1940. He lived now at 9 rue Richepanse, Paris, and had taken up his previous employment as a clerk. To support this story he was provided with a Carte d'Identité issued by the Paris Préfecture de Police on 16th April, 1941, a Feuille de

[1] 'Brossolette was, without doubt, the man who, amongst all those I have met in my life, made the greatest impression on me.'

Démobilisation issued in Marseilles on 2nd September, 1940, and a Permis de Conduire issued in Paris on 12th June, 1934. He was also furnished with a current French ration card issued in the name of Thierry.

Finally, Yeo-Thomas received his orders, which read:

SEAHORSE OPERATION ORDER

1. Seahorse to investigate with Colonel Passy . . . the potentiality of Resistance groups in the 'Zone Occupée'.
This investigation will comprise:

(a) A thorough examination of the set-up, especially with regard to its effectiveness.
(b) An inquiry into the nature of existing groups and their relation to the present central staff, known as Etat-major Zone Occupée.
(c) The consideration, in conjunction with the Forces Françaises Combattantes staff officers, of the means for establishing a system of joint control, firstly in France and secondly in relation to a future inter-allied command.

2. An especially important function, from the point of view of S.O.E., is to decide, as near as possible, the real capacity of individual organizations to furnish men and equipment, and carry out precise tasks or directives emanating from London but issued by local commanders.
On the basis of the above an approximate estimate of the requirements of these groups in the way of equipment, communications, arms and explosives will be furnished.
3. Special attention should be paid to the Communistic Organization, known paramilitarily as F.A.N.A., in order to ascertain:

(a) whether it is seriously willing to fall in with the F.F.C. plans for a local general staff, or, if not, whether use could be made of the organization on the basis of liaison rather than direct control;
(b) whether we may be able to implement the progress and action, especially on the side of training and ability.

Rather a tall order, don't you think?

CHAPTER V

THE SEAHORSE IS AMPHIBIOUS

In those days operations took place between the end of the first quarter and the beginning of the last quarter of the moon, preferably when the moon was at its fullest. Yeo-Thomas calculated that he would be leaving between the 17th and the 28th of February. As the day approached he was surprised that he did not feel frightened. Instead he found himself thinking of José Dupuis, the schoolteacher friend to whom he had sent a postcard on leaving Pointe-de-Grave. Sure that she at least was loyal and hoping that she listened into the French news from London, he sent her a message by the B.B.C. '*De Tommy à José. Nous reboirons bientôt du bon vin de Chignin.*' [1] During holidays before the war he had drunk this wine with her in the village near Chambéry after which it was named, and he was confident that she would understand the message if she heard it.

Meanwhile plans had been slightly changed. Brossolette had already left for the field and Passy and Yeo-Thomas were to follow him.

On the morning of 24th February Tommy was warned that the operation would take place that night. He had a farewell lunch with Barbara, who by now was a civilian working for the B.C.R.A. At three o'clock he left Dorset Square for 10 Duke Street, where he picked up Passy. They were driven through the cold misty countryside to Tempsford in the Midlands, where they arrived about five o'clock.

After a cup of piping hot tea they went through all their kit under the vigilant eyes of an accompanying officer. The clothing which they were going to wear in France was examined for tell-tale English labels and the pockets turned out to make sure that they did not contain any forgotten bus tickets or British-stamped envelopes. No objection was made to the Countess Grabbe's sachet which Yeo-Thomas still wore round his neck. When they had changed from their uniforms into their civilian suits they put in the now secure

[1] 'From Tommy to José. We'll soon drink again good Chignin wine.'

pockets their false French identity papers, their money, their benzedrine tablets and other appurtenances. In case of sudden need Yeo-Thomas placed his cyanide tablet in his waistcoat pocket while Passy concealed his inside a small signet ring with a swivel top. They were dined by the C.O., who produced a bottle of excellent burgundy.

The two agents then put on their strip-tease suits, rubber helmets and spine pads. An outer thigh pocket carried their revolvers and other special pockets their compasses and knives. To their already cumbersome gear they attached their parachutes. With all their armour on they were driven out to the waiting Halifax bomber whose shape loomed up eerily through the mist. The accompanying officer wished them luck by saying 'merde'. They climbed clumsily into the aircraft, because the hole was not very large and their parachutes made ingress difficult.

Inside there was not much room for them to sit because of the packages piled up all around. Each package was protected with sponge rubber and heavy canvas and had its parachute attached. The packages, inside one of which were Passy's and Tommy's suitcases, contained arms, wireless transmitting sets and explosives.

The despatcher, a sergeant, busied himself upon last-minute jobs. The engines started up, the aeroplane vibrated and began to move slowly forward. Because there were no windows or openings, Yeo-Thomas could not see out, but he could feel that they were taxying up to the end of the runway, where the aircraft would turn into the wind. The aircraft stood still. The engines broke out into a roar and then quietened down again. The pilot opened the throttle, and the great Halifax began to move forward once more, gradually going quicker and quicker. Soon a light, thin feeling beneath his legs told Yeo-Thomas that they were airborne.

In those days there were two nights in the world, one which we believed to be the right kind and the other the wrong kind. It was from the right kind of night to the wrong kind of night that Yeo-Thomas was going, so that the wrong kind of night might again become the right kind of night. A thought similar to this occurred to him as he sat there among the packages unable to talk to Passy because of the noise of the engines. He was wondering what it would feel like to be surrounded by Germans, to walk in familiar places

28

and to know that all around him were enemies, the constant perception of whose presence might lend an appearance of rectitude to their purposes.

About half an hour later they were over the French coast. Soon the bursts of flak could be heard above the drone of the engines. The pilot took avoiding action, mounting, diving, swerving. Suddenly there was silence, the machine side-slipped wildly, and for a second Yeo-Thomas thought that they were going to have to bale out. Abruptly, however, the engines roared into life again and the aircraft went steadily on. Shortly afterwards they began to circle and Tommy knew that the pilot must be looking for the pinpoint and the lights of the reception committee. But although they kept there, there was still no sign from the despatcher, and at last the circling stopped and the sergeant came forward and shouted in Tommy's ear:

'Low cloud over your pinpoint. Pilot can't find it. We're going home.'

Yeo-Thomas passed the message on to Passy. Angry at the anti-climax, they sat in silence. They passed through searchlights and more flak as they re-crossed the French coast, but both of them were too dejected to feel afraid. At 4.30 a.m. they were back in Tempsford, so short a distance separated the wrong from the right sort of night. Tired out, they went to bed and next morning, on instructions from Headquarters, returned to London.

On Friday, 26th February, they made another attempt. The aircraft took off shortly after midnight in the pale light of the waning moon. Apart from a little flak over the French coast, the flight was uneventful. At about 3 a.m. the despatcher came to tell them that they were over the pinpoint, which was near Lyons-la-Forêt in Normandy. He opened the hatch, round which he had already arranged the packages, ready to be pushed out after the agents had jumped. Passy and Yeo-Thomas climbed over and hooked up the static lines which would pull open their parachutes as they fell through the hole. (In operations over France the drops were too low to permit the use of self-opening parachutes.)

Passy, who was to jump first, got into position with his back to the engine and his legs dangling through the hole. Tommy sat opposite him, ready to swing in as soon as he had jumped. Below him he could see the lighted torches of the reception committee, twinkling like an incandescent necklace. The red lamp went on. Seeing his companion stiffen, Yeo-Thomas edged nearer the hole. The despatcher's arm went up, the lamp turned to green and Passy disappeared. Surprised at his own fearlessness, Tommy swung his legs into the hole and gave a push. He felt the rush of air in the slipstream and then the slight jerk of his parachute opening out as he started to float down.

Slightly to the right and underneath him he could see the monster flower of Passy's parachute shining in the moonlight. The air was crisp and cold. The light of the torches came rushing up to meet him. He touched the ground, rolled over, undid his harness, stood up and drew in his breath. He had fulfilled the vow which he had made in 1940 in front of the American memorial at Pointe-de-Grave. He had returned to France. Seahorse had arrived.

A man came rushing up to him and vigorously shook his hand. '*C'est vous, Shelley?*'

'*Oui,*' Yeo-Thomas replied, a little puzzled by the vocative but realizing that it was more prudent to agree than to ask for or attempt explanations. (He discovered later that this name, which was to become famous throughout the whole of French Resistance, was a second code name about which no one had told him.)

By now the packages were coming down, braked by their pretty balloons of puffed-up parachute. When they had landed Passy and Yeo-Thomas helped the reception committee to carry them to a small wood a few hundred yards away, where they were concealed in a pit specially dug to receive them. Then they took off their stripteases and handed their flasks of rum round to their almost frozen hosts.

'*Allons, mes enfants, au travail?*' the leader of the reception committee said.

This leader was Jacot, one of the original members of the Resistance Movement known as the Confrérie de Notre Dame, and he spoke with the authority gained by experience. The members of the reception committee were to remain behind to bury the packages. Passy and Yeo-Thomas, accompanied by a guide, would proceed on bicycles to the safe house fifteen kilometres away where they were awaited. Curfew, however, was at midnight and they had no right to be out after this hour. As there was always the danger of running into a German patrol on the road a story had been concocted in case of mishap. They were to say that they had been at a wedding party at which they had stayed too long through being slightly drunk and were out after curfew because they had to be back at work in Rouen the next morning. In order to lend plausibility to this explanation it was essential they should carry nothing compromising on their persons or in their suitcases.

Accordingly Passy and Yeo-Thomas handed over their pistols. They said that there was nothing compromising in their cases, which, groping in the darkness, they removed from the package which had contained them.

'On no account must you make any noise,' the guide said. 'If I make a sign you are to dive into the nearest ditch or bush.'

There were carriers on the bicycles for their bags. That on Tommy's was fitted with an extensible elastic fixture which went round the case and clipped back on to the carrier. The bicycle itself had been made for a man of over six foot and, as Yeo-Thomas was only five foot eight, he had to climb on to a pile of stones in order to mount.

The guide, putting a finger to his lips, moved off. Passy followed and Yeo-Thomas came last. They had gone only a hundred yards when Tommy's case fell off with a resounding crash. Alarmed, the guide looked round, put his finger to his lips again and hissed for silence.

Yeo-Thomas got off his bicycle. But when he attempted to fasten his case on again he found that the elastic of the strap had perished and was beyond repair. The only thing he could do was to lay the suitcase across the handle-bars with one end against his chest and the bottom on the top part of the frame. Then he had to find another pile of stones in order to mount again. Lurching over the ruts, he found it almost impossible to balance the case and at the same time reach down with his too short legs to the distant pedals. At the first big bump the case banged against the bell on the handle-bars and made it tinkle. The guide looked round again angrily. Yeo-Thomas dismounted once more and tied his handkerchief round the bell while his companions waited impatiently. Then he had to find a mound in order to be able to mount again. Almost

31

immediately the leader thought he heard a suspicious noise and he signed to them to dive for cover. This happened several times. After each alert Yeo-Thomas had to hunt for another pile of stones or a mound.

By the time they reached the outskirts of Lyons-la-Forêt Tommy's chest was sore, his fingers half-crushed and his legs aching. The guide signalled to them to dismount and hide in the shadow of a wall while he went forward on foot and reconnoitred. After a little he returned and motioned them on. Once again Yeo-Thomas had to climb on to his uncomfortable machine, but this time the ride was short. Soon the leader stopped in front of a small door which opened immediately. They pushed their bicycles through it and leaned them against a wall. Their guide led them into a brightly lighted room, in the centre of which was a huge table covered with food.

Their hostess was a young and attractive woman called Madame Vinet. She was the wife of the local chemist, who was a member of the reception committee. The rich meal of Bayonne ham and galantine with truffles surprised Yeo-Thomas, accustomed to the dreary rations of Great Britain. There was also a delicious cider to drink and to end up with a glass of old calvados. It was only afterwards that Tommy learned that the Vinets, although living sparingly themselves, had spent their savings on the black market in order to give their helpers from England what they considered to be a fitting welcome. When the members of the reception committee turned up and handed the two agents the revolvers which they had taken the risk of carrying on their persons, Yeo-Thomas was moved almost to tears. Solemnly they all stood up and drank a toast to victory. He discovered, however, when Passy and he went up to their room, that their own journey through the night had not been devoid of serious danger: in the darkness Passy had taken by mistake and carried on his bicycle a case containing a wireless transmitter, hand grenades and explosives.

Next morning, when Passy's suitcase had been retrieved, they and Jacot set out by bus for Rouen. The bus, belonging to the local hotel and driven by producer gas, was a rickety affair, with worn seats and broken springs. Their fellow passengers, mostly peasants on their way to town to sell their produce on the black market, did not talk much, perhaps because they were afraid that the three strangers on the bus might be German agents. Smelling of onions, sweat, garlic and stale wine, they sat, meanly purposeful, like characters in a short story by Guy de Maupassant. In silence too, Yeo-Thomas gazed out at the Normandy countryside which he had known since boyhood and which he had not seen for so long.

Their first rendezvous was with Brossolette in Paris. To help pass the two hours which they had to wait in Rouen before their train left, Jacot took them to a café. On their way Yeo-Thomas had his first sight of the occupying troops: on the pavements where Madame Bovary's best dress had billowed in the breeze in beautiful syntax strutted the SS in black uniforms with skull and crossbones; on the cobbles over which the curtained cab had clattered tore the tyres of tremendous Teutonic trucks. The high peaked caps and shining riding-boots of the officers brought such fury to Tommy's expression that Jacot had to warn him: '*Faites attention, Shelley. S'ils vous voient les regarder comme ça, vous vous ferez arrêter.*' [1]

In the café the customers were badly dressed, dowdy and depressed. The drinks were ersatz: Campari tasted like Cinzano and Cinzano like Noilly Prat. Later, on a walk round the town, Jacot told them of further changes: there was no longer any milk in France and to ask for a *café crème* might indicate suspicious unfamiliarity with contemporary conditions; there were meatless days and days when even substitute alcoholic drinks were not served except in black-market restaurants. He explained to them how to use their ration and tobacco cards.

The Paris train was crowded with the same sort of wooden-faced people they had seen on the bus, so familiar with tragedy that they were bored by it. The two agents and Jacot travelled first-class, avoiding the compartments marked '*Nur für Wehrmachts-angehörige*'.[2] Their journey was uneventful.

They arrived at the Gare St. Lazare at 8 p.m. The station was blacked-out. Passengers were scurrying through the darkness to catch the forlorn suburban trains. Groups of Feldgendarmerie moved menacingly up and down in the obscurity.

---

[1] 'Look out, Shelley. If they see you looking at them like that you'll be arrested.'

[2] 'Reserved for Wehrmacht.'

There were also German soldiers in the métro, entering by the exit stairs and pushing out of the way the civilians whom they met. Their discipline, however, was good: even in the first-class compartments, in which all military travelled free, other ranks saluted officers. At Villiers, where Jacot and the two agents changed, there were more troops on the platform of that already dismal junction. By the time they came out under the cold bright stars at the Porte Dauphine Tommy was beginning to be able to look at the enemy without glaring.

Brossolette was waiting for them in the rue de la Faisanderie, in a flat which belonged to another school-teacher, Madame Claire Davinroy. Her apartment was considered as specially safe, as the rest of the building was occupied by members of the Gestapo, who would be unlikely to expect such temerity on the part of the subversive. Brossolette, to avoid recognition, had dyed his white streak of hair.

After dinner it was decided, as an additional precaution, to split forces and to organize other safe houses to which they could move if the need arose. Yeo-Thomas, who arranged to meet Passy and Brossolette at the Porte Maillot next morning at eleven, was taken to a nearby flat belonging to Roland Farjon, son of the ex-vice-President of the Senate. Monsieur and Madame Farjon welcomed him warmly and invited him to stay as long as he liked. But as they had young children and were already running great risks to help the Resistance, Tommy declined and, thanking them, said that he would seek another lodging next day.

In the morning he breakfasted with his hosts in an ice-cold room on ersatz coffee without milk, grey-brown bread and approximate jam. This meagre table of the rich made him realize how much greater must be the privations of the poor. As he left to take his first walk in occupied Paris, Yeo-Thomas was more than ever conscious of the urgency of the work he had undertaken.

It was as yet only 8.30 a.m. and the sky was grey, but with a promise of sunshine later. As he walked along the rue de la Pompe towards the Trocadéro, he made rules for himself: he must get used to working surrounded by the enemy, he must study the habits of the police, watch out for new regulations and merge himself as much as possible with the French population.

The silence of the streets struck him at once. There was almost no motor traffic except for German staff cars or lorries. An occasional French car snorted along, belching flames from its cylindrical producer-gas containers. Instead of taxi-cabs there were vélo-taxis. These consisted of one- or two-seater wooden or wicker trailers fitted behind cycles or tandems on which the husky drivers pedalled. There were also numerous bicycles, with number plates. Then he noticed the Jews with yellow stars sewn on to their clothes. They and most of the other people on the pavements looked shabby and unhappy and cold. Almost everybody was wearing wooden-soled shoes. Paris seemed even sadder than the last time he had seen it, with the black smoke swirling down in oily coils from the sky.

In the rue de Passy there were long queues of miserable shivering women outside apparently empty food shops. Yeo-Thomas walked into a bistro on the Place and ordered a coffee. It was served of course without milk and to sweeten it there was liquid saccharine in a bottle. The usual assertive know-alls were lined up along the counter, but instead of running France at a few million removes they were talking about food. A man with a small yellow pool in his eye had managed to acquire ten pounds of potatoes. A man with a face like a petulant Clemenceau had received half-a-pound of butter. There was no talk of the Germans. For the mean muttering men the disaster had already receded into history. Disgusted, Yeo-Thomas paid and went out.

When he reached the end of the street he turned down towards the métro station from which he could look down at his father's flat. It was more than two years since he had last heard from the old man and he gazed at the familiar windows with affection. Then he turned and walked up the rue Franklin towards the Trocadéro. Rounding the bend, he was startled to see a cordon of French and German police drawn up across the street. His first inclination was to turn and walk back in the opposite direction, but he knew that he could not do this without arousing suspicion. Mastering his fear, he pulled out his false identity card and approached the police.

The police were working in pairs, one French and one German. When his turn came Yeo-Thomas showed his card. He trembled inwardly as both policemen glanced at his photograph and read through his description. He did his best to look unconcerned while they examined him closely. Was there, after all, something wrong with his card? Had S.O.E. slipped up? Then the German policeman said 'Gut'. He was handed back his card and allowed to walk on.

Confident now that his identity card was a first-class forgery, Yeo-Thomas moved on, but not too quickly, in case the police might still be watching him. A pale sun was beginning to pierce the sky. In spite of the swastikas flying from requisitioned buildings the city still looked beautiful. Tommy's heart grew bold and happy. He was back in Paris, not yet in uniform it was true, but that would come. His content vanished when, approaching the Avenue Victor Hugo, he ran into a second police barrage.

The short distance between the two barrages seemed significant. Had the Gestapo already got wind of his arrival or were they after some other agent? To his consternation he saw three or four men being pushed into a waiting Black Maria. Fearful but again feigning indifference, he approached the policemen. Once again he was allowed to pass.

Good agents always arrived punctually at their rendezvous, as hanging about attracted attention. Yeo-Thomas reached the Porte Maillot at eleven o'clock exactly and so did Passy and Brossolette. They went at once to 102 Avenue des Ternes, where relations of Brossolette's, the Peyronnets, lived. Madame Peyronnet, whose flat was to become a regular meeting-place for the agents, at once found a safe house for Passy in the nearby rue Marcel Renaud and for Yeo-Thomas at Neuilly in the rue Casimir Pinel. The rue Marcel Renaud opened on to the busy rue Demours, in which their comings and goings would be unlikely to be noticed, and the flat, on the ground floor and giving on to a courtyard itself backing on to that of an adjacent building, would be easy to escape from if the police arrived suddenly. Tommy's safe house was in a luxury flat belonging to the blonde and attractive French cinema star Jeanne Helbling. This flat was on the first floor and it too overlooked a courtyard, escape from which would be easy. Brossolette was to remain with Claire in the rue de la Faisanderie. Apart from these three flats they gradually located a number of subsidiary apartments to which they could retreat if any of their present safe houses became 'blown'.

Work was begun immediately. While Passy busied himself with

intelligence matters, Yeo-Thomas got in touch with agents already sent to the field to organize parachuting and landing operations and the storage of weapons and explosives. These agents were Schmidt, Ayral, Fassin, Pichard and Deshayes. Brossolette established contact with the various Resistance Groups with whom their mission chiefly lay.

In order to accomplish their operational orders, it was decided to:

1. Ascertain the strength, the geographical distribution and the nature of each Resistance Group in the Occupied Zone.
2. Explain to the leaders of each Group and obtain their acceptance of the principles of organization to which they would be required to conform upon incorporation in the Secret Army.
3. Separate in each Group Intelligence from Action and the Military side from the Civil side.
4. Prepare the Co-ordination of the paramilitary bodies, after having organized them on sound bases with proper General Staffs.

This was an immense task. There were many Groups in France of whose existence and location they were ignorant; all had to be included if their co-ordination was to be effective. They had to distinguish between Resistance Groups proper and purely intellectual associations. Prior to their departure for the field it had been assumed that names like *Voix du Nord*, *Le Cerle* and *La Ligue* represented Resistance Organizations. It was found that they did not. *Voix du Nord* was a clandestine publication expressing the opinions and aspirations of not very active resisters, while the last two movements were of purely political or masonic origin. A common denominator had to be found before the values and merits of the real Resistance Groups, embryonic as yet, could be assessed. After a process of elimination the following five important Groups emerged:

1. Organisation Civile et Militaire.
2. Ceux de la Libération.
3. Ceux de la Résistance.
4. Libération.
5. Front National.

Their first meeting was with Colonel Touny, the leader of the Organisation Civile et Militaire. An ex-regular cavalry officer, he was a tall, powerfully built man in his middle fifties. He was assisted by a Commandant Berthelot and Roland Farjon, who had sheltered Yeo-Thomas on his first night in Paris. Both Touny and Farjon were later arrested and died.

The Organisation Civile et Militaire was found to be the most complete and highly organized of all the Groups and to possess the best security. With members at all levels in the Société Nationale des Chemins de Fer, the Postes, Télégraphes et Téléphones and other public services, it would be able seriously to harass the Germans on 'D' day. Although non-political in structure, the views of its followers inclined towards the right. From its highly organized paramilitary branch, strong in the north and the centre, it was hoped to recruit high-grade cadres and troops for the Secret Army. The effective membership of this Group was estimated at 40,000.

Shortly afterwards, Passy, Brossolette and Yeo-Thomas made their first contact with the Communist Party in the person of a young man called 'Joseph'. Oval-faced, clever and courageous, Joseph was a representative of the Communist Intelligence branch, known by the code letters F.A.N.A. Although they all got on well together, their first meeting did not resolve many problems. When it was suggested that a W.T. link should be established between F.A.N.A. and London, Joseph replied that the party's communications were already overwhelmed with transmissions. As there were then no communications between F.A.N.A. and London, the supposition could only be that there were plenty between F.A.N.A. and Moscow. When Joseph complained that the Communists were not receiving any arms from the Allies, Yeo-Thomas proposed that they should first send men to London to be trained in their use. Joseph promised to do so but the men were never sent. The non-political Yeo-Thomas anticipated Mr. Ernest Bevin by at least three years in arriving at the conclusion that the Russians wished to keep their adherents as far removed as possible from contact with those who subscribed to other ideologies. Another meeting, destined to be more successful, was arranged for a later date.

On 7th March they met M. Lecompte-Boynet, the professor-like Chief of Ceux de la Résistance. This was an almost solely paramilitary organization, particularly strong in Paris and with branches in the Champagne, Vendée and Cotentin areas. Its members, recruited from all classes, were opposed to political intrusions, seeking, if not a new heaven, at least a new earth. Although at present only about a thousand strong, their cadres and their troops were good and ready for action. Their Intelligence had already done valuable work for M.I.6. M. Lecompte-Boynet agreed immediately to obey the instructions of the Inter-Allied Staff. He calculated that he would have at his disposal on 'D' day between 25,000 and 30,000 troops.

Their next meeting was with the leader of Ceux de la Libération, M. Coquoin, who was accompanied by his assistant Médéric. This was a solid Group, again mainly paramilitary and anti-political. Chiefly concentrated in and around Paris, it had offshoots in the Nièvre, Cher, Allier and Brittany. On its staff was the Managing Director of the 'Transports Routiers', an organization which controlled all road transport in France. In this way the Group obtained valuable information about the transport of German troops, which was carried out largely in commandeered vehicles. Of these the Germans had, as a precaution against invasion, already concentrated stocks in motor transport parks which would be sabotaged by members of the Group when the time came. The Group had also trustworthy agents among the Police, the Fire Brigade and the Garde Mobile, who could be counted upon to take charge of operations on 'D' day. These promises were all kept. The potential of this Group was estimated at 35,000 men.

M. Coquoin readily accepted the instructions which Passy and the others gave him. But Colonel Schimpf, the chief of the paramilitary organization whom they met later in a flat on the Avenue de l'Opéra, was a die-hard of the 1914–1918 war and took more convincing. He favoured a more dramatic use of the Secret Army and was all for blood with plenty of thunder. Eventually he reluctantly agreed to obey what at heart he considered very boy-scout orders, but he did not live long enough to implement his word: within eight months he was arrested and died later in Buchenwald. Coquoin was killed at the end of 1943 and the jovial, effervescent and impetuous Médéric was betrayed in 1944 and swallowed his cyanide tablet.

Contact with its baldish chief, M. Périgny, showed that

Libération was mainly occupied with intelligence work, the greater part of which was carried out by the subsidiary *Voix du Nord* under the direction of M. Van Wolput. As in the case of its parent, Libération of the Unoccupied Zone, founded by M. Emmanuel Astier de la Vigerie, its paramilitary organization, only recently started, was almost negligible; indeed, the commanding officer himself was unaware of the number, quality or location of his troops. With Libération were also incorporated the Confédération Générale du Travail, the Confédération Française de Travailleurs Chrétiens and the Comité d'Action Socialiste; the last-named and the Communist Party were the only two survivors of the pre-1940 political parade,

It was Joseph who introduced the three agents to Ginsburger, also a Communist. Ginsburger in turn invited them to attend a meeting of the 'Comité Directeur' of Front National. On 18th March, Passy, Brossolette and Yeo-Thomas sat, at a pre-arranged hour, on a bench near the bandstand in the Luxembourg Gardens; there they were met by a bearded and secretive agent-de-liaison. After they had been made to double several times on their tracks they were led to the Luxembourg Station, where they caught a train for Sceaux. On their arrival at Sceaux, after more tortuous perambulations, they were conducted to a small villa where they found the Directorate awaiting them. The members were Ginsburger, Professor Joliot Curie, Max André, Chanoine Chevrot, Lenten preacher at Notre Dame and Curé of St. François Xavier, and a religious known as Father Philippe. If the lion wasn't exactly lying down with the lamb, the weaned child seemed to have put his hand in the cockatrice's den.

Ginsburger presided at the meeting. His opening speech was a foretaste of discourses which were later to become familiar: the Franc-Tireurs et Partisans, the paramilitary organization of the Communist Party, were the most powerful Group in the Resistance; therefore all the other Groups should unite under the control of the Front National.

For, as Yeo-Thomas was later to point out in a very able report, the Front National was, in effect, the Communist Party. The apparently anodyne umbrella name had been chosen for the same purpose of concealment as inspired Hitler to include the adjective 'Socialist' in the official title of his oligarchy. The Communists knew that, with their record of trouble-making in 1936 and of disloyalty in 1939, they could not hope to unite under their own fiery label the bourgeois and Catholics. Their tactic was simple, and their reasoning not altogether invalid. Unity was strength, and as their Group was the strongest in the Resistance, it was the duty of the lesser Groups to amalgamate with theirs. Under the name of 'Front National', governed by an obviously representative directorate, they would federate the smaller Groups and bring them without their knowledge under the control of the Communist Executive, whose true identity could be withheld from the curious under the plea of wartime security.

That the Franc-Tireurs et Partisans formed the strongest and most effective Resistance Group could not be denied. Already their shock troops numbered between 25,000 and 30,000. They claimed to carry out roughly 250 attacks and to kill between 500 and 600 Germans every month. These acts had resulted in reprisals, and losses among the rank and file of the Group had been heavy. Such casualties were, however, compensated several times over by the numerous recruits subsequently enrolled. But there was a factor which the Communist leaders did not assess correctly: many of these recruits were not Communists and, as Yeo-Thomas pointed out in his report, 'joined the movement because they were unaware of the existence of any other and because they wanted to hit back at the Germans'.

This swelling of the ranks had lessened the security of the Group. Careless talk had enabled the Gestapo and the Vichy Police to penetrate the organization. To counteract this the Franc-Tireurs et Partisans had been split up into small hermetically sealed cells. As a result the Group had become unwieldy and the communication of orders a lengthy and laborious process. Possessing many leaders of tiny units, the Movement was almost entirely lacking in cadres.

The eventual strength of the Franc-Tireurs et Partisans was estimated at 100,000 men.

In France, as in most countries, the Communist Party derived the greater part of its membership from discontented workers in the industrial centres: its rank and file were to be found in the lower levels of the metallurgical industries, the French National Railways, the Post Office and other administrations. But although most of them had adhered to the Party since before the war, it was not until after the invasion of Russia by Germany that they were given resistance directives by their leaders. It was clear, therefore, that the Franc-Tireurs et Partisans were directly subordinate to Moscow. Moscow, however, did not contribute any funds and, in order to obtain material assistance, the leaders had to place their troops officially at the disposal of General de Gaulle. Yeo-Thomas summed up the situation thus in his report: 'From my contacts with them I imagine that the rank and file are really patriots and only interested in a free France, whereas the heads have other ideas in mind and are planning well ahead, in fact, so far ahead as the period which will follow the "Gouvernement Provisoire".' Subsequent events were to prove him right. The avowed aim of the Communist Party was the mass uprising of Frenchmen on 'D' day; their real purpose was the expansion of the Party to such a size that it would dominate all others after liberation. Meanwhile B.B.C. newscasters continued to jeer at Frenchmen who feared the 'Communist bogey'.

At this meeting of the Directorate of the Front National the Communists present, while professing political impartiality, tried to impress upon the three agents that the Communist Party was the only pre-war political party still in existence and that its members had always resisted actively. They maintained that it was they who had unified resistance and represented its opinion. In that case, Passy and Brossolette asked, why were none of the other four Resistance Groups represented on their Committee? The plain question was put to the Directorate: were they or were they not going to participate on the same terms as the others in the co-ordination of the Resistance Movements? A reply was promised for a later date.

The first steps had now been taken to the formation of a unified Secret Army. As efficiency rather than numbers was desired, it was intended at first to limit its ranks to 20,000 well-trained troops. This Army would be commanded by a common General Staff known as the 'Etat-major de la Zone Occupée'. Each individual Resistance Group would, through its chief, be required to accept formally the following conditions:

1. That the officers composing the E.M.Z.O. would be appointed regardless of their Group of origin.

2. That such officers would be appointed on the grounds of their personal merit and not on the basis of proportional representation.

3. That all directives would come from Great Britain in accordance with the plans laid down by the Inter-Allied General Staff.

4. That all troops belonging to the Secret Army would, no matter what their origin, obey the orders of those set in authority above them (*sic*).

No effective Secret Army could, however, be mustered until steps had been taken to counteract 'La Relève' or the Compulsory Labour Service. Under order of the occupying authority all Frenchmen between the ages of 19 and 32 had been registered and were being sent to Germany, to work in factories or in the Organisation Todt. Some had even been sent to the Russian front. Although many Frenchmen had avoided registration or had taken refuge underground, combined German and French police forces were combing town and countryside for deserters. In Paris there were continual round-ups in the streets, and men whose papers showed that they were between 19 and 32 years of age were put in lorries and shipped to Germany immediately. Every week 20,000 men were taken from Paris in this way. If, as was stated to be the case, the age limit was to be raised to 42 and then to 55, all hopes of a Secret Army would vanish.

On 14th March, 1943, Yeo-Thomas reported this fact and his fears to London, and suggested a solution. Men must be encouraged by propaganda to evade this conscription. They could, however, do so only in one of two ways: either by leaving the country or by living clandestinely. As for the majority the first alternative was impracticable, there remained chiefly the second. But to live clandestinely the outlaw required both money and forged ration cards with which to obtain food. Both must be provided by the Allies if the potential members of the Secret Army were to be given the means of avoiding deportation to Germany. And the money, he insisted, must be 'on a generous scale and not in driblets'. It was thus that what was later known as the 'Maquis' had its origin.

During their negotiations with the leaders of the Resistance Movements, Passy and the others kept in touch with London. Telegrams for transmission had to be taken to the agent-de-liaison, who, in turn, handed them on to the W.T. operator. This was a dangerous task for all concerned. The messages, printed in code on thin paper, were carried in an article which could be easily destroyed in case of necessity, such as a packet of cigarette papers or a match-box. But it was the W.T. operators who ran the greatest risks, as the Gestapo sent special direction-finding vans round the streets and country roads to pick up their transmissions. Consequently the operators had to vary their emplacements ; and, transporting their sets in suitcases, they were always liable to be stopped by the German police and required to open their valises.

While Yeo-Thomas went about his business in Paris he took special precautions against being followed. Shadowing, he dis-covered, was generally carried out by teams of which one member would pass on to another the description of the suspect. In order to vary his appearance he purchased several hats of different shapes and colours and scarves of various patterns and changed both hats and scarves several times a day. He also learned that a sleuth is trained to recognize his prey by his walk. Sometimes, therefore, he wore shoes with steel tips, sometimes shoes without tips and oc-casionally he put under the heel of one foot a wedge of cardboard, thus completely changing his gait.

The morale of the population, although undernourished, poorly clad and suffering from lack of heating, he found good on the whole. While the rich could resort to the black market, where a meal cost 800 francs and a pair of shoes 450, ordinary men and women, earn-ing from 1,800 to 2,500 francs a month, suffered terrible privations. In spite of their misery few were active collaborators. The mass avoided all contact with the Germans, looking the other way when they passed through the street. The old political parties and 'les cons illustres' of Third Republican Governments had been dis-credited. All patriots were Gaullists. General Giraud had few followers.

He visited José Dupuis, his school-teacher friend, in her flat at 39 rue de la Felicité. Alternately laughing and sobbing, she told him that she had received the postcard which he had sent from the Pointe-de-Grave and heard his B.B.C. message. She was still teach-ing at her girls' school in the *premier arrondissement* and her thirty pupils were all patriots. She begged him to give her something ac-tive to do even though it were dangerous. Yeo-Thomas engaged her at once, to help him to build up a small circuit of his own by means of which he could keep in touch with his contacts. Eventu-

44

ally she became his second-in-command. The risks which she ultimately ran were considerable, as she was easily recognizable, being five foot ten.

Yeo-Thomas had still plenty of work to do; there were the final details of the amalgamation of the various Resistance Movements to settle, and the Groups in the provinces had to be visited. Pending the arrival in Paris of Moulin and General Delestraint, who had been delegated by de Gaulle to command the unified Resistance, Passy set off to inspect the Somme, the Nord and the Pas de Calais. Yeo-Thomas, accompanied by Pichard, went to visit the Organisation Civile et Militaire on the Nièvre, the Cher and the Allier.

Train journeys were always dangerous on account of the frequent check-up made by the German and French police. Yeo-Thomas and Pichard travelled first-class for the same reason that they always wore good clothes and smart hats: an appearance of prosperity suggested profitable collaboration with the Germans and rendered them less liable to interrogation. Their journey however was not to be without risk. Just as their train was about to leave Paris a Frenchman whom Yeo-Thomas had known in pre-war days entered their compartment. He was, Tommy remembered, both pro-German and anti-British. Deciding not to go and stand in the corridor in case his abrupt retreat might arouse suspicion, Yeo-Thomas buried his face in his newspaper. Eventually, laying down the paper, he turned to look out of the window. As he raised his head he saw the man look at him and give a start. Gazing out of the window he could feel that the man was still staring at him. He turned again and their eyes met. Yeo-Thomas gave no sign of recognition and began to talk to Pichard. The man leaned forward and touched him on the knee.

'*Monsieur, votre visage m'est familier,*' he said. 'Haven't I met you before the war?'

Yeo-Thomas looked him full in the face.

'*Je pense que vous faites erreur, Monsieur,*' he said. 'Perhaps I look like somebody you know or maybe you've seen me somewhere else, but I'm sure I've never seen you before.'

His bluff succeeded. The Frenchman agreed that he must be mistaken, although he maintained that Tommy's resemblance to an acquaintance of his was startling. After that they talked about the curious and constant recurrence of 'doubles'. Yeo-Thomas was glad when the train reached Nevers.

After lunch in the house of a family which Pichard used as a letter-box they met Courvoisier, an ex-regular N.C.O. of the Zouaves who was the local Resistance leader. A dynamic, bull-necked man, he had as his assistants the Secretary of the Préfecture and the Director of the local waterworks. Yeo-Thomas spent three days in the area, visiting the reception committees and the resistants.

The Group numbered 2,000 and had well-organized Intelligence, Supply and Operational branches. Among their members they included the 350 local gendarmes and their Commandant. These policemen protected the reception committees during operations; as they were able to move about the countryside without arousing comment they also carried messages, transmitted orders and reported on German troop movements. Invited by the Commandant to meet the senior N.C.O.s and introduced as 'le Capitaine Shelley de la Royal Air Force', Yeo-Thomas gave them a short lecture. Because of the harm already wrought to Resistance by the Giraud affair he emphasized the necessity of recognizing de Gaulle as the only leader of the French. The men were visibly heartened at hearing such an opinion expressed by a British officer.

Later, after visiting M. Jeanneney, ex-President of the Senate and pre-war second personage of France, Yeo-Thomas returned to Paris and reported the result of his mission. The austere Passy, the learned and militant Socialist Brossolette and the jovial, humorous and Conservative Yeo-Thomas had now become intimate friends. Shared danger and a common purpose sought for other ends than personal profit bind bonds more lasting than those which derive from the pitiful commercial pursuits of peace. A house that is founded on shared dividends accruing from the sale of zip fasteners shall not so surely stand.

On 23rd March, 1943, they learned that their efforts to unite the paramilitary organizations of the various Resistance Movements had been successful. Colonel Passy's conditions had been accepted by all the Groups. On 26th March there met in Jeanne Helbling's flat in Neuilly the following leaders: Colonel Touny of the Organisation Civile et Militaire; Lecompte-Boynet of Ceux de la Résistance; Coquoin of Ceux de la Libération; Périgny of Libération; and

Ginsburger of the Front National. All were accompanied by their assistants and, in the presence of Passy, Brossolette and Yeo-Thomas they signed an agreement which had already been approved by their directing committees.

Réunis le 26 Mars 1943 en zone occupée les chefs ou représentants mandatés, ci-dessous, de la zone occupée:

'O.C.M.';

'Libération', organe de résistance, notamment du Comité d'Action Socialiste, de la Confédération Générale du Travail et de la Confédération Française de Travailleurs Chrétiens;

'Front National';

'Ceux de la Résistance';

'Ceux de la Libération'

renouvellent collectivement l'assurance, individuellement donnée déjà par chacun de ces groupements, de leur entière confiance dans le Général de Gaulle et le Comité National pour réaliser l'union de tous les français de la Métropole et de l'Empire, pour libérer la France et redonner la parole au peuple français.

Avec le Général de Gaulle et le Comité National Français ils sont résolus:

à poursuivre la lutte contre l'ennemi par tous les moyens et particulièrement les armes à la main; à abattre toutes les dictatures, celles de Vichy comme celles de Berlin et de Rome, et de quelque masque qu'elles se parent; à rétablir les libertés républicaines en rompant, par une profonde rénovation politique et administrative, avec les faiblesses du régime passé aussi bien qu'avec l'arbitraire de Vichy; à promouvoir des réformes économiques et sociales décisives.

The style was perhaps a little bit pompous, and employed many words to say what perhaps could best have been said in a few; that all the French Resistance Movements backed General de Gaulle.

The sincerity of those who signed was proved by each Group agreeing to:

1. Contribute officers and men to the Etat-major de la Zone Occupée and the Secret Army.

2. To obey instructions transmitted by the E.M.Z.O. as received by it from the Inter-Allied General Staff in London, passing through General de Gaulle.

3. To furnish a true and accurate estimate of their cadres and troops.

4. To pool their possibilities under the control of General de Gaulle, acting in accordance with the Inter-Allied General Staff.

Agreement was also reached on the future employment of the Secret Army. Its members would not be used as regular troops, at least not until after liberation. Quality rather than numbers must be the aim; a few well-trained and tactically placed men would be of more value than unarmed hordes. On 'D' day picked troops from the Secret Army would be supplied with priority targets;

troops not so employed would act as guerillas, attacking isolated detachments of the enemy, but would not attempt to deal with armoured formations or large organized units.

But before a truly effective Secret Army could be brought into being its men must be armed. The leaders of the various Groups pointed out that at present their men had almost no arms at all and that their W.T. communications were practically non-existent. The necessary equipment, they insisted, must be supplied by London. At the same time help must be given to potential recruits to enable them to avoid deportation in the labour drafts to Germany.

There was also the scarcely less important question of medical supplies: drugs, antiseptics and surgical instruments would be required in large quantities. Professor Pasteur Valéry-Radot, a descendant of the famous bacteriologist whose name he bore, had worked on this problem and had prepared a list of his requirements. The three agents undertook that these would be parachuted before 'D' day.

On 12th April Moulin and General Delestraint, whom de Gaulle had delegated to command united Resistance, arrived in Paris from the Unoccupied Zone, where they, too, had been co-ordinating the various Movements.

Jean Moulin, a small dark man with laughing eyes, had been Prefect of Chartres at the time of the Armistice. There, unlike some of his colleagues elsewhere, he had been dignified and courageous in his attitude towards the invaders. Refusing to sign a declaration that the rotting corpses found lying in and around the town had been the victims of *French* atrocities, he had been imprisoned by the Germans and tortured. Rather than yield he had cut his throat with a razor. This attempt to destroy his life had been discovered before it had succeeded and he had been taken to hospital, where he recovered. On his discharge he had been dismissed by Vichy and accorded military honours by the Kommandantur because of his bravery. In September, 1941, he had landed in England. If Moulin had survived he would almost certainly have been the first post-war Prime Minister of France.

Delestraint was a regular officer of the French army who had made a big impression on the British. Although forceful and fearless, Yeo-Thomas considered him unsuited to clandestine warfare;

later, when arrested and questioned, he was to pull out of his pocket two sets of identity papers.

Another meeting was called, at which Moulin and Delestraint were introduced to the Resistance leaders, to whom they expounded their plan for the construction of the E.M.Z.O. and the Secret Army. Moulin, who rather overshadowed Delestraint, began by increasing the basic figure for troops from 20,000 to 50,000 men. But to achieve this strength, he insisted, every Movement would have to contribute its best men. Furthermore, behind these 50,000 there would have to be held a reserve of 100,000 men. In the meantime the 50,000 men would be organized into compact units and trained like a regular army. And being trained like a regular army, Moulin was careful to point out, meant other things besides being taught the art of killing: it meant learning discipline, how to salute officers and how to stand to attention—in other words, the much-derided and not yet exploded spit and polish.

Naturally the leader of the Communist Franc-Tireurs et Partisans objected. He drew attention to the fact that the immediate transfer of his shock troops to the Secret Army would mean the cessation of their present activities. The more acts of sabotage his men committed, he maintained, the better trained and the more aggressive they became. There was also the propaganda value of such acts to be considered. He was reluctant, under such conditions, to divert any portion of his troops to the Secret Army. While he was still willing to place his men at the disposal of General de Gaulle on 'D' day, he could not curtail their activities in the meanwhile. The meeting broke up without a solution to his objection having been found, although Moulin seemed to meet him half-way by agreeing to ask the Inter-Allied General Staff for a list of interim sabotage targets, against some of which Communist troops would be employed.

The leaders of the other Movements all agreed to concentrate on building up a Secret Army for 'D' day. All leaders were unanimous in insisting that the invasion should take place before the end of the year.

During his last few days in Paris, Yeo-Thomas established contacts for the future visit which he was sure he would have to make. With Passy and Brossolette he met the leaders of the French Trades Unions. Saillant, who had replaced Jouhaux as president of the

Confédération Générale du Travail, and Tessier, president of the Confédération Française de Travailleurs Chrétiens, were both opposed to a revival of the old political feuds after liberation. At the time, no doubt, their feeling was sincere; in spite of what St. John says, the only time that it is really easy to love our neighbour seems to be when he is helping us to hate another neighbour.

Tommy also went to visit his father in his flat at 3, rue des Eaux. As instructed by José Dupuis, he rang the bell five times. His father showed no astonishment when he opened the door. '*Entrez, Monsieur*,' he said, as though his son were a stranger. Then, when he was sure that there was nobody to overhear him, he asked: 'What the bloody hell have you been doing for the last two years? You ought to have been here long ago.' He did not speak of his own imprisonment in Fresnes: he was, he said, doing a little resistance work on his own account. Both father and son were too wise to ask each other for details. After giving the old man some tea, cigarettes, coffee, sugar and money and promising to come and see him again as soon as he could, Yeo-Thomas left as discreetly as he had arrived.

On 14th April word was sent from London to the three agents that they would be picked up on the night of the 16th by a Lysander, from a field near Lyons-la-Forêt. They set out at once from the Gare St. Lazare, taking with them an American pilot called Ryan who had been shot down from a flying fortress and sheltered by a friend of Professor Pasteur Valéry-Radot. Ryan had a fractured shoulder, which had been reset by the Professor, and could speak no French. He was told that if anybody spoke to him on the train his reply must be limited to an evangelical '*oui*' or '*non*'.

They travelled in two groups to Pont de l'Arche: Passy, Brossolette and another agent in one compartment, and Yeo-Thomas, Ryan and Dutertre of the Lyons-la-Forêt reception committee in another. During the journey nobody attempted to speak to Ryan, who pretended to be reading a French newspaper. In the buffet at Pont de l'Arche, fumbling for, and at first failing to find, his wallet, Yeo-Thomas committed his only indiscretion. 'Where the hell's my money?' he said in English. Fortunately there were a lot of people talking noisily in the buffet and his remark was not overheard.

From Pont de l'Arche they took a small local train to Fleury-sur-Andelle, whence they made another uncomfortable journey by bicycle to Lyons-la-Forêt. They reached the village after dark. Passy and Brossolette were again sheltered by the Vinets and Yeo-Thomas and Ryan in a neighbouring farmhouse. All next day they remained indoors. Ryan, unaccustomed to clandestine life, kept talking loudly in his unmistakable American accent and on more than one occasion had to be silenced by the farmer's wife.

At 10.30 p.m. Yeo-Thomas and Ryan climbed into a van drawn up in the farmyard and hid behind sacks of potatoes. Dutertre sat in front with the driver. After an hour's bumpy journey the van stopped and they got out. They found themselves on a deserted country road beside a road-mender's hut, into which Tommy's suitcase was pushed. Beside the road a field shimmered like a lake in the moonlight. The stars twinkled brightly in the sky. They hurried across the magic field and lay down in a copse, where they were presently joined by Passy, Brossolette, Vinet and Jacot.

Yeo-Thomas says that he was both happy and frightened while he lay waiting for the Lysander to arrive. He was happy to have accomplished so much and frightened lest a last-minute accident should ruin everything. So much depended upon so little. The district was heavily patrolled. The Lysanders might not turn up. The Germans might hear the hum of the approaching aircraft. Helpless in the huge indifference of the night, the three most-sought-after men in France lay fearful in the copse.

Soon, however, there was a buzzing sound in the air. Dutertre, Jacot and Vinet rose and ran on to the field, where torches had been fixed to three sticks arranged in the form of an L. Jacot flashed the recognition sign and the Lysander replied. The aircraft circled, landed, came down the longer branch of the L against the wind, turned along the shorter and came to a standstill with the wind behind it. A second Lysander hovered overhead.

In less than three minutes Passy, Brossolette, Yeo-Thomas, Ryan and their suitcases were in the gunners' cockpit and the Lysander was airborne again. An hour later they landed at Tangmere, back once more in the right sort of night.

Next evening the B.B.C. French service sent out for the first time the message: '*Le petit lapin blanc est rentré au clapier*'. The little white rabbit had returned to his hutch.

CHAPTER VI

WITH HUTCH IN THE HUTCH

THE message was true in a double sense, for Colonel Hutchison was still commanding 'R.F.' Section. The section had grown and was to grow more: Captain Alex Murray had come from Costa Rica; Captain Thackthwaite, later to be awarded the O.B.E. for his work in the field, enlivened the drudgery inseparable even from clandestine organization by reciting undenominational clerihews. Flight Lieutenant Whitehead, shortly to win the M.C. for bravery, was to join from Tommy's former Polish squadron. The moon period was on, operations were in full swing and supplies had already been sent to some of the reception committees which Yeo-Thomas had visited.

It is possible that Yeo-Thomas's unceasing insistence upon the necessity of priority for the needs of French Resistance may have exasperated some of his superiors who had neither his knowledge nor love of France. Without losing any time he sent in a detailed report of the results of his mission. All day long he bombarded brigadiers, colonels and air commodores with written memoranda and spoken words emphasizing the importance of creating an effective Secret Army in France. He shot off his mouth at conferences, he counselled strategists and intimidated politicos, and always his arguments were the same. An invasion of the Continent could not be carried out expeditiously without the aid of a Secret Army already established on French soil. A Secret Army could not be found already established on French soil unless explosives and arms and money were sent to France. Therefore explosives and arms and money must be sent to France. A Secret Army could not be mustered unless able-bodied young Frenchmen were helped to evade the Compulsory Labour Service. Therefore able-bodied young Frenchmen must be helped to evade the Compulsory Labour Service. General de Gaulle was the acknowledged leader of all patriotic Frenchmen. Therefore all those who supported General Giraud were knaves, buccaneers and fools. The French were afraid that the British and the Americans would amputate a part of their colonial empire after the war. Therefore the British and the Americans must immediately and publicly state that they had no intention of amputating a part of the French colonial empire after the war. It was impossible for W.T. operators in the field, tapping out their messages with one ear cocked for the rumble of a German D.F. van, to do otherwise than send mutilated messages. Therefore W.T. operators in the field must be excused for sending out mutilated messages. To Yeo-Thomas it was all as simple and logical as 'Socrates is a man; therefore Socrates is mortal', and if he repeated his arguments a little too often for some people's liking it was perhaps because he suspected that some of his superiors shared only Socrates's mortality.

On 20th May General de Gaulle asked to see him. Ushered into an immense room, Yeo-Thomas saw the immense General seated at an immense desk. He saluted. De Gaulle rose, held out his hand and said formally, as though he had learned the little speech by heart:

'*Je vous félicite de votre mission. Le Colonel Passy m'a fait votre éloge. Je vous remercie de ce que vous avez fait pour la France. Quelles sont vos impressions?*' [1]

Naturally Yeo-Thomas took advantage of this invitation to attempt to convert the General himself to Gaullism. When he had finished, the General said gloomily from the depths of his belly:

'*Moi je n'y suis pour rien, mais il me semble qu'en dépit de tout ce que disent les gens il y a en France quelque chose qui s'appelle le Gaullisme.*' [2]

It was said of General de Gaulle that he was temperamental and intransigent; both accusations were probably true. He was however first and foremost a patriot: entirely without personal ambition, his one idea was to serve France, and he didn't mind how much he offended red-tabbed Wykehamists in the process. The fact that his famous speech of 18th June, 1940, was at the time more courageous than prophetic only emphasizes his nobility. It is now the fashion to accuse him of fascism. If a belief in the necessity of discipline is fascist then General de Gaulle is a fascist; but in that

[1] 'I congratulate you on your mission. Colonel Passy has been singing your praises. I thank you for what you have done for France. What are your impressions?'

[2] 'I, myself, have nothing to do with it, but it seems to me that in spite of all people say there's something in France called Gaullism.'

case so also is Mr. Aneurin Bevan. At any rate the General knew how to recompense a British officer who had helped France: on 29th May he sent Yeo-Thomas the Croix de Guerre with palm.

There is a rule that no British officer can wear a foreign decoration without the sanction of high authority. When Yeo-Thomas applied for permission to wear the Croix de Guerre, the Air Ministry refused, on the ground that, in its opinion, General de Gaulle lacked the right to grant such a decoration. Embarrassed, because his French friends were already inquiring why he was not wearing the ribbon, Yeo-Thomas pointed out that he had seen in an illustrated paper a photograph of General de Gaulle bestowing the Croix de Guerre upon naval officers and asked why the Air Ministry refused to the General a power credited to him by the Admiralty. Eventually, upon the insistence of Colonel Hutchison, permission to wear the decoration was granted.

While on leave in Somerset he learned that he had also been awarded the Military Cross. He went and bought the white-and-purple ribbon, which Barbara sewed on his tunic. On his return to London his friends of the B.C.R.A. gave a dinner in his honour to celebrate the granting of the British decoration.

Next day the officer representing the Air Ministry at S.O.E. sent for Yeo-Thomas. 'There's been a mistake,' he said. 'You were recommended for the M.C. all right, but for some reason the Air Ministry has refused to sanction it. I'm afraid you'll have to take down that ribbon.' This time even Hutch's high-power 'phoning was of no avail, and it was not until nearly a year later that the award was approved.

Once again Tommy was in an awkward situation. He had to visit the French almost daily, and if he appeared without his M.C. ribbon it would, in view of the previous blocking of his Croix de Guerre, make him look ridiculous and be bad for British prestige. In the end he had to resort to the tactics of deceit which he had learned in the field. He kept at the office a spare tunic with an M.C. ribbon sewn on it; this tunic he wore when visiting the French. On all other occasions he wore a tunic without this ribbon, and if while wearing it he met the French he explained that he had not yet had time to decorate appropriately all his uniforms. To such subterfuges do bureaucrats reduce the brave.

Meanwhile Moulin reported that good progress was being made with the Secret Army. General Delestraint had got matters well in hand. The Occupied Zone had been divided up into six districts each with its Regional Military Officer and Air Operations Officer ('Bureau des Opérations Aériennes'). The so-called Unoccupied Zone had been similarly divided and staffed. Each Zone was commanded by a senior officer, in charge of both military and air operations and directly responsible to General Delestraint.

Then suddenly disaster overtook them. On 9th June Delestraint was arrested by the Gestapo; on 20th June, Moulin, Larat and other important officers were also arrested. In less than a fortnight the Secret Army had lost its two top men and many of its most competent leaders. Every effort had to be made to rescue those who had been arrested and to enable the seriously damaged circuits to carry on. Fortunately only a few weeks previously two new men had been sent out, 'Z' to take charge of the Occupied Zone Secretariat and Bingen that of the Unoccupied Zone; it was decided that they should also administer the Secret Army until suitable replacements for Moulin and Delestraint had been found.

By August it was clear that, in spite of optimistic reports received from 'Z' and Bingen, things were going from bad to worse. Although parachuting and the landing operations were proceeding smoothly and co-ordinates of new grounds were being regularly received, little or no information was being received from the paramilitary side. The Regional Military Officers complained that they were receiving no help from the various Resistance Movements. Abandoning a plot for the capture by Médéric and himself of Admiral Doenitz, Yeo-Thomas accepted gladly when it was suggested that he should accompany Brossolette to the field on another mission of inspection. Centralization of authority had proved dangerous and must be replaced by a more horizontal hierarchy.

This time Yeo-Thomas was given the cover name of Tirelli. A fresh set of false papers had to be prepared and another personal history memorized.

The code name for his new mission was Marie Claire; this was the name of a pre-war French woman's weekly which informed correspondents upon the propriety of such acts as a young wife walking about the bedroom in the presence of her husband with the tops of her stockings hanging down. The questions asked of Yeo-Thomas were slightly less domestic:

OPERATIONAL INSTRUCTIONS MARIE CLAIRE

1. Marie Claire will proceed as a member of a joint S.O.E./B.C.R.A. mission and will act as such. He will be responsible to his own H.Q. and will report to them on return.

2. He will inquire into and report upon the state of the Resistance Movements in the Occupied Zone; their degree of training, their strength, their morale, the state and distribution of their armament, and in general their effectiveness for the activities envisaged.

3. He will report upon the personalities in charge of the various component parts of the organization, and will make recommendations as to other personalities to fill vacant or weak places in the organization.

4. He will impress upon the Resistance Groups the importance of sending to Britain the returns of strengths which have been asked for.

5. He will discover the time-lag necessary between the receipt of instructions by the H.Q. of any region and their receipt by local groups.

6. He will discover the degree of mobility of sub-units and the time taken for their movement.

7. He will endeavour to discover how far the plans already sent to the field have been permeated to the lower ranks and to assess how far they have been compromised.

Once again it was a tall order.

CHAPTER VII

MISSION MARIE CLAIRE

THIS time it was to be a Pullman operation: there was to be no parachuting. Yeo-Thomas and Brossolette, who had just returned from Algiers, were to be landed like a couple of company directors by Lysander near Angoulême.

They took off from Tangmere at 11.30 p.m. on 18th September and once again, huddled in the cockpit, they were afraid that their journey was going to be abortive. It was cloudy and foggy over the Channel and the sea was invisible. Then the flash of German anti-aircraft fire lit up the clouds and made them look like monster pink powder-puffs. The excitement, however, was brief. The Lysander rocked, shot up, swerved, twisted and turned and then went steadily on.

Soon the pilot told them on the 'inter-com' that they were over Poitiers. About 1.25 a.m., flying low, they caught sight of the three lights of their reception committee. When the regulation signals had been exchanged the aircraft began to circle. Below them lay the landing ground, bordered on either side by a stream shining with inconsequent loveliness in the moonlight. As soon as the aircraft came to a standstill Yeo-Thomas and Brossolette threw out the packages and then climbed out themselves. A leading French Communist called Mercier climbed in, and within five minutes of landing the Lysander was airborne again.

Almost immediately a second Lysander appeared and landed. Two more agents got out after they had thrown out more packages.

The packages created a problem for the members of the reception committee, who had not been expecting so many and had only one car at their disposal. The agents, after sorting out their own suitcases, had to wait behind bushes and were guarded by two men with Sten guns, while the packages were driven to a ruined and unoccupied house fifteen miles away and concealed there.

About 3 a.m. the car returned. The car was a front-wheel drive Citroën, into which nine passengers had to be crammed. Once again they had to run the risk of being caught out after curfew, which was at midnight, and as they were in a car they could not quickly take cover. They resolved that if they met a German patrol they would fight their way through it. The possibility of such an encounter was considerable, as they had forty miles to go.

Three-quarters of an hour after they had started their near rear tyre burst while they were driving through a village, and they all had to get out. Changing the wheel was, in spite of their precautions, a noisy operation and it was necessary to keep a sharp look out. The two men with Sten guns guarded the car, one in front and one behind. Brossolette and Yeo-Thomas hid in the shadow of a big farm door and the other two agents on the opposite side of the street. Those who were changing the wheel worked speedily, but in the silence of the night the noise seemed deafening. They had to fear not only the arrival of a German patrol but also discovery by unfriendly villagers. Anxious and impatient, Yeo-Thomas suddenly saw pink lines of light from one of the shutters in a house opposite. The shutters opened slowly and a man's head appeared. Yeo-Thomas stepped out of the shadow and pointed his Colt threateningly. The shutters slammed shut at once and the light went out. Yeo-Thomas could only hope that if the man were a collaborator there was no telephone in the house.

Even when the wheel had been changed and the jack removed their troubles weren't over. The spare tyre turned out to be soft and a frantic search failed to reveal a pump among the tools. There was nothing to do but to climb into the car again and hope that the tyre would hold out under their heavy weight. They chose the lesser danger of driving quickly because they were afraid of being stranded far from their destination. The tyre had a slow puncture and as the miles went reeling past the bumps became heavier and heavier. By the time they reached the safe house they were riding almost on the rim of the wheel.

The safe house was a long low building with a flattish roof, called in that part of the country a 'mas'. While they were eating the copious meal which had been prepared for them the agents learned that this was their hosts' first Lysander operation. The members of the reception committee were thrilled by their success. They complained, however, that so far not nearly enough arms had been parachuted to them.

Next morning Brossolette and Yeo-Thomas breakfasted on specially-baked white bread and a mixture of young wine and brandy called 'Pinaud des Charentes'. At lunch they had to give an account of the insufficiently publicized British war effort and explain why the Americans had tried to replace de Gaulle by Giraud. A few months later the 'mas' was successfully attacked by a strong German detachment and of their eleven hosts only two survived: one had thirteen bullet wounds in his body and the other six through his stomach and an arm blown off.

At four o'clock in the afternoon Lepointu, the survivor who lost his arm, drove Brossolette and Yeo-Thomas to Châteauneuf. From there they caught a train to Angoulême, where, because of the curfew, they had to wait hours in a rainy night under a leaking roof on a platform for the Paris train, which left at half-past one in the morning. There were no seats in the train and they had to stand all the way. They arrived at the Gare d'Austerlitz at seven o'clock and telephoned at once to Madame Peyronnet, using a previously arranged convention.

Established once more at 102 Avenue des Ternes, their first concern was to get into contact with 'Z' and with Pichard, now Senior Air Operations Officer for the Occupied Zone. In each case this was done by means of a letter-box, which was the name given to a person willing to receive messages, verbal or written, and pass them on from one agent to another. Often, to increase security, two intermediary agents-de-liaison were used: one, who knew only the sender, carried the message to the letter-box; and the other, who knew only the recipient, collected it. Before his return to England at the end of his previous mission Brossolette had already fixed up such a letter-box for 'Z'; and at the same time Yeo-Thomas had made arrangements with Madame Bosc, proprietress of a small restaurant in the rue Richepanse, to act as a letter-box for himself.

As soon as they had arranged these appointments with 'Z' and Pichard, Brossolette and Yeo-Thomas got down to the job of strengthening their circuits, which had been weakened by the recent wave of arrests. José Dupuis was asked to find two capable agents-de-liaison and two more safe houses. Madame Peyronnet's daughter, Poucette, aged sixteen, was engaged to carry messages on her bicycle. She in turn recruited a Danish physical culture teacher, Suni Sandöe, a fearless stocky woman with Scandinavian blue eyes, who placed not only her services but her flat at 11 rue Claude Chahu at their disposal. Madame Denise Martin, the wife of a solicitor, and her sister Nicole Bauer also volunteered to help them. Nicole Bauer, nicknamed Maud, became another cyclist messenger and she in turn brought in the plump little Jacqueline Devaux and her flat in the rue Leverrier. An attractive Canadian, Diana Provost, married to a Frenchman, allowed her flat in the rue du Colonel Moll to be used as a meeting place. All these women risked, in the event of discovery, torture and death.

The new flats were especially welcome for, with the Gestapo hot on the tracks of Resistance, it was necessary to possess a wide choice of retreats in case of emergency. Arms, food, clothes and money were concealed in those safe houses so that it was easy immediately and permanently to leave a threatened dwelling-place for one that was secure.

The Gestapo had a habit of waiting in blown flats for the arrival of unwarned agents, and for this reason Brossolette and Yeo-Thomas arranged to meet as many contacts as possible outside in the street. In this way they could make sure that they were not being followed and could also watch their approaching contact to ascertain that there was nobody who looked like a sleuth on his trail. If an agent were sure that he was not being followed he would carry a scarf or a newspaper in his hand; if he had reason to suspect that he was, the scarf would be round his neck or the newspaper in his pocket, and in that event the two agents would pass without speaking. At all such meetings the two people concerned approached the rendezvous from opposite directions. In case, because of some unforeseen contingency such as an air-raid alarm, he missed an appointment, each agent arranged to pass a certain part of the city at a certain hour every day; the points and the times varied according to the day of the week and they were staggered, so that the time and point for Monday of one week became the time and point for Tuesday of the next.

Because they were so familiar with the details of the cover stories they had used on their previous mission, Brossolette and Yeo-Thomas continued to use their old false names. Thus Tommy, while able to become Tirelli at a moment's notice, remained Thierry. In his dealings with the French Resistance Movement, he maintained his former name of Shelley; this name had now become famous throughout the French underground and, in spite of the risks attached to its continued use, he judged, without conceit, that it would prejudice paramilitary morale if he were to abandon it. For Brossolette Tommy was 'Cheval', and for Tommy Brossolette was 'Polydor'. These private names were the symbols of their unspoken affection for each other.

At 9.15 on the morning after their arrival in Paris they started out on foot to a flat in the rue de la Pompe where 'Z' had given them a rendezvous. On their way they passed the bookshop which Brossolette had owned at the beginning of the war. 'Z' received them in a magnificent drawing-room with double doors with glass panels and chandeliers dripping crystal icicles. They sat on Louis

XV chairs while 'Z' explained to them that he had chosen this palace of brittle splendours because it was only a hundred yards distant from the Secretariat situated in the same street.

This lack of elementary security alarmed Brossolette and Yeo-Thomas. 'Z', a brave man who had been seriously wounded by flak in his first attempt to parachute into France, ridiculed their protests. It was at once clear that 'Z', accustomed since the arrest of Moulin and Delestraint to exercise with Bingen supreme authority over the Resistance Movements, resented their mission as a reflection upon his competence.

Continued conversation showed that the situation was out of hand: little had been done to implement the decisions of the Allied General Staff; careless security, due to over-confidence, was jeopardizing the whole structure of Resistance; and Bingen, head of the Secretariat of the Unoccupied Zone, seemed to be spending most of his time in the Occupied, where in fact he was at present.

Arrangements were made to meet 'Z' and Bingen at the same flat next day, and a meeting was requested with Colonel Morinaud, recently sent out to supervise the Regional Military Officers. Arrangements were also made for regular contact through an agent-de-liaison. Brossolette and Yeo-Thomas particularly insisted that all messages should be verbal and in no case should a communication be committed to paper. 'Z's agent-de-liaison was to come to 102 Avenue des Ternes every evening at five o'clock punctually. If anything were wrong a pot containing a plant would be placed outside one of the windows of the flat, in which case the agent would not enter the house. Such possible lack of contact was provided for by agreement to meet every morning at ten o'clock in the rue de Sèze: 'Z' would enter the street from the Boulevard de la Madeleine and Brossolette and Yeo-Thomas from the rue Tronchet.

On Thursday, 23rd September, they again met 'Z'. Bingen was also present and, when questioned about the organization in the Unoccupied Zone, was vague. Neither 'Z' nor Bingen was able to reply to questions about paramilitary matters. Brossolette and Yeo-Thomas left the rue de la Pompe filled with foreboding.

That same evening the agent-de-liaison failed to keep his appointment at five o'clock. At ten o'clock there was a ring at the door which Madame Peyronnet answered. Their caller was the agent-de-liaison, accompanied by the concierge. The go-between, stopped by the concierge and asked where he was going, had replied that he was going to visit a Monsieur Shelley who lived with the Peyronnets on the third floor. Afraid that the intruder might be a burglar, the good lady had insisted on accompanying him. This placed Brossolette and Yeo-Thomas in an awkward position, as they had already given their names to the concierge as MM. Boutet and Thierry, bombed out of their homes in Nantes. Luckily the woman was devoted to the Peyronnets and did not ask any questions. When she had gone the agent-de-liaison handed Yeo-Thomas an envelope addressed to 'M. Shelley' and containing a typewritten list of appointments with names and places set out in detail. Yeo-Thomas told the go-between to inform 'Z' that Brossolette and himself would call upon him in the rue de la Pompe at ten o'clock next morning.

At 9 a.m. on Friday, 24th September, Brossolette and Yeo-Thomas met Pichard, whose report confirmed their fears about the insecurity of the Secretariat. Pichard complained that he was getting no assistance from 'Z', that his funds were always delivered to him late and that 'Z' was fostering antagonism between the Air Operations Officers (Bureau des Opérations Aériennes) and the Resistance Movements. Before taking action against 'Z', however, Brossolette and Yeo-Thomas decided to obtain confirmation of those statements from other agents. Pichard also stated that he feared for the safety of Morinaud, who had lately missed several appointments.

One hour later they again saw 'Z' and Bingen, to whom they protested violently about the breach of elementary security committed by their agent-de-liaison on the previous evening. While promising that in future all their communications would be verbal, 'Z' and Bingen maintained that Brossolette and Yeo-Thomas overrated the dangers of clandestine activity. Angered by the insinuation that they were scared, Brossolette and Yeo-Thomas pointed out that two of the men employed by 'Z' and Bingen—Alain, who was Georges Bidault's W.T. operator, and Nard—were insecure because they had been blown, and requested that they be returned to London in accordance with instructions already given. This 'Z' refused to do on the grounds that the two men in question were too valuable to lose. Neither he nor Bingen appeared to be perturbed by the fact that Morinaud had not been seen for several days. After requesting an interview with the Regional Military Officers and the Air Operations Officers, Brossolette and Yeo-Thomas left. In the street they passed Nard, who, contrary to all regulations, gave them a sign of recognition.

Fortunately they had their own means of getting in touch with the Resistance Leaders. Interviewed that day, Coquoin (Ceux de la Libération), Lecompte-Boynet (Ceux de la Résistance), Colonel Lacroix (Organisation Civile et Militaire), Joseph (Franc-Tireurs et Partisans), Colonel Aymon (Libération) confirmed their worst fears. The only progress achieved since their previous visit had been the nomination of regional movement heads. Sub-regional and district set-ups were still in the same chaos as in April. Regional Military Officers had no contacts and local leaders often refused to receive their visits. The conflict between the Air Operations Officers and the Movements was rapidly becoming an open breach. Instead of a united General Staff innumerable committees met irregularly and bewildered the few who listened to them by their piddling and pettifogging pronouncements. It was superabundantly clear that 'Z' and Bingen possessed neither the authority nor the competence to replace Moulin and Delestraint.

Broken-hearted, Brossolette and Yeo-Thomas returned to 102 Avenue des Ternes. At five o'clock the agent-de-liaison again failed to turn up. At ten o'clock he still hadn't put in an appearance. Alarmed by the memory of the go-between's previous *gaffe*, they decided that it would be safer to leave the flat at once: Brossolette went to stay with Claire in the rue de la Faisanderie and Yeo-Thomas moved to Jacqueline Devaux's flat in the rue Leverrier.

Next day Maud was sent to find out if the Peyronnets' flat was still safe. At 6 p.m. she met Yeo-Thomas at the Etoile and told him that the agent-de-liaison had been arrested the previous evening carrying a piece of paper on which was written: 'Mme P, 3 étage, 102 Avenue des Ternes'. Surprisingly, however, the go-between had stalled for time before pretending that he was engaged in black-market transactions; he had told the Gestapo that he had been going to the flat, which he had never visited before, in search of a potential customer. Because of this delay the Gestapo had not raided Madame

Peyronnet's flat until six o'clock that morning. Fortunately the concierge had been loyal and the Peyronnets, although severely interrogated, had been able to convince their inquisitors that they were in no way connected with subversive activities but had been attempting to procure black-market supplies for friends. A search of the flat had revealed no trace of Brossolette's and Yeo-Thomas's occupation. 102 Avenue des Ternes could, however, no longer be used as a safe house, as the Germans would be certain to watch it for some time.

On Sunday, 26th September, the news was very much worse: 'Z' and Bingen informed them that the Secretariat had been raided the day before and all the previous four months' courier and incoming and outgoing telegrams, kept in the office contrary to regulations, seized. Lists *en clair* of prominent Resistance supporters, among whose names figured those of M. Jeanneney and M. Farjon, had also been removed by the Gestapo. Nard and other important officers had been arrested. 'Z' himself had been arrested but subsequently released, and Alain had had a narrow escape. In spite of the magnitude of the calamity 'Z' and Bingen appeared unconcerned.

A few days later they learned that Colonel Morinaud had indeed been arrested and had swallowed his cyanide tablet rather than run the risk of weakening under torture. This severe blow had decapitated the Regional Military Officers in the Occupied Zone.

The hunt was on in earnest now and to bamboozle pursuers of their own persons Brossolette and Yeo-Thomas again changed residences: Brossolette went to stay with the Danish physical culture teacher Suni Sandöe, and Yeo-Thomas returned to Jeanne Helbling's flat in Neuilly, where he became M. Tirelli.

It was fortunate that they decided to take matters into their own hands because the W.T. operator to whom Yeo-Thomas had entrusted his signal of 26th September had to go into hiding before he could transmit it; and the message did not arrive in London till 14th October. Demoting on their own authority 'Z' and Bingen, Yeo-Thomas and Brossolette took command and attempted to stop the rot. They called a meeting of Air Operations and Military Officers to settle the differences between the Bureau des Opérations Aériennes and the Resistance Movements. This was successfully held on 6th October, under the chairmanship of Colonel Mangin, the son

64

of the famous general and now Senior Military Officer in the Occupied Zone. From him Brossolette and Yeo-Thomas learned that the Gestapo possessed a full list of the names, including naturally their own, of all agents sent out during the September moon period.

There were at that time 32,000 Gestapo agents concentrated in Paris on the drive against Resistance. Even such a threat failed to impress the nonchalant 'Z' and Bingen. Both they and the new go-between with which Yeo-Thomas had provided them continued to turn up late for rendezvous or to miss them altogether. In the end the inevitable happened and the agent-de-liaison was arrested on account of his own carelessness.

Arrests continued to be made in ever-increasing numbers. The two agents had to take special precautions against being followed. Bingen arrived one day at a rendezvous with no fewer than three men trailing him: Brossolette and Yeo-Thomas drew them after themselves and lost them by each jumping into a different vélo-taxi on the Place St. Augustin. Another sleuth Yeo-Thomas shook off in the métro by getting out at a station and jumping back into the train just before it left; yet another he drew down into the basement of the Printemps departmental store and dodged out of the employees' entrance while the shadow was blocked by a group of shoppers.

There was still much to be done: proper contacts had to be provided between the Regional Military Officers and the Resistance Movements; the morale of both Air Operations Officers and the Military Officers, seriously weakened by dissensions and arrests, had to be strengthened; security had to be tightened up by decentralization; and the organizations in the provinces had to be visited and compelled to obey the directives received from London.

To carry out even the preliminary arrangements for such a scheme meant making and keeping appointments at a time when rendezvous were particularly dangerous. The courageous José, Maud, Denise, Jacqueline and Claire were used to maintain contacts with the many agents whom Brossolette and Yeo-Thomas were then directing. And even they were not enough. Through José Dupuis they recruited three young men recommended by a patriotic priest: Horace, a slim boy of twenty, who became Yeo-Thomas's personal agent-de-liaison; Josseaume, aged 25, who, as 'Agenor', was to perform a similar service for José; and another youngster of 24 who was to be Brossolette's go-between.

While waiting for 'Z' to secure the presence of the Regional Military Officers at a meeting of the Comité Militaire, Yeo-Thomas decided that in view of the heat of the chase it would be prudent to procure a third false identity. Through M. Coquoin of Ceux de la Libération he met the Commissaire de Police of the 17th Arrondissement, who provided him with a genuine identity card and a birth certificate in the name of Gaonach. The advantage of the new card over his two others was that its authenticity could be proved, as it was registered at the Préfecture de Police. But even the owner of a valid identity card must be able to prove that he lived somewhere; and so, through the agency of M. Huret of Molyneux, Yeo-Thomas rented in the name of Gaonach a flat at 33 rue de la Tourelle near the Porte de St. Cloud. It was a spacious and well-furnished apartment, with several means of exit: situated on the first floor, it had a servants' staircase and the windows of a back bedroom gave on to the roof of a shed from which it would be easy to jump into the street behind. As the tenant of the neighbouring flat was a German colonel, personal assistant to General von Stulpnagel, Military Governor of Paris, it was a little like a tart trying to acquire an appearance of respectability by living next door to the Archbishop of Canterbury. When he had stored ammunition, revolvers, grenades and food in this new retreat, Yeo-Thomas explained to the concierge that he would not be taking up residence immediately as he was an engineer by profession and travelled a great deal. He also prepared her for the visit of his friend M. Boutet, a bombed-out refugee from Nantes.

He was soon to be glad of his acquisition, for proofs of the Gestapo's vigilance increased. One morning, opening the shutters of his bedroom in Jeanne Helbling's flat in Neuilly, he noticed somebody peeping through a discreetly drawn curtain in a window of the house opposite. The next morning the watcher was still at his post and a man in a greenish beige raincoat was loitering industriously at the corner of the street. Much as he disliked leaving Jeanne Helbling alone when danger was threatening, Tommy had no option but to step out of the house immediately by the back door. At dinner that evening in Les Mousquetaires in the Avenue Malakoff his hostess told him that the man with the raincoat had remained at the corner of the street most of the morning and then had vanished. There had been no signs of any other watchers since.

Brossolette, too, felt that it was safer to keep on moving, and changed from Suni Sandöe's flat in the rue Claude Chahu to Claire Davinroy's flat in the rue de la Faisanderie. He stayed there a couple of days and then Yeo-Thomas and he, feeling that the net was drawing closer and anxious not to get their friends into trouble, moved to the new flat in the rue de la Tourelle. A few days later Claire failed to keep an evening appointment with Yeo-Thomas at the Etoile. Disturbed, because Claire was always punctual, Yeo-Thomas went and telephoned her flat from a small café to which it would not matter if the call were traced. *'Bonsoir, chère amie,'* he said. An obviously disguised woman's voice replied: *'Bonsoir, chéri. Viens tout de suite. Je t'attends.'* *'Oui,'* Tommy answered and hung up. It was clear that Claire had been arrested and that the Gestapo was waiting in her flat to trap any of her friends who might call upon her.

Brossolette, who had known Claire since childhood, was deeply distressed when he heard the news. Through a friend of his, Madame Marcelle Virolle, they soon obtained the details. An agent, whose code name was Gulliver, had recently been arrested. From the concierge of the house in which he lived the Gestapo had learned that his flat had been obtained for him by a Madame Claire Davinroy who lived in the rue de la Faisanderie. At six o'clock they had raided Claire's flat: in addition to 125,000 francs stored there by Yeo-Thomas, incriminating documents had been found on her desk and she had been arrested. All that day a Gestapo man in plain clothes had walked her little white dog up and down the street in the hope that it would show pleasure if any of her friends approached.

The danger didn't end with their escape from it at poor Claire's expense. As a result of Gulliver's arrest almost his whole circuit was rounded up; and one night the documents at the 'Centrale', where signals were encoded and decoded, were seized. Confident that all the guilty were already in prison, the Gestapo left the papers unguarded overnight, intending to collect them the next day. One of the circuit's agents-de-liaison, however, a woman called Berthe, had not been caught: learning of the raid, she removed the documents, with the complicity of the concierge, hid them in a safe house in the rue Jasmin and informed Brossolette and Yeo-Thomas that she had done so. When Pericles, Gulliver's assistant and Marcelle Virolle's brother, returned from London, they told him what had happened and forced him to go into hiding, as they had heard that the Gestapo was searching for him and possessed his description. Pericles then informed them that among the papers now concealed in the rue Jasmin were details of the as yet unused German VI emplacements, and Yeo-Thomas said that he would go and get them. Having obtained the key of the flat from Berthe, he discovered that the house was already being watched by the Gestapo. He consulted the telephone directory and ascertained that a doctor lived at the same address. Accompanied by two of Pericles' friends he went to the house after dark, intending to tell anyone who tried to stop him that he was ill and going for medical advice. Luckily, however, there was nobody watching the house when they arrived and they were able to transfer the two suitcases containing the documents to another safe house in the same street. There they destroyed the unimportant papers and transported by métro those dealing with the new secret weapon to Pericles in his flat on the Boulevard Montparnasse.

This, of course, was only a sideshow; their real business was to put French Resistance on a sound footing again. At last, after a month of dangers, depressions and excitements, a meeting of the Comité Militaire was held on 27th October. Colonel Touny (Organisation Civile et Militaire) presided; also present were 'Z', M. Coquoin (Ceux de la Libération), Colonel Aymon (Libération), Joseph (Franc-Tireurs et Partisans) accompanied by another delegate to represent the umbrella Front National, and Maître Arighi (Ceux de la Résistance). Colonel Morinaud having been arrested, there was nobody except Bouloche, Paris Regional Military Officer, to represent the Regional Military Officers. Pichard, chief Air Operations Officer, had been brought in to voice the complaints of the Bureau des Opérations Aériennes.

It was a stormy meeting. Both 'Z' and Colonel Touny protested against the new decentralization decree that Regional Military Officers should in future receive their orders direct from London. They claimed that the Comité Militaire was the proper channel for the reception and downwards transmission of such orders. Bouloche maintained that it was his duty to communicate all directives immediately to his subordinates. Coquoin and, rather surprisingly, Joseph agreed, as also did Pierre Kaan, the spectacled and professorial-looking secretary of the Comité. Yeo-Thomas clinched the argument by pointing out that if Colonel Morinaud had been the only man to know London's directives all Resistance in the Occupied Zone would have come to a standstill when he was arrested. In future, he ruled, the Comité Militaire, while it would be kept informed of all that transpired, would not be empowered to pass orders to lower echelons. He also insisted that, in order to prevent a recurrence of the strife which Brossolette and he had just settled, clearly stated details of the functions of the Air Operations Officers should be sent to all regional leaders and departmental heads.

Heartened by Joseph's support, Yeo-Thomas tried to persuade him to go to England for training; Joseph was keen to go but did not think that the Party would allow him. In this conjecture he was right. Joseph, Yeo-Thomas found, always tried to carry out London's instructions, but the complicated construction of the Communist organization made co-operation difficult. Because of the slowness of communications imposed upon the Franc-Tireurs et Partisans by their horizontal hierarchy the greater number of the parachute operations arranged for them failed. Apart from Joseph, almost all their leaders were arrogant and, asserting that most of the victims of the Gestapo were Communists, claimed for their Movement the title 'Le Parti des Fusillés'. While there could be no doubt of their heroism, their martyrology was certainly swelled by the fact that the Germans always described all their opponents as 'Communists'.

Forced to keep on the move, Brossolette and Yeo-Thomas found a new safe house in the Latin Quarter, in the rue de Rennes; and almost immediately they had to vacate it because of their suspicions of Horace, Yeo-Thomas's new agent-de-liaison, who knew the address and brought messages there. Tommy had noticed that Horace was often late for appointments and made flimsy excuses.

To test the boy he sent him on an errand to a house outside Paris which he knew to be empty and of which he also gave Horace the telephone number. Reporting in the evening, Horace said that he had been to the house and, having found nobody there, had made inquiries and arranged to return the next day. Unable to describe the house when asked to do so, he finally admitted that he had never visited it but had telephoned instead and got no reply. Suspecting him of treachery, Yeo-Thomas was going to kill the boy, but, on the intercession of José Dupuis, dismissed him with a warning.

For they could afford to run no unnecessary risks: the Gestapo had their descriptions and the Abwehr counter-espionage was on their tracks. Other agents were being arrested within an hour of having spoken with them. To ensure comparative safety Yeo-Thomas was driven to meet some of his contacts in hospitals, a trick he learned from Joseph. He would pass the contact without recognition at the intersection of two streets, turn and follow him at a distance of fifty yards to the hospital, enter the visitors' gate and talk with him in the grounds. Punctuality at such meetings was, of course, essential, a point not realized by 'Z', who still continued to give trouble and would arrange rendezvous in dangerous places like the Gare St. Lazare.

The morale of Resistance, Yeo-Thomas learned from those he met, was low and from a cause which he at the moment was powerless to remove. Although the Air Operations Officers had now built up a network of 600 grounds, although every month 150 reception committees stood by, possibly only five operations would be attempted in a moon period. As a result of this paltry parachuting the Secret Army was not being equipped and, for want of explosives, important targets were not being sabotaged.

The reason, of course, for the lack of air operations was that the R.A.F. did not think that they could spare the planes. Yeo-Thomas accuses his masters of a lack of imagination. The load of one Halifax bomber dropped to a reception committee and handled by the right men could, he claims, have done more damage to the German war machine than the loads of 250 bombers dropped in a raid. Repeated air bombardments had failed seriously to hinder the work of a ball-bearing factory at Annecy; three saboteurs, with explosives and the complicity of one or two of the workers, so damaged the machinery that the factory never produced another ball bearing during the rest of the occupation.

The story of the 'Barrage de Gigny' even more properly illustrates his contention. At the time of the Allied invasion of Italy the Germans used the Saône to transport submarines in sections, motor torpedo-boats, artillery, tanks and ammunition, thus keeping the railways free for troop movements. Many heavy and accurate air raids would have been required to arrest this traffic; with floating mines dropped in containers and assembled afterwards a small group of Resistance men blew up the locks at Gigny and blocked this waterway for many months.

The harm done to Resistance morale by this lack of supplies was perhaps greater than that not done to the Germans. The saboteurs knew that the scientific department of S.O.E. was producing time bombs with magnets which could be clamped on to the hulls of ships, explosive coal which could be introduced into German stocks and altimeter switches which, when inserted into aircraft, blew off the tail when the plane reached a certain height. They knew also that the reason they were not receiving sufficient quantities of such instruments was because all available British bombers were being concentrated on massive and often unsuccessful raids. The amount of arms that was being dropped in a month could equip only a hundred men of the Secret Army. It was small wonder that Brossolette and Yeo-Thomas found it difficult to convince Resistance leaders that their efforts were being appreciated in London.

This scarcity of arms was serious because lately the potential of the Secret Army had been increased by a new factor: the Maquis, to which all who desired to avoid compulsory labour in Germany were forced to resort. Of this vast and new body Brault was the national chief. Known to Resistance as 'Jerôme', he flitted about the country like a will-o'-the-wisp, organizing all Maquis which were not specifically Communist.

Brossolette and Yeo-Thomas met Jerôme at a safe house in the Avenue Rapp. What he told them convinced Yeo-Thomas more than ever that here was the material for an effective fighting force. But once again he learned that the men lacked arms, equipment, clothing and cash. In order that he might accurately compute their wants he arranged to meet Jerôme at Cahors on 2nd November and accompany him on his inspection of the groups in that area.

But before he left Paris he had another narrow escape. Arriving early for a mid-day meeting with an agent in a flat on the Boulevard Péreire, he had time to investigate the district before keeping his appointment. A couple of blocks from the safe house he saw a Citroën with German police marks drawn up in a side street. From his seat at the wheel the driver, who was in the car, could observe the house to which Tommy was going. Passing in front of the café which formed the ground floor, Yeo-Thomas entered the house, climbed the stairs and listened at the door of the flat in which he had his rendezvous. Suspicious because of the silence, he returned to the street and crossed the railway. At ten minutes to twelve he came back and, as the car was still in the side street, went into the café and ordered a drink. At twelve o'clock exactly the car drew up in front of the house and four men in civilian clothes got out. Almost immediately the concierge was bundled into the car, which drove off again, leaving behind three men who disappeared into the house. Paying for his drink, Yeo-Thomas left the café and, on his way to cross the railway, passed the car as it came towards him to take up its former position in the side street. It was obvious that the flat had been blown and that the three men who entered the house were waiting in the flat to arrest him when he kept his appointment. Shocked by this very close shave and by the thought of what his arrested contact must then be suffering, he began to think that it was a good thing that he was leaving Paris for a short time.

On 2nd November he took care to see that he was not trailed when he went to catch the train. Nor did he take any chances when he arrived at Cahors in the small hours of the next morning: instead of leaving the platform by the official exit he dropped on to the track, walked in the shadow of a stationary goods train and got out of the station without giving up his ticket. His precaution was probably wise: Jerôme, who was waiting for him in the darkness with a car, informed him that Sicherheitsdienst officials had been waiting at the exit from the platform and closely scrutinizing all arrivals.

Over a meal Jerôme told him more about the Maquis: his groups in the Occupied Zone contained 6,000 men, he said, and those in the Unoccupied Zone 12,000. And, because quality was more important than quantity, *ne devenait pas maquisard qui voulait*: before being admitted to the Maquis proper, candidates spent from four to six weeks in holding camps, where they were screened and tested.

That day, accompanied by Jerôme, Yeo-Thomas inspected two camps in the Département of the Lot. The first was reached shortly after dawn. At the approach to the camp their car was met by the officer in charge, a wiry young man wearing a leather cap, a corduroy jacket and breeches and carrying a Sten gun. Stopping in a rutty lane, they got out and made their way across rough ground, through bushes, trees and rocks. Twice challenged by outposts, they arrived on a high plateau to find twenty-five variously clad and accoutred men standing to attention while the tricolour, with the revolutionary Croix de Lorraine superimposed upon its now conformist red, white and blue, was hoisted slowly into the cold morning air. The orders for this moving little ceremony were rapped out in military style and executed with promptitude and precision.

The thirty men in the camp were disciplined, well fed and happy. Divided into groups of five, each commanded by an N.C.O. ('Sixaines'), all the armament they possessed between them consisted of one Sten gun with a hundred rounds, three French rifles with five rounds each and ten revolvers with ten rounds each: there were no grenades at all. The available arms were used by all in turn for instructional purposes, drill, weapon-stripping and field-craft exercises by night. Lack of ammunition prevented target practice. The 'Q' side was well handled and accurate accounts were kept. Food was purchased from sympathizers in the surrounding villages. Although small *coups de main* were permitted against collaborators, looting was forbidden and severely punished. All were eager, but complained of their puny armoury.

In the afternoon they visited a similar group of thirty men whose sole armament consisted of one rifle and ten rounds of ammunition. Many of the men in this group were; ex-soldiers of the Infanterie Coloniale and were wearing their old uniforms. Such were particularly chagrined by the knowledge that if they were attacked they could defend themselves only by flight to another district.

Returning to Cahors, Jerôme and Yeo-Thomas caught the night train to Lyons. As Jerôme had pressing business elsewhere, he delegated to a friend the duty of driving Tommy in a motor van to a country shop near Poncin in the Département of the Ain, where he was introduced to two members of the neighbouring Maquis as 'le commandant anglais Shelley'. This Maquis was also, he found, situated in an almost inaccessible position among trees and boulders. It could be approached only by two narrow, steep and slippery paths, both guarded by outposts in telephonic communication with the headquarters hut. The camp consisted of sixty men living in five huts, camouflaged so as to be invisible from the air. An ex-regular army officer was in command. The armaments, although inadequate, were more ample than those of the camps in the Lot: ten Sten guns with a hundred rounds each, twenty rifles with twenty-five rounds each and a few grenades. There was also a resident doctor with medical supplies. Recently the men of this camp had successfully raided the larder of the Vichy quartermaster-general's stores at Bourg and felt strong enough to resist reprisals threatened by the police of the Groupe Mobile de Réserve. In combination with some 400 men in a neighbouring Maquis they were planning an operation against the armaments factory at Le Creusot.

Yeo-Thomas left this camp more than ever convinced that these mobile, spartan and well-trained bodies of men could, properly armed, render valuable assistance to the Allies on 'D' day. Already the news of the presence of a British officer had gone round the district, and on the way into Bourg the driver of the van told him that the members of other neighbouring Maquis had requested the honour of his visit. Tommy had, however, more pressing work to do in Paris, and on his arrival at Bourg at half-past eight he went straight to the station.

As the train for Paris did not leave till half-past eleven he had three hours to wait on the draughty platform: he judged it imprudent to go to a restaurant in the town because there was a strong Gestapo detachment in Bourg. Tired and sleepy, he sat on a crate and leaned against the wall. Soon there were so many people on the platform that it seemed impossible that each of them could have a personal destiny. Apart from some boys from a Vichy Youth camp, most of them were middle-aged men and women with hard-hating, mean, acquisitive looks on their shiny, brainless faces. Alert only in their misinterpretation of the world, purposeful in their essential purposelessness, clutching their umbrellas and their black-market purchases, they looked like figures on a canvas by Breughel: all God's children without wings. The warmth from their crowded bodies began to ooze in a damp mist along the platform and the smell of their stale sweat and dirty feet soon made it seem like summer.

At half-past ten it was announced that saboteurs had wrecked the line and that the Paris train had been withdrawn, but still the people continued to wait. Perturbed by the delay and cut off from his friends of the Maquis, Yeo-Thomas went to make inquiries of the station-master, to whom he justified his anxiety by saying that his wife was dying in Paris. The station-master told him that if the repair gang finished their work on the line promptly there might be an early morning train which would get him into Lyons in time to catch the nine-o'clock train to Paris. Promising not to arouse possibly vain hopes by communicating this information to the other travellers, Yeo-Thomas went and dozed standing up in the waiting-room, as his crate had already been annexed.

Hours later, but while it was still dark, an obsolete and rusty engine pulled alongside the platform a clattering assortment of archaic carriages. Each carriage was painted a different shade of green, which made the train look like a badly-darned stocking. The seats were all wooden and most of the windows were broken. Too cold to sleep, Yeo-Thomas curled up in a corner after taking a swig of Mirabelle from his flask. At half-past six the train started with a jerk. The engine puffed, grunted, wheezed, whistled and roared; the carriages bumped as though rolling on square wheels; slowly, lumpily they trundled through the empty early morning world towards Lyons, which they reached at half-past eight.

At Lyons, after swallowing two cups of acorn coffee, Tommy bought a first-class ticket for Paris: in this way he could travel in any class dictated by convenience and the requirements of safety. Aware that his description had been circulated to the Lyons Gestapo, whose particularly pitiless chief had already been pointed out to him by Jerôme, he kept a sharp look-out. Although there were two German Feldgendarmes standing near the ticket inspector, he approached them without great apprehension, knowing that their stupidity had earned them the nickname *têtes de veau primées*.

75

The two policemen barely gave him a glance. Reassured he made his way along the dismal, dingy platform. After all, he argued, even if he had been trailed from Paris to Cahors and thence to Lyons, the motor van in which he had travelled the previous day had not been followed and the Gestapo could not know where he was.

It was perhaps this confidence coupled with the weariness resulting from three sleepless nights which prompted his next act of temerity. Except for the first-class compartment reserved and labelled '*Nur für Wehrmachtsangehörige*', the train was packed, and he was unable to find a seat. In the reserved first-class carriage only one compartment was occupied, by a somnolent German general and one of his staff. Too tired to contemplate standing, Tommy climbed into the neighbouring carriage, passed through the narrow connecting passage into the reserved carriage and entered an empty compartment. Closing the door and pulling down the blinds, he stretched himself out on the seat and fell fast asleep.

Twenty minutes later, when the train was running through the lovely green countryside, he awoke to find a German railway policeman standing over him and shaking his shoulder. Tall and fair, with close-cropped hair and a long pointed nose, the policeman wore a black uniform with silver piping on the tunic and the usual eagle and swastika on his sleeve.

'*Afez fous la bermission de foyager dans la foiture réservée bour la Wehrmacht?*' [1] he asked in heavy, cold-in-the-head German French.

'It's the first I've heard of it being the carriage reserved for the German army,' Yeo-Thomas said.

'*Fous n'afez bas foo la blaque qui est dehors sur le côté de la foiture?*' [2] the policeman asked severely.

Yeo-Thomas looked at him with feigned surprise succeeded by apparently dawning comprehension.

'No, Monsieur, and now I'm beginning to understand how I didn't see the notice. You see, I got into a carriage and worked my way here along the corridors. I'm sorry, but that's how it happened.'

'*Montrez-moi fos biéces d'identité.*' [3]

---

[1] 'Have you permission to travel in the carriage reserved for the Wehrmacht?'
[2] 'You didn't see the notice on the outside of the carriage?'
[3] 'Show your identity papers.'

Tommy was travelling under the name of Gaonach, and carried his identity card behind a celluloid window in a special wallet; facing it, and behind another celluloid window, was a photograph of a naked girl, specially placed there to distract the inquisitive.

'You see, Monsieur,' he said, handing the policeman the case, 'I am an engineer and I work for the German Todt Organization.'

But the policeman was no longer interested in M. Gaonach, Ingénieur. Breathing steamily, the whites of his eyes swelling out to the size and appearance of shelled eggs, he stood gazing glassily at the bare beauty.

'You see, I am an engineer and I work for the Todt Organization,' Yeo-Thomas repeated.

'*Oui, j'ai foo,*' [1] the policeman said, still goggling clammily at the wrong photograph.

'I've been inspecting some work for the Todt Organization around Lyons,' Yeo-Thomas went on. 'I was sent specially from Paris, but I've been held up everywhere by this infernal sabotage. I tell you, Monsieur, I'd like to get my hands on those bad Frenchmen who don't seem to realize that Germany is their best friend.'

It was laid on a bit thickly, perhaps, but the policeman had been too wrapped up in the photograph to notice.

'That is a very nice case indeed,' he said, reluctantly returning the wallet.

'As I say, I'm very tired,' Yeo-Thomas said. 'For three nights I haven't slept.' He handed the policeman a cigarette and lighted it for him. 'I tell you, Monsieur, I'd like to get my hands on those rascals of saboteurs.'

The policeman, still with a reminiscent look in his eye, agreed that it was a pity that so many Frenchmen should be misguided; then he came back to the matter in hand, but this time his tone was friendly.

'*Fous ne boufeʒ bas rester ici,*' [2] he said. 'If the General saw you I'd get a reprimand. But wait here for a few minutes while I see what I can do for you.'

Before long the policeman was back again. He told Tommy that a few carriages further up the train he had found a man travelling

[1] 'Yes, I've seen.'
[2] 'You can't stay here.'

first-class with a second-class ticket and had turfed him out; he had ordered the other occupants of the compartment to see that nobody took the vacant seat, as he was going to bring along a loyal Frenchman who worked for the Todt Organization.

'*C'est barceque fous êtes un ami de l'Allemagne que j'ai fait cela bour fous*,'[1] he said.

'*Monsieur, vous savez que je suis de coeur avec vous*,'[2] Yeo-Thomas said.

Although his new travelling companions didn't welcome the friend of Germany the policeman had declared him to be, Tommy was too tired to care and fell asleep immediately. He lunched in the restaurant car at the same table as three young Frenchmen who told him that as the line had been sabotaged between Dijon and Lyons the train was making a detour. They also said that he might be surprised to learn that arms and explosives were constantly being parachuted into France. Yeo-Thomas replied that he did not believe them, as it was impossible for such operations to take place under the watchful eyes of the Germans. He was surprised to discover that his companions had a very good idea how these droppings were carried out. After lunch he went back to his compartment and dozed while his fellow passengers continued to regard him with disapproval.

Late in the afternoon, returning to the restaurant car for tea, he was informed by the attendant that there was no more room. Protesting that he was hungry and thirsty, Yeo-Thomas tipped the man and asked him to take another look. The attendant walked away down the car, turned and beckoned to Tommy, indicating the only vacant seat. Approaching, Yeo-Thomas was horrified to see that the man opposite whom he was to sit was the ill-famed chief of the Lyons Gestapo, who had already been pointed out to him by Jerôme. He knew that the official had heard of him and suspected that he might even have seen his photograph. But to retreat, especially after having insisted on being found a seat, would have aroused suspicion, and he had no option but to sit down at the same table as this highly dangerous person. Pretending to be gazing out of the window, he covertly observed his new neighbour: a duelling

[1] 'It is because you are a friend of Germany that I am doing this for you.'
[2] 'Sir, you know that I am with you entirely.'

78

scar ran down one side of his hard, clean-shaven face; through gold-rimmed spectacles two steely blue eyes were quite openly fixed upon himself with icy hostility. Yeo-Thomas says that he felt 'as though a gimlet were being screwed into his head'. He was glad when the waiter brought the bread, ersatz jam and tea so that he could avoid the man's gaze by looking down at his plate. Then, to his dismay, the Gestapo chief began to talk to him in a slow, precise French.

'*Vous venez de loin, Monsieur?*'

'I've come from Lyons, Monsieur,' Yeo-Thomas answered, terrified. Was the man suspicious? he wondered. Had he identified Shelley? Or, recognizing a familiar face, was he trying to place him? He knew that it would be no use telling such a perspicacious official any lies about M. Gaonach, Ingénieur, working for the Todt Organization; nor would the photograph of the naked girl be likely to beguile so seasoned an inquisitor. At that moment the train passed some overturned carriages and trucks, clearly visible from the window. 'Seems to have been a bit of trouble here,' Tommy said, seeking safety in an obviously dangerous topic.

'These unfortunate events are always happening.' The tone was cold, the eyes colder.

'I am surprised, Monsieur, that the German army has not yet found an effective means of dealing with such acts.'

'Sabotage is like the black market,' the Gestapo man said. 'It has so many heads that we cannot strike them all off at once. But rest assured that the German Army will master both these evils in the end.'

They continued to talk together. When they had paid their bills Yeo-Thomas forced himself to wait until the Gestapo official had risen and left the table with a curt '*Auf Wiedersehen*'. Following him closely, Tommy discovered that he was travelling in the same carriage as himself.

Still afraid that the German might have identified him, he spent the next two hours standing up in the corridor, determined to leap out on to the track if a move were made to arrest him. To allay suspicion he returned to the restaurant car for dinner, although he was careful not to choose the same service as the Gestapo official. When the train reached the Gare de Lyon at half-past eleven he got out on the wrong side of the carriage, left the station unobserved and took a vélo-taxi to the rue de Chevreuse. From there he walked to the rue Leverrier, where he spent the night in Jacqueline Devaux's flat.

Next morning he met Brossolette, who informed him that there had been more arrests during his absence. Pichard had had a number of narrow escapes; and Marcelle Virolle and Pichard's sister had become so compromised that they would require to be exfiltrated to England. For the next few days Yeo-Thomas took up the old round of meeting contacts and shaking off sleuths. At night he forgot his peril by listening to such programmes as Itma, in which some deliberately complicated intellectuals found the unfriendly fog of the neo-impressionists. But it did for the soldier in 1939–1945 what Bruce Bairnsfather did for his father in 1914–1918. Among the B.B.C. messages there was also a *tendresse* from Barbara, sent '*du moineau au lapin*', 'from the sparrow to the rabbit'.

Among those recently arrested had been poor Roland Farjeon, leader of the Organisation Civile et Militaire in the north of France. About to visit this region and replace the lost chief by Deshayes and another agent called Piquier, Yeo-Thomas learned with surprise that he had been called back to London.

Both Brossolette and Yeo-Thomas were depressed by this news. During the eight weeks that they had been together they had succeeded in tightening up French Resistance: they had settled the differences between the Regional Military Officers and the Air Operations Officers and acquired great influence over both; they had inspired and earned the respect of the various Resistance Leaders. This was not astonishing: Brossolette was a very distinguished, able and courageous man; and Yeo-Thomas's prestige as a British officer was enhanced by his bravery and by his love and understanding of France. Their presence was sufficient to assure the heads of Resistance that the difficulties and needs of their Groups were known and would be passed on to Headquarters. They decided, therefore, that one of them must always remain in France: as soon as Yeo-Thomas had made his report in London he would return and relieve Brossolette.

On 10th November word came through that Tommy would be picked up by Lysander in the neighbourhood of Arras. With a heavy heart he said good-bye to Brossolette and went to the Gare du Nord carrying two suitcases: in one were his clothes and in the other, under a layer of packets of cigarettes and slabs of chocolate, the documents dealing with the new German secret weapon which had been salvaged from the Gulliver disaster. Marcelle Virolle and Pichard's sister, who were to be exfiltrated by the same operation, accompanied him; all three travelled in separate compartments and the journey was without incident. At Arras they met outside the station and went in search of the corset shop in the rue Saint Auber where they would be put in touch with the local Resistance authorities: upon Tommy's asking for an outsize brassière he was to be invited to pass into the back-shop, where he would hand over one half of a bisected hundred-franc note of which the tradeswoman already held the other. Unfortunately, he went first to the wrong shop, from which the lady in charge, anxious to do good business by selling a super *soutien-gorge*, allowed him to escape with difficulty. However, the next shop he tried proved to be the right one and from there they were passed on to a perfumery, owned by a Madame Fraser, a Frenchwoman who had married a Scot. After having dined with this cheerful and intrepid lady, Yeo-Thomas passed the night with a gentlemen's outfitter called M. Doutreme-puich who, understandably, preferred to do business under the name of 'Marcel'.

Next morning Deshayes, who was in charge of the air operations in the district, arrived to say that a message had come over the B.B.C. postponing the Lysander pick-up on account of bad weather. Accordingly Yeo-Thomas filled in the time by visiting, in the company of Deshayes's ruddy-faced assistant Thierry,[1] the local Resistance groups. At Amiens he found the men divided up into units of five, each headed by an N.C.O., with no lateral communications with other sixaines and receiving all communications vertically from their leader. (In spite of this security measure forty-eight men of this group were arrested the day after his visit.) He also inspected other groups around Lille and noted their requirements.

On 12th November he learned that the pick-up might be transferred to Tours. There was also more disturbing news: an agent-de-liaison came to inform him that a number of arrests had taken

[1] Not to be confused with Yeo-Thomas's cover name.

place in Paris and that among those rounded up had been a contact with whom Brossolette had an appointment for the next day. Unable to ascertain whether Brossolette had been warned or not, Yeo-Thomas decided to go to Paris and make sure: in view of the possibility of the Lysander operation being transferred to Tours he had to take his luggage with him.

On arriving at the station he remembered that on the inward journey from Arras to Paris the baggage of all passengers was ordinarily searched by the military authorities: he could not afford to take such a risk carrying a suitcaseful of documents relating to Vergeltungswaffen (V1s and V2s) and their emplacements. Then, just as he was about to turn tail, he caught sight of two German Luftwaffe officers walking along the platform towards the train: following them was an orderly pushing a barrow stacked with a mountain of valises and trunks. Tagging along on the outskirts, Yeo-Thomas watched the orderly load the officers' luggage into the carriage and saw, as he had expected, that there was no room in the compartment for so much baggage: a great deal of it had to be piled up at the end of the corridor, where the orderly, who was accompanying his masters, mounted guard over it. Yeo-Thomas got into the same carriage and sat down on his own suitcases in the corridor beside the German soldier. As soon as the train started he lighted a cigarette and then, as though by afterthought, offered one to the orderly, who accepted.

'*Danke schön,*' said the orderly.

Tommy gave him a light.

'You are very kind,' the orderly said in bad French.

'It is always agreeable to share with someone pleasant,' Yeo-Thomas said.

The chief tragedy of the 1914–1918 war consisted, as a cynic not inaccurately remarked, in the number of people who weren't killed in it; and, when you look round the lounge of any fashionable hotel, you'll see that that goes for the 1939–1945 war as well. The smooth, deceitful men who have misinterpreted history and made the muddles are rarely required to go down into the arena and throw and receive the javelins. Because Yeo-Thomas was no more responsible for the pre-war ineptitudes of democracy than the Bavarian orderly for the threats and thefts of National Socialism they were soon conversing amiably. Although Tommy's kindliness was inspired by a very practical purpose it was difficult for him not to like the ordinary, stupid, bewildered, guiltless, decent little German soldier when he pulled out photographs of his fair-haired children and of his humble, badly dressed, pudding-faced wife, who certainly didn't know the difference between oligarchy and parliamentarianism.

'I've got children too,' Tommy said.

'War is bad for children,' the orderly said. '*Auch für Soldaten.* For soldiers too, war is bad.'

'War is bad for everybody,' Yeo-Thomas said.

'*Ganz richtig,*' the orderly said. 'You are right.'

Tommy took out his flask of Mirabelle.

'We must drink to the health of our families,' he said, raising the flask to his lips. When he had pretended to take a deep draught, he wiped the top of the flask with his sleeve and handed it to the soldier.

The orderly took a good pull. He accepted another cigarette. For a little they puffed away together in silence. Then Yeo-Thomas rose, ostentatiously opened the suitcase containing the secret documents, took out a slab of chocolate and handed it to the soldier.

'*Für Kinder,*' he said in his best German. 'For your children.'

Chocolate was scarce in Germany, even for the troops, and the German was overwhelmed. Putting his arms round Tommy's shoulders he gazed at him tenderly with eyes full of tears which were not entirely Mirabelle.

'*Vielen Danke,*' he said. '*Mille mercis.* I think that you are a good man.'

'On the contrary, I am a bad man,' Tommy said. 'Listen, I am in trouble.'

'Good men as well as bad men can be in trouble.' The German's broken French made him seem more than ever like an overgrown child, symbolic of humanity's frightful uncomprehending misery; but Yeo-Thomas had to go on lying to him if he was to achieve his very necessary purpose.

'You see, it is difficult for a Frenchman to make a living these days,' he said. 'To provide for my wife and children, I am forced to do things which I do not like: black market, in other words. In

83

this suitcase here I have cigarettes and chocolates which I am taking to sell in Paris. I don't like doing this sort of thing, but, as I say, I've got responsibilities. And if the police and the customs search my case the goods will be confiscated. And what's even worse I'll be arrested and my family will starve.' Out came the flask again; and, after taking another fake swig, he handed it to the German, who emptied it. 'You do see that I am in difficulties, don't you?' He gave the German another cigarette and then a whole packet.

'*Vielleicht ist es nicht so schwer,*' the orderly said with a large alcoholic grin. Lifting up a couple of his officers' valises he signed to Yeo-Thomas to slip the suitcase from which the chocolate had been extracted in beneath them. 'Now I do not think that the police will say much to you.'

And when the police and the customs authorities arrived a few minutes later they did not have much to say to Yeo-Thomas, although they went through all his pockets and examined his papers carefully: his second suitcase, containing only his clothes, was found to be in order. As he had foreseen, the German officers' luggage was not examined.

The rest of the journey he passed in happy companionship with the now befuddled orderly. When they reached the Gare du Nord the soldier returned the suitcase containing the documents to Yeo-Thomas, who helped him to unload the officers' baggage. To avoid too close scrutiny by the Gestapo men, who, like the hotel porters in the old Caledonian Railway advertisements, met all arrivals, Tommy accompanied the orderly to the exit, where the two friends parted after loud expressions of mutual goodwill.

Taking a vélo-taxi to the rue Claude Chahu, Yeo-Thomas found that his journey had not been in vain: Brossolette was in Suni Sandöe's flat, and, unaware of the arrest of his contact, would probably have stepped into a Gestapo trap the next day. They talked for a little together and, listening-in to the B.B.C., Tommy learned from a cryptic message that his operation had been retransferred to the Arras area. Having again promised to come out and relieve Brossolette in two months' time, Tommy left before curfew and went to spend the night in Jeanne Helbling's flat in Neuilly.

The following morning he arranged for José Dupuis to help another circuit during his absence and for Maud to act as Brossolette's agent-de-liaison. At one o'clock he left again for Arras and was seen off by Jeanne Helbling. During the journey he looked out of the train window with sadistic pleasure at the evidences of successful sabotage: four ammunition trains had been derailed during the previous few days and the tracks were littered with damaged carriages and trucks, overturned guns, light tanks and lorries. Beneath the leaden November purgatorial sky gangs of German soldiers and French civilians were clearing up the wreckage.

Arriving in Arras in the late afternoon he again saw Thierry, who gave him a list of the pressing needs of the local groups: among the grisly paraphernalia paradoxically required for the preparation of peace were automatics for sector officers, silent pistols, daggers, grenades, rifles and ammunition; benzedrine tablets, woollens, windjackets, torches, batteries, food and money were also wanted. A chance meeting with Piquier, Regional Military Officer for the north of France, confirmed the urgency of giving Resistance the tools without which it could not accomplish its task. Once again Yeo-Thomas realized that it was essential that the authorities in London should satisfy the requirements of the heroic men who were risking most painful forms of death in order to liberate their country.

The rest of the time he spent with Madame Fraser and M. Doutremepuich waiting to learn the date of his exfiltration. As before, he was nervous, aware of the danger and consequences of a last-minute slip. His fears were increased when Deshayes informed him that the whole area was cordoned off and that German patrols, especially interested in the contents of suitcases, searched all whom they met on the roads after dark. M. Bisiaux, the local undertaker, had, however, found a rather macabre solution to the problem: Marcelle Virolle, Mademoiselle Pichard and Yeo-Thomas were to be driven to the landing ground shut up inside a motor hearse; apparently it was normal to transport a corpse at night for a funeral the next day.

On Monday, 15th November, a telegram was received to say that the operation would take place that night at a ground called Charente, some twenty miles distant. Tommy's luggage, which now included the presents of a Rolls razor from Madame Fraser and a black tie to wear when he should return to France in R.A.F.

uniform from M. Doutremepuich, was sent to be stored in the hearse. In the evening the operation was, according to custom, confirmed by two B.B.C. messages. About eight o'clock, after a drink of champagne, the two girls left for the hearse, which had been parked in a dark back street; Yeo-Thomas followed a little later, with his Colt in readiness in his shoulder holster. A sharp wind blew through the narrow cobbled alleys: the weather was bitterly cold, the sky was overcast and the moon did not shine through the clouds. It began to look doubtful that the operation could succeed in such conditions.

Inside the hearse Yeo-Thomas was handed a Sten gun and a couple of grenades. Then the back was shut and they were in darkness. As the girls' teeth were soon chattering with cold Tommy gave them some brandy from his flask. Unlike a coffin the three passengers could not be clamped down and as soon as the hearse began to move they were thrown from side to side. The bumpy road jolted the Sten gun against Yeo-Thomas's thighs and bruised them. Boxed up in blackness they lurched uncomfortably across a timeless and invisible world. Then terror struck them all as the hearse stopped abruptly and they heard the heavy tread of Feldgendarmerie patrol-men's feet. There was the sound of throaty German questions, of quick Gallic replies, of more questions. Then there was silence. Gripping his Sten gun, Tommy watched the blackness where the door was, prepared to shoot should the soldiers attempt to search the hearse. The big boots trudged away and the hearse moved on again.

A little later there was another stop, but this time the questions were asked in a muffled voice and the man who had asked them jumped up in the cab beside the driver. They were now under the protection of Resistance men who were patrolling the road for the last five miles. Soon the hearse stopped again, the back was thrown open and, cramped and stiff, the two girls and Tommy climbed down into a farmyard. Entering the house they were greeted by the farmer's wife, who had prepared for them a meal of vegetable soup, steak, fried potatoes, cheese and fruit, with wine, coffee and brandy. Half a dozen sturdy armed peasants watched them with interest while they ate: realizing that this was the first time that these men had seen a British agent, Yeo-Thomas spoke to each man individually and at length and thanked him for the risks he was running on their behalf.

The operation about to be undertaken was even more hazardous than Tommy had imagined. In a private conversation Alex, the hatchet-faced leader, explained to him that the Germans in the district were particularly vigilant. Twenty armed men had, therefore, been placed round the farm in such a way that nobody could come within 500 yards of it without being observed. Ten of those men would withdraw and cover Yeo-Thomas and the girls when they left for the airfield. Around the landing ground itself there were ten more men concealed in bushes and another six men were patrolling the approaches. If the passengers were caught it would be only after Alex and his helpers had been killed. Alex went on to apologize for the French defeat in 1940 and promised that Resistance members would do their utmost to be worthy of their liberation. He ended on a formal sentence of respect: '*Mon Commandant, c'est un grand honneur pour nous tous d'assurer la protection d'un officier anglais, surtout d'un anglais si grand ami de notre pays.*' [1] To show his gratitude for this touching little speech Yeo-Thomas gave Alex his platinum cuff links as a souvenir.

But too much remained to be done to spend the rest of the night in protestations of fidelity. Deshayes came in and said that he had checked the direction of the wind and driven into the ground the stakes marking the places for the men to stand with lighted torches. The peasants filed out carrying their rifles at the trail. About midnight Alex and Deshayes led Tommy and the girls to the airfield.

It was pitch black outside and icy cold. The earth was frozen and crunched under their steps. They passed through a gate and, as they were traversing a field, a man with a Sten gun at the ready emerged from a hedge, spoke a few words with Alex and stepped back into the shadow. They passed through another gate, crossed a ditch and, after being silently challenged several more times, reached the landing ground.

While Alex went to inspect his men Yeo-Thomas and the girls waited in the darkness. The sky was still cloudy and the moon was not shining. The cold wind swirled around them, numbing their

---

[1] 'Commandant, it is a great honour for us to be able to protect an English officer, especially an Englishman who is such a good friend of our country.'

feet and their hands and making a moaning, whistling noise in the eerie silence of the night. Five miles away at most were German troops. Might they not be much nearer, creeping on their bellies through the black fields? But even in his discomfort and anxiety Tommy was able to realize the much more terrible dangers to which their helpers were exposed: even if he and the girls got away, Alex, Deshayes, the farmer and his wife and the others might still be tortured and shot if any trace of the operation were discovered. Once again he determined to do all that he could to help such brave people.

Imperceptibly almost the sky began to clear; the moon shone through the clouds, lighting them and making them look like a silver shawl. As the earth detached itself from the sky the landing ground became visible and Yeo-Thomas was able to distinguish their luggage heaped up in readiness for loading into the plane. As the light increased a faint buzzing was heard, and soon the Lysander could be seen above them, gleaming like a moth caught in the head-lamps of a car. The recognition signals were flashed; the torches were lighted; the aircraft circled and came to a standstill within twelve yards of where Tommy and the two girls lay; the cockpit door was thrown open; two men got out and their luggage was thrown out after them; the customary champagne and perfume were passed in to the pilot; within four minutes the three passengers and their luggage had been picked up and the aircraft was climbing up into the sky again.

It was uncomfortable in the cockpit, with three passengers and fourteen packages or suitcases crammed into a space designed to hold one man and his machine-gun. With a girl on each knee, Yeo-Thomas was unable to reach up and close the cover of the cockpit, which had been inadvertently left open, nor were the girls able to do so. As usual, they ran into flak over the French coast, but they encountered no German fighters; the passage was rough and both girls were sick, but in little more than an hour they were back in England, where Major Johnson was waiting to welcome them at the aerodrome.

Next day Yeo-Thomas was ordered to report at the Air Ministry in Horseferry Road, to give an account of his experiences. Dressed once more in his uniform, he was shown into a room in which an

Air Commodore with a square brick-red unspiritual face sat behind a large desk. Tommy stood to attention and saluted this highly paid officer, who eyed him critically and with disapproval.

'You are improperly dressed,' the Air Commodore said.

Conscious that he had polished highly both his shoes and buttons, Yeo-Thomas glanced down to see if one of the latter was undone.

'I'm sorry, Sir, but I can't see what is wrong.'

'Don't you read your Air Ministry Orders?'

'When I can; yes, Sir.'

'In that case you ought to know that you should no longer be wearing those V.R.s [1] on your lapels; it was in A.M.O.s last month.'

Familiar as he was with the stupidity of officers promoted from their peacetime obscurity to conduct a war they didn't understand, Yeo-Thomas was flabbergasted. Did the braided oaf really imagine that while a man was facing torture and death he had the opportunity of keeping himself informed of the permutations of badges and phylacteries? Too angry to realize what a good story he had to tell to his friends, he answered coldly:

'Last month, Sir, I was in Occupied France and did not receive A.M.O.s.'

But the Air Commodore was dyed in the wool.

'Don't let it happen again,' he said gruffly.

And that wasn't all: a few days later Tommy found in the letter-box of his flat a typewritten envelope placed there by an anonymous neighbour critical of his apparently exclusively administrative war service; the envelope contained a white feather and a sheet of paper on which was printed in capitals: COWARD.

Unlike the unimaginative Air Commodore's rebuke, this insult was at least a tribute to his security.

[1] Brass letters standing for Volunteer Reserve, and till then worn by all non-regular Air Force officers.

CHAPTER VIII

THE GOSPEL ACCORDING TO ST. THOMAS

THE hutch now contained a lot of new rabbits: the staff of 'R.F.' section had been increased; Lieutenant-Colonel L. H. Dismore was in command and there were no more pink slips ordering immediate conference. One thing, however, was still the same: the award of Tommy's M.C. had not yet been confirmed and he was once more forced to adopt his two-tunic technique. Offered a D.S.O. for his second mission, Yeo-Thomas angrily refused; all that he wanted was his M.C., and that only so as not to appear a fool before the French. The lean, efficient, good-humoured and deservedly popular Dizzy tried to kill two birds with one stone by recommending him for a bar to his contested M.C.

Fresh from his nerve-racking experiences in the field, Yeo-Thomas became outspokenly critical of complacency at home. While he admired the energy of the many who wholeheartedly devoted themselves to the performance of necessary routine, he suspected that there were a few whose main ambition was to pump themselves up into full colonels and group captains. Others he considered doctrinaire xenophobes, fearful of arming underground foreign allies because the procedure had never been outlined in the military manuals. Perhaps because of his interview with the imbecilic Air Commodore he was especially disapproving of the Air Ministry. Night after night, he pointed out, Frenchmen were risking their lives to wait for arms and supplies which were seldom or never dropped to them; and they could not understand how Great Britain, with all her publicized air power, could not do more to satisfy their requirements. Co-ordinates of landing grounds were necessary and these had been given, but it was unreasonable of the authorities to exact measured surveys from those who were continually exposed to the vigilance of the enemy. For the Lysander pilots and for the majority of those engaged on parachuting operations he had the greatest admiration; he was, however, impatient with those who circled round pinpoints and returned home, *re infecta*, with the excuse that the torches marking out the ground had not been bright enough. In a lecture given to both R.A.F. and U.S.A.A.F. crews he emphasized the dangers and the difficulties faced by reception committees:

'. . . When you go on operations you run the normal flying risks while you are over England. When you are over the Channel or enemy territory you run additional risks but only for a restricted number of hours. If you are shot down and captured you become a prisoner of war. If you get back to base you find a hot meal awaiting you and a comfortable bed in which you can immediately go to sleep. Unless there is an air raid you will not be disturbed and you will have nothing more to worry about until you go on your next operation. You have warm clothing and comparatively comfortable quarters. You get your pay, you get leave and, if you do a good job, you get a gong or promotion.

'Now look at things on the other side of the Channel. The man in the reception committee often has to travel many miles on foot or on bicycle in order to reach the landing ground. There is a curfew in France and he has to get to and from the ground without attracting attention, or he will be arrested. During the moon period he has to do this night after night, and often he has to wait many hours in vain for an operation which may have been cancelled at the last moment. He can never catch up on the sleep he misses because during the day he has to earn his living, working as a farm labourer, a mechanic or a clerk. And when he is working he lives under the hourly threat of a visit from the Gestapo. He gets no pay for his resistance work, no promotion, no gongs. If he is caught he is not treated as a prisoner of war but as a spy, and is tortured and shot. And not only will there be no pension for his dependants but he has to face the fact that his wife and children may also be tortured and shot. . . .

'When you do not find the reception committee waiting for you you think that they have been careless; you do not stop to wonder why they are not there. You fail to understand that a sudden change in the German Order of Battle may make a ground which was safe one day impossible to use the next. While you fly fuming back to your base it does not strike you that the whole reception committee may have been arrested. You complain about the weak lights.

Don't you understand that it is difficult to secure batteries in occupied territory? Do you realize that those obtainable are mostly of inferior quality? Do you know that a man may have to bicycle twenty or thirty kilometres in order to obtain one battery?'

To Tommy it was all such elementary pot-hook stuff that even an air commodore ought to have been able to understand it. To a congregation of vice-admirals, brigadiers and air vice-marshals he gave a detailed account of the situation in France. For the space of three hours he cried out aloud: 'Great is de Gaulle of the French.' With all the eloquence he possessed he pleaded the cause of the Resistance Movements, stressing their need for arms and equipment. He gave proof of the results which could be achieved with adequate supplies. 'Our present puny efforts are as likely to succeed as a man trying to fill a swimming-pool with a fountain-pen filler,' he thundered at the pews of wayward brass. Jutting out his chin, he besought the R.A.F. to divert from bombing more than sixteen aircraft to serve the reception committees. If they withheld the necessary assistance they would be responsible for the loss of thousands of lives when invasion took place. The sermon failed and he was told that the bombing plan was far more important; it was like trying to convert a bench of bishops.

It is to his credit that it was almost exclusively with his superiors that he quarrelled. On only one occasion, when he was interviewing candidates for the 'Jedburghs', did he lose his temper with a subordinate; Jedburghs were teams of Allied officers who were to be dropped behind the German lines just prior to 'D' day to take command of Maquis and Secret Army groups, and the qualifications required were high. An Army lieutenant, with dirty buttons and a greasy service cap, entered the room without knocking.

'G'morning,' he said, strolling up to the desk and failing to salute.

'Mr. X, you will please go outside and come in properly.'

Puzzled, the sloppy soldier retired and came in again, this time after knocking.

'G'morning,' he said, still without saluting.

'Mr. X, GO OUTSIDE THAT DOOR AND COME IN PROPERLY.'

The product of football pools, free thought and progress went out, knocked, came in again and saluted slackly and wearily. Yeo-Thomas roared at him:

'You are the most outrageous thing I have ever seen in officer's uniform. Go outside and come in smartly or you will regret ever having come here.'

Lieutenant X did as he was told and put a hint of zeal into the performance.

'You realize that we are looking for officers with a good knowledge of French?'

'Yes, Sir.'

'Do you qualify?'

'I think so, Sir.'

'*Parlez-vous français?*'

'*Ung peutee.*'

Lieutenant X, it was clear, had volunteered merely in order to obtain a free railway voucher to London.

'Mr. X, you are a disgrace to your uniform: your tunic looks like a sack; your buttons are filthy. We are looking for real officers and I reject you. See that you leave my presence smartly and properly. Dismiss!'

The anecdote is interesting for two reasons: it disproves the legend, current in the Army, that the R.A.F. is a breezy egalitarian free-for-all where aircraftmen borrow the group captain's staff car to take the air vice-marshal's girl friend out to dinner and send in the bill to the air commodore afterwards; and it shows the value that Yeo-Thomas, an irregular soldier, placed on parade-ground formality. A strip was torn off Lieutenant X, not because Yeo-Thomas himself was always respectful when he insulted his superiors, but because the 'brown job' lacked what Arthur Bryant calls so neatly 'the spirit of proud subordination which makes an army'. Jedburghs, who if captured were liable to be treated as spies and tortured and shot, required to be courageous; therefore, they required to be disciplined. Such at least was Tommy's argument. Of the eight officers he interviewed that day he chose only two, one of whom he tried to dissuade because of the man's family obligations: Captain Hay, who was to die in action, and Captain Desmond Hubble, whom he was to meet again in Buchenwald.

Meanwhile in France the situation was deteriorating, and the weather wasn't making things easier. Networks of trained agents were being wiped out by the Gestapo and their French collaborators. M. Bollaert, who had been sent out to replace Jean Moulin, as General de Gaulle's personal representative, was having difficulty in exercising his authority; and both he and Brossolette were in such constant danger that it was decided to exfiltrate them immediately. Of two Lysanders sent to pick them and others up one had to turn back because of bad weather and the other was shot down in flames over the French coast. The house in which Bollaert and Brossolette had been sheltering while waiting for the operation to take place was raided within an hour of their leaving it. Heavy fogs made another operation temporarily impossible: on one night alone nine aircraft crashed. And when at last the fog over France lifted, England was still blanketed. Unable because of security regulations to refer to the weather in a signal to the field, Yeo-Thomas tried to explain to Brossolette in a message sent over the B.B.C. the reasons for the delay: '*Du Cheval à Polydor: nous mangeons toujours de la purée de pois, mais nous aurons du dessert.*' [1] As the French always refer to English fog as 'mashed peas', Brossolette understood and replied that he would try to return by a sea operation organized by another branch of the service. Tommy signalled back that exfiltration by sea was much too dangerous at that time of the year and counselled patience and discretion till the next moon period, when another Lysander would be sent. '*Le Cheval n'oublie jamais ses amis,*' [2] he assured Brossolette by the B.B.C.

But the January moon period proved as unsatisfactory as the December: the lost aircraft were not replaced, some of those remaining developed engine trouble and only three Lysander operations took place, in the south of France, where it was impossible to pick up Bollaert and Brossolette. His friend was still in danger and he had been unable to help him; and men and women who had pinned their faith on the Allies were being badly let down. With meagre means at their disposal the Secret Army and the Maquis would be wiped out long before they could attain their potential.

[1] 'From Cheval to Polydor. We are still eating mashed peas, but there's a sweet in the menu.'
[2] 'Cheval never forgets his friends.'

Yeo-Thomas was so discouraged that he made up his mind that once Brossolette was safely back in England, he would send in his resignation.

It was in this rebellious mood that he took the train to Oxford to see Major-General Sir E. D. Swinton, whom he knew well and to whom he told his troubles, railing at the Air Ministry for refusing to provide sufficient aircraft. The General heard him patiently and, probably because he was familiar with Tommy's impulsive character, very sensibly pointed out to him that a squadron leader was not in a position to know the whole pattern of the war and that his superiors might have reasons for their policy which he ignored. But Yeo-Thomas stuck to his guns: he wasn't talking from hypothesis or hearsay; he had been and seen and learned, and he *knew* that those in authority were underestimating the value which a properly equipped French Resistance would represent on 'D' day.

'There is only one man who can decide on such an important point, and that is the Prime Minister,' General Swinton said. 'Would you dare to face him if a meeting could be arranged?'

Yeo-Thomas most certainly would.

The General took Tommy at his word: a letter was sent to Mr. Churchill, to be handed to the Prime Minister personally by Mr. Brendan Bracken.

On 1st February, 1944, Yeo-Thomas was summoned to No. 10 Downing Street to meet the Prime Minister at 3 p.m. Introduced by Major Desmond Morton into the long room where Cabinet meetings took place, Yeo-Thomas found Mr. Churchill seated alone at the middle of a long table facing the windows. The Prime Minister had his chair tilted back, one knee pressed against the table, and was, not surprisingly, smoking a cigar. Nervous but determined not to show it, Yeo-Thomas came to a halt and stood smartly to attention in front of the man whom he most admired in the whole world. Mr. Churchill looked at him critically.

'I'm a busy man and I have no time to waste,' he said. 'But when I get a letter from Ole Luke Oie I know it is about something of interest. He says you know France better than any other Englishman. I doubt it. What have you got to say? I can give you five minutes.'

It must have been rather like pleading against time for mercy with God the Father. Tommy knew that he had the proper arguments, but he was terrified that in his haste he might omit the most convincing. He started in right away on the Secret Army and the Maquis. He spoke of their appalling lack of arms and equipment. He spoke of the need for aircraft to drop supplies. He told the Prime Minister about the brave men and women risking torture and death, carrying messages through the crowded, police-ridden streets of Paris and waiting for agents in the darkness in the windy wilderness of central France. Panting, breathless, he threw a potted version of the whole sad story at Mr. Churchill and hoped that his hero would understand. His hero did.

'Sit down,' Mr. Churchill said and, when Tommy had sat down: 'What is the organization of the Maquis like?'

Yeo-Thomas told him in detail, not forgetting to mention the group with one rifle between thirty men.

'They will need clothing besides arms?'

'Yes, Sir.'

'What sort of clothing do they need?'

'Thick woollen socks, underwear, gloves, wind jackets, strong heavy boots.'

'How many of each?'

'That, Sir, depends upon the number of aircraft at our disposal for dropping supplies.'

'How many aircraft are required to step up your operations effectively?'

'At least a hundred, Sir; more if possible.'

'I shall see that you get a hundred to start with.'

Yeo-Thomas dotted his 'i's and crossed his 't's.

'Thank you, Sir; but it is necessary for the hundred aircraft to be serviceable and to do at least two-hundred and fifty sorties in every moon period.'

'I shall see to that. If the hundred aircraft do not do the requisite number of sorties you will have to be given more machines.'

Sure now that he was making headway, Yeo-Thomas started off again. He told the Prime Minister all he knew about the situation in France. He told him about the sabotage and the fearful martyrdom endured by ordinary humdrum folks. Perhaps in his excitement he repeated himself, for Mr. Churchill interrupted him again.

'Have you written reports about these things?'

'Yes, Sir.'

The Prime Minister turned to Major Morton.

'Why have they not been passed to me, Morton?'

'I don't know, Sir; I shall find out.'

'Yes, and see that I have them immediately.'

Mr. Churchill turned back to Yeo-Thomas. Unerringly picking out the essentials, he asked a number of questions which Tommy described as 'dead on'. 'What a mind, what versatility!' he says. The Prime Minister, of course, was a man very much after Tommy's own heart; and I rather think that Yeo-Thomas must have pleased Mr. Churchill, who looked at him with the hint of a smile and said:

'You have chosen an unorthodox way of doing things and you have short-circuited official channels; it might mean trouble for you, but I shall see that no such thing happens.'

There and then the Prime Minister dictated notes on what Yeo-Thomas had told him and an order to the Air Ministry to put a hundred aircraft at the disposal of 'R.F.' section. He had just finished when M. Astier de la Vigerie, whom Yeo-Thomas had already met several times, entered.

'Squadron Leader Yeo-Thomas has been pleading on behalf of France, Monsieur de la Vigerie, and I have been listening,' Mr. Churchill said. 'I am going to increase substantially the number of aircraft doing parachuting operations to the Resistance, and greater supplies and more armament are going to be sent.'

Yeo-Thomas went out of No. 10 Downing Street walking on air; he had spent fifty-five minutes with the Prime Minister, that great man to whom he rightly attributed the preservation of Western civilization. Something of this vicarious glory must still have been shining from him when he got back to Norgeby House, where 'R.F.' section was now installed, for he was immediately visited by some very senior officers, who prudently congratulated him upon his initiative.

The wand which Mr. Churchill had waved was a powerful one: within forty-eight hours 'R.F.' section had at its disposal twenty-two Halifaxes, twelve Liberators, thirty-six Stirlings, six Albemarles and a number of small aircraft for pick-up operations; other planes were to operate from North Africa. 'R.F.' section went hard at it, sending telegrams to the field to reception committees and ascertaining the requirements of the various regions.

The only fly in the ointment was that they had not yet been able to bring back Bollaert and Brossolette. And it was impossible to get in touch with them because, in spite of Tommy's categorical warning, they had decided to come home by sea and were now in hiding somewhere near the coast. Then the inevitable happened, and it fell to poor Major Johnson to tell Yeo-Thomas of their arrest.

'Tommy, old man, this is going to shake you,' he said and then he told him.

Yeo-Thomas was stunned. Bollaert he had known, but Brossolette he had loved as men can love only those with whom they have shared discomfort and extreme danger. The whole man was physically present to him as he stood there in Johnson's office. The thick eyebrows, the piercing dark brown eyes which could gleam with kindness or glare with anger, the black hair parted in the middle and brushed straight back from the high forehead, the long, thin fingers, the strong hands, the hooked nose, the expressive, sensitive mouth, he loved them because he had been able to give them companionship in their essential loneliness in the world, and because their loneliness had companioned his when he was facing the hatred of cruel men. And Brossolette's friendly voice he heard too, as he had last heard it in Suni Sandöe's flat when he had gone to warn him of his contact's arrest: *'Alors, Cheval, qu'est-ce qu'il y a? Je vous croyais à Arras et sur le point de partir.'* [1]

'Any details?' he asked when he had recovered his self-control. 'What happened? Was he betrayed?'

There were no details as yet, Johnson said. All that they knew was that Bollaert and Brossolette had been arrested in Brittany while attempting to get away by boat.

Dismore, Johnson, Thackthwaite, that nice D.S.O. Fife and Forfar Yeoman Murray-Prain, the bubbling little Kay More, the lanky energetic Clarke, Alex Murray, Whitehead and the sweet and sensible Barbara all did their best to comfort him. But it was no good. Even when he learned that Brossolette had not been identified and was in Rennes prison under his false name of Boutet it was

---

[1] 'Well, Cheval, what's the matter? I thought you were in Arras and just about to leave.'

still no good. For Tommy knew that in prison Brossolette would not be able to procure any hair dye and that sooner or later the telltale white streak would begin to show; and when that happened the Gestapo, who knew all about the white lock, would identify Brossolette and begin to torture him. Ashamed of his own safety in England, he felt that he had betrayed his friend when he had left him alone in France, and it was in vain that Dismore reminded him that he had been ordered to return home. I don't think that Tommy very often reads the Bible, but there is a lament in the Old Testament which expresses his grief: 'O Absalom, my son, my son. Would God that I had died for thee, O Absalom, my son.'

There was, he knew at once, only one thing that he could do: he must return to France and rescue Brossolette before the white streak of hair had time to show. And quite apart from that particular purpose there seemed to be every justification for his going: with the capture of Bollaert and Brossolette French Resistance had again been decapitated and demoralization might once more set in, as it had after the arrest of Moulin and Delestraint; he knew all the heads of the Resistance Movements and all the cogs in the complicated machine of underground intrigue; he had acquired great authority over Regional Military Officers and the Air Operations Officers. Without excessively flattering himself he was sure that there was nobody else who could so adequately replace Bollaert and Brossolette. 'D' day was approaching, and when it broke his presence in the field might prove of great use to the Allies.

But the arguments with which he convinced himself did not so readily convince his superiors. His superiors knew what he knew and chose to pretend that he didn't know: that the Gestapo was informed of his activities and possessed his description and that there was every likelihood of his being captured. This they told him; they refrained from pointing out that it would be disastrous if anybody so well informed as himself about Resistance and staff planning were to break down under torture and talk. But Tommy guessed what his chiefs were thinking and he soon found a way of overcoming both their spoken and their unspoken objections.

He realized that his masters were right to entertain those fears; the bravest of men could not be certain that he would not talk under torture, especially if the executioner were subtle enough to suggest as he gave another twist to the thumbscrew that the war was not being fought about the Holy Ghost after all, but about exports and imports.

With the Gestapo constantly on the alert it was impossible to guarantee that he would not be arrested; talking could be avoided with certainty only if torture could be avoided; and torture might be avoided if, in the event of capture, he were able to pass himself off as a member of the crew of a British aircraft who had been compelled to bale out over enemy-occupied territory and who could consequently claim treatment as a prisoner of war. His cover story, of course, would require to be unshakable because the Gestapo, with its customary thoroughness, possessed the Air Force List containing the names of all those engaged on operational flying. Accordingly, through the agency of Wing Commander Redding, liaison officer betw en S.O.E. and the Air Ministry, he got in touch with Squadron Leader Dodkin, whose name was on the operational list, but who had been grounded and would not be required to fly again. Tommy spent several hours with Squadron Leader Dodkin, whose life story he learned and whose serial number he suggested that he should assume. In the end his chiefs accepted the manœuvre and identity discs were struck for him in Dodkin's name.

Once more he had to learn new codes and conventions. He had also to provide himself with additional aliases and memorize their particulars, because the Dodkin cover could be used only in the event of arrest. He sent a B.B.C. message to José Dupuis, '*de Tommy à Hélène . . .*' to advise her of his return. Realizing the very real danger into which he was going, he made a will, without telling Barbara. But Barbara guessed his forebodings because she shared them; she tried to reassure him by not reassuring him, and her own anxieties she bore alone. Not much has been said in this book about the gay, gentle and lovely Barbara, although her silent courage gives her a special part in the story: Tommy says that without her sympathy and love he could not have endured.

Although it was usual for the B.C.R.A. to have a French representative on missions chiefly concerning themselves, because of the exceptional circumstances they agreed to Tommy going alone as a bipartite delegate of Britain and France. '*Mais cette mission ne peut constituer en aucune façon un précédent,*' Commandant Manuel wrote to Dismore. *'Je ne suis d'accord qu'en raison de la personnalité d'Asymptote.'* [1] For Asymptote was the not very Dick Barton code name which Yeo-Thomas had been given for his third mission, and of which the titanic terms of reference were as follows:

OPERATIONAL INSTRUCTIONS FOR ASYMPTOTE

1. Asymptote will be responsible to his H.Q. and will make a full report on his return. This will not preclude him from sending an interim report during his mission.

2. He will inquire into and report upon the state of the Resistance Movements in the Occupied Zone, their degree of training, strength, morale and preparedness. He will see how far the distribution of arms has progressed and whether this distribution has been and is being made with due regard to the order of priority of plans as sent to the field with the Regional Military Officers.

3. He will see whether the general tightening up of security which he recommended during his last mission has been implemented.

4. He will contact the Regional Military Officers and ascertain whether they are getting adequate support and assistance from the Regional Movement Heads. If, in his estimation, this is not the case, he will approach them or their chiefs and exert all his efforts towards increasing and improving relations with a view to ensuring the maximum co-operation at all levels.

5. He will contact the Air Operations Officers and take similar steps to those in (4) above. In addition he will endeavour to ascertain the quantities and employment of stores already delivered to the field.

6. He will endeavour to discover how far the plans already sent to the field have been set on foot and whether the teams selected to execute them are properly briefed and trained.

7. He will investigate current sabotage activities with a view to ascertaining whether instructions from H.Q. are reaching the proper people and are being followed. He will be provided with the list of targets of first priority and will check up in the field on the efforts being made to attack them. He will endeavour in every way to increase all sabotage activities on the lines directed by H.Q.

8. He will contact such officers of the Maquis organizations as are nominated to him by Jerôme and will, as far as is practicable, inquire into the strength, armament, resources and morale of Maquis groups not covered by the Missions Cantinier, Xavier, Union and Citronelle (if then in the field).

9. It will be for Asymptote to decide, according to the situation which he finds in the field and his estimate of his own personal security, or of his contacts, which, if any, of the foregoing tasks should be deleted from this programme.

10. He will investigate any matters not specifically mentioned in this *Ordre de Mission* which he judges to be of importance to the prosecution of the war, and make comments and/or recommendations in consequence.

I doubt if he noticed that clause No. 9 constituted a let-out from the task which he had persuaded his chiefs to impose upon him, or

[1] 'But this mission must not be regarded in any way as a precedent. I give my consent only because of Asymptote's personality.'

that clause No. 10 almost cancelled the let-out. It was of Brosso-lette, lonely in a cell in Rennes, that he was thinking when he left for Tempsford on the night of 24th February, 1944. Brossolette was a man of courage and of vision and his own familiar friend. Brossolette would never have failed him, and he would not fail Brossolette. He must rescue Brossolette before his true identity was revealed by the white hair on his head beginning to show.

CHAPTER IX

MISSION ASYMPTOTE

ONCE again he was travelling third-class, and he was to parachute. Because of the necessity for rescuing Brossolette before his identity was discovered, Tommy had elected to jump in the dark rather than wait for the next moon period. He was accompanied by a saboteur whose code name was Trieur and whose first trip this was.

They were to be dropped near Clermont-Ferrand, about 250 miles south of Paris, and had a long way to fly. There was the usual flak over the French coast, but the rest of the journey passed without incident.

The procedure was the same as on his first mission with Passy and Brossolette: when they were nearly over the pinpoint the despatcher hooked up their static lines and opened up the hole. Trieur looked nervous and Yeo-Thomas, who was to jump first, tried to cheer him up by giving him the thumbs-up sign as he swung his legs into the trap. Below it was inky black, and it was some time before Tommy could see the twinkling lights of the reception committee. Then he felt the despatcher's hand on his shoulders, the red light went on, the aircraft made a wide turn and ran in over the ground; the green light went on, he pushed himself out through the hole, whirled round in the slipstream, floated and, because of the lack of moonlight, began to count. Dropped from a height of 500 feet he had been told that he would touch the ground when he had reached twenty; instead his head hit it with a bang at thirteen and he was knocked unconscious for two or three minutes. He was still dizzy and shaken when he unfastened his parachute; getting up with difficulty, he found that he had sprained his left ankle.

His discomfiture was increased when the aircraft made its second run overhead and he had to dodge its dropped containers as they came hurtling down. He was helped to cover by the Air Operations Officer Evêque, whom he had already met in London. Trieur had landed safe and sound in the next field. Fortunately, the farmhouse where they were to spend the night was only half a mile distant, and Yeo-Thomas was able to hobble there painfully.

Next morning, although his ankle was still swollen, he determined to leave for Paris that afternoon: not until he was there could he get in touch with Abeille and Archer, who were in charge of the Brittany region, and with whom he hoped to be able to arrange a means of helping Bollaert and Brossolette. The farmer drove him and Trieur over rutty tracks covered with ice and put them in a bus which took them at a breakneck speed over even more slippery roads to Clermont-Ferrand. There they met and dined with Alain Bernay, the Regional Military Officer. Because of his hurry to get to Paris, Yeo-Thomas refused Bernay's invitation to remain with him for a few days and visit the local groups, and Trieur and he caught the half-past eleven train to the capital.

It is a favourite device of unoriginal film producers to translate to the chant of revolving railway train wheels the not particularly profound problems of their puppets: 'CAN I BE A BUSINESS GAL AND STILL BE A GOOD WIFE TO AL?' By the rules of such facile onomatopoeia Tommy ought to have heard the train wheels singing: 'BROSSOLETTE, BROSSOLETTE, BROSSOLETTE'. He heard nothing of the sort, nor did he require to: indeed, he sought relief from thinking about Brossolette in tipping off to the as yet untried Trieur some of the dodges which the saboteur would have to employ if he were to remain for long undetected in Paris.

As soon as he arrived in Paris he handed Trieur over to Maud, who passed the saboteur on to Jacqueline Devaux, who found him a flat. From Maud Tommy learned that Bollaert and Brossolette were still in Rennes prison, and that the latter was still believed to be a M. Pierre Boutet. Maud had established contact with some of the German officials and, by bribing the guards and passing herself off to them as Boutet's mistress, had managed to send him food, wine and clothing in which were hidden messages to which Boutet had replied when sending out his linen to the laundry; by this means she had ascertained that Bollaert and Brossolette were relatively unmolested and that the latter's lock of white hair had not yet begun to show.

His first night in Paris Tommy spent with the Peyronnets, whose flat in the Avenue des Ternes was again considered to be comparatively safe.

The next day, while waiting to contact Abeille and Archer, he got in touch, through the ever-faithful José Dupuis, with Pichard and with Clouet des Pesruches, who, under the slightly less Boulevard St. Germain pseudonym of Galilée, was Air Operations Officer for the Touraine. From them he was able to obtain a clear idea of the situation in the Paris, Seine et Marne, Tours and eastern France areas. Partly because the recently stepped up parachutings had not yet been going on long enough for their impact to be felt throughout the country, the morale of Resistance was low. There were four main reasons for this: the weariness of constantly waiting and constantly disappointed reception committees; lack of arms; a growing belief that the Allies had no real intention of ever invading the Continent; and the increased vigilance of the Gestapo, now aided more and more by Darnand's Militia and the Lafont Organization. It was the old story, with a few new drop scenes, and Tommy told his new version of the other old story to contradict it: parachuting operations were being formidably increased; Jerôme was now in London demonstrating the great potentiality of the Maquis; and the invasion *would* take place.

Not wishing too greatly to inconvenience the Peyronnets, whose flat had already been watched by the Gestapo, Tommy spent his second night in Paris in Jeanne Helbling's flat in the rue Casimir Pinel in Neuilly. Through his hostess he was able to contact Abeille and Archer. Abeille, who before the war had been a Prefect, immediately placed the whole of the Brittany organization at Tommy's disposal for the rescue of Bollaert and Brossolette. But before determining upon a given course of action Yeo-Thomas decided to go to Rennes and conduct a preliminary investigation on the spot.

He left for Rennes on 1st March, taking Maud with him. With a local lawyer, who was a member of the Resistance, he discussed the possibility of getting Brossolette transferred on a trumped-up charge from Rennes prison to another prison in the south of France where he would be forgotten about by the Rennes authorities and whence they could ultimately secure his release on the basis of wrongful arrest. In the end they abandoned this plan, which failed to take into account Bollaert and which would be a lengthy process involving the suborning of at least two Gestapo officers and the manufacture of an imaginary but convincing misdeed. Because of the danger of Boutet's real identity being discovered, time was the essence of the problem which could, therefore, be solved only by force.

He then went to reconnoitre the prison and its precincts. Almost opposite the main entrance there was a grocer's shop, whose owner was a member of one of the Resistance groups and who numbered among his customers most of the French and some of the German prison officials. From the grocer Yeo-Thomas learned that the greater part of the prison had been handed over to the Germans and only a few cells left free for the French; the main entrance was heavily guarded; all the gates were closed and at each gate was posted a sentry with a light machine gun which could be trained on every avenue of approach; a direct telephone line connected the guard-room of the prison with that of an SS barracks not more than 600 yards distant. Tommy made a careful reconnaissance, found where the telephone line ran and where it could most easily be cut.

He saw at once that a frontal attack would be foredoomed to failure, but he soon hit upon a plan which he thought would stand a chance of success. When the telephone wire connecting the two guard-rooms had been cut, ten men from the local Resistance groups would keep watch from points of vantage situated in houses opposite the prison and would cover all approaches to the main gate. Three other men, of whom one would speak German perfectly and the other two fluently, would present themselves in German uniform with Sicherheitsdienst badges to the sentry at the main entrance; to him they would show forged instructions, supposedly emanating from the Paris or the Rennes Gestapo Headquarters and ordering the prison authorities to free Bollaert and Brossolette for transfer. Once in the guard-room, where it was the custom for those in charge to verify such documents by telephoning to the Headquarters from which they purported to have been issued, the three disguised men would overpower the guards, who, when not on sentry duty, so the grocer had said, always removed their belts and hung their weapons on the wall. The man who spoke perfect German would then return to the sentry at the main entrance, tell him that all was in order and ask him to open the gate so that a car, which would be waiting outside, could be brought into the yard in order that the prisoners might be picked up without attracting the attention of passers-by; the driver would back in and stop the car in such a position as to prevent the sentry from closing the gates again. Meanwhile the two other men would proceed into the prison proper, taking with them the corporal of the guard, whom they would threaten to shoot immediately if he did not obey their orders. Bollaert and Brossolette would be brought out of their cells, put in the car and driven to a second car which would be waiting round the corner from the grocer's shop. While the second car took them to a safe hiding-place in the centre of the town, the first car would continue south, leaving an obvious trail behind it.

The plan seemed a good one, but it could not be put into action immediately: three German-speaking Resistance members, two cars and petrol had to be found; and, owing to a recent lack of parachuting operations in Brittany, Sten guns, pistols, hand grenades and ammunition would have to be brought to Rennes from a remote region.

Full of energy and confidence, Yeo-Thomas returned to Paris and put the preparations in train. In the meantime he carried on with his official work: he held conferences with Sapeur and Commandant Palaud, who were responsible for the paramilitary organization of Paris, with 'Z' and with the leaders of Front National, Franc-Tireurs et Partisans, Ceux de la Libération, Ceux de la Résistance, and Organisation Civile et Militaire. Because of the repeated hold-ups by German police in the métro, and because vélo-taxis were rare, he had to do a great deal of walking: seven or eight contacts a day in places as widely separated as the Porte Maillot, the Boulevard St. Michel, the Trocadéro, the Porte de St. Cloud, the Parc Monceau and the Place de la Nation laid a considerable strain on his as yet imperfectly healed left ankle. He had also to take the usual precautions against being followed and to make sure that his contacts were not being trailed when he met them. For the Gestapo was more than ever alert: Pichard and Clouet des Pesruches were being hotly chased and José Dupuis had become so blown that she had had to be sent into the country for a month's rest. In view of this constant danger, Tommy kept changing residences; but wherever he passed the night there was also a radio, and once a week a cryptic message came over the B.B.C. to assure him that Barbara had not been a casualty in the little blitz to which London was then being subjected.

He was staying in Suni Sandöe's flat in the rue Claude Chahu when he was informed that all was now in readiness for the attempt to rescue Bollaert and Brossolette from Rennes prison. Deciding to go to Rennes on the night of 21st March, and anxious to assure himself before he left that the air operations in the Touraine were running satisfactorily, he made an appointment for that morning with Antonin, a new agent-de-liaison lent to him by Pichard; Antonin was to bring him any messages he might have received from a girl called Brigitte, who was Clouet des Pesruches' go-between, and to be prepared to pass on to Brigitte any instructions which Yeo-Thomas had for Clouet des Pesruches. The appointment had been fixed for eleven o'clock at the Passy métro station, situated, unlike most others, on a bridge above ground; Antonin was to walk down the steps on the left and Tommy was to come up them on the right; they were to cross in front of the newspaper kiosk next to the ticket office and to feign surprise when they met.

At eleven o'clock precisely Yeo-Thomas passed the kiosk, but Antonin was not there. Ordinarily Yeo-Thomas would not have broken his security rule of never waiting for an unpunctual contact, but it was imperative that instructions should be passed to Clouet des Pesruches at once, in case he was detained in Rennes longer than he anticipated. He therefore went down the steps on the other side of the station and came up again, using the same steps as before. Having ascended the first flight and still seeing no sign of Antonin coming towards him, he hesitated as to whether to pay a surprise visit to his father, whose flat was only 100 yards distant. Deciding to put duty before pleasure, he continued up the steps, meeting a crowd of people coming down from the train which had just arrived and feeling fairly safe in the other crowd which was climbing the steps towards the station. As he drew level with the last flight leading up to the ticket office five men in civilian clothes pounced on him, handcuffed him and began scientifically to search his pockets. Just then Antonin, escorted by another two Gestapo men in civilian clothes, passed by on the other side of the steps, looked at Tommy and was led away.

'*Wir haben Shelley*,' [1] Tommy's captors shouted with glee.

CHAPTER X

HE WAS NOT WONDERFUL BY MISTAKE

As soon as Yeo-Thomas had been handcuffed, two of the Gestapo men set about pushing back the excited crowd: they forbade access to the station and threatened to shoot anybody attempting to approach their prisoner. For a few minutes Tommy, tightly gripped by his captors, stood in a small arena of steps, hemmed in by a throng twenty yards above him and twenty yards below him, and reading on the spectators' faces fear or pity or the shamefaced loathing with which men contemplate misfortunes which they try to believe can never happen to themselves. This tableau, however, was of brief duration: he was quickly hustled up the steps, through the crowd, and propelled into a Citroën with a uniformed driver which had been waiting at the corner of the Boulevard Delessert. He was made to sit in the back with two policemen on either side of him. As soon as the car started these two men began to take it in turn to punch him in the face. 'Shelley,' they cried, '*Wir haben Shelley. Englischer Offizier. Terrorist. Schweinehund. Scheisskerl.*'

[1] 'We've got Shelley.'

This horrible little litany of imprecation continued until they reached the Gestapo Headquarters in the rue des Saussaies, and so did the cruel blows. Tommy's head felt twice its normal size and the blood from his lacerated face was pouring down over his shirt and suit. He says that he was surprised to find himself 'thinking in a completely impersonal manner just as though it were another person being beaten up, and it was a very extraordinary feeling'. It must have been. What was even more extraordinary was that during this painful passage to prison he was able to wonder whether the attempt to rescue Bollaert and Brossolette would still be made and to think out what he was going to say when he was interrogated.

It was clear that the Dodkin story would no longer serve in its entirety: the fact that the Gestapo men had greeted him as Shelley seemed to indicate that Antonin had talked. (He learned later that the agent-de-liaison had been arrested while carrying in his pocket, contrary to all regulations, a piece of paper marked: SHELLEY PASSY 11.) It was obvious, therefore, that the Germans would know that the otherwise unimpeachable identity papers in the name of Gaonach which he was carrying were false. The Gestapo knew and had long known that Shelley was a British officer, but they did *not* know the name of the British officer. If they discovered his real identity and failed by normal methods to make him speak they would certainly arrest his father and torture the old man in his presence. Dodkin then he would have to be, and not a baled-out Dodkin: the absence of the identity discs stamped with this name and hidden beneath the floorboards of Suni Sandöe's flat would perhaps add to rather than detract from the credibility of the tale, as a British officer would be unlikely to carry such compromising property on his person while actually engaged in the field. All this he thought out while his face was being battered in the car.

When they reached their destination he was yanked violently out of the car and, with a pistol pointed at his back, was propelled into the lift. His abrupt arrival in an office on the third floor astonished the three men sitting there. '*Wir haben Shelley,*' the leading policeman shouted as Tommy was pushed into the room. At this the three men rose from their chairs and began to punch him and kick him, knocking him against desks and cupboards and walls. They stopped only when he had been beaten into semi-insensibility.

Then they locked the door, stripped him naked and made him stand on a telephone directory. Enraged by the discovery of his tear-gas pen and the revolver in a special holster strapped to his thigh they started in on him again. '*Schweinehund, Scheisskerl*,' the thugs shouted as they slapped his face and kicked him in his bare groin with their heavy boots. They tore from his neck the small brown canvas sachet which the Countess Grabbe had given him at the beginning of the war and laid it on a desk beside the other objects which they had removed from his pockets: among these were his identity papers, the keys of four of his apartments of which he had been intending to return three to the owners before he left for Rennes, and two monocles which he had worn to disguise himself. The discovery of the last particularly infuriated his tormentors, for they flung them on the floor and trampled on them. The spectacle was so ridiculous that Tommy laughed aloud in spite of his pain: this earned him another beating up.

This new battering was scientifically administered to him as he stood heels together, arms handcuffed behind his back, naked on the telephone directory: as a blow made him sway sideways, a punch on the jaw, the nose or the ear or a kick in the stomach restored his equilibrium. 'I don't know how long I was kept in this position,' Yeo-Thomas says. 'To me it seemed hours, but in all probability it was only an hour and a half.' Although so dazed that the room was swimming before his eyes, he was still able to think fairly clearly. Two desires were in his mind: to avoid betraying his friends and to escape from his agony. He could do both if only he could get at the signet ring containing the poison tablet which the thugs had omitted to remove from his left hand. Sooner or later, he felt, they would be bound to unhandcuff him, and then he could slide open the top of the ring, swallow the tablet and put himself beyond treachery and pain.

He was still standing on the telephone directory when a tall, broad-shouldered man with cold steel-grey eyes and a cruel mouth entered the room. Tommy's tormentors stood sharply to attention, extended their arms in the Nazi salute and said '*Heil Hitler!*'

'*Heil Hitler!*' said the newcomer, returning the salute and stopping in front of Yeo-Thomas, who even on his perch was a head shorter. Looking down at the prisoner, the tall man spat in his face and gave him a crashing slap on the cheek which sent him careering against the wall. Unable to use his hands Tommy collapsed on the floor, where the tall man kicked him every time he tried to get up. Tommy let his body go limp to minimize the effect of the kicks. '*Schweinehund, salaud, terroriste,*' the brute cried in bilingual rage, as he bent down, pulled Yeo-Thomas to his feet and flung him into a chair.

Very deliberately the new thug drew up another chair and sat down in front of Tommy, staring at him with his expressionless icy eyes. Tommy describes the man's eyes as being like 'twin daggers, trying to pierce his brain'. Knowing that the man's purpose was to make him lower his own eyes Yeo-Thomas looked him full in the face. Once again the heavy fist crashed on to his lips and nose, drawing streams of blood. '*Tu as compris, ordure?*' the man asked in correct but guttural French. 'Now you know where you stand, you bloody swine.' Tommy did not answer.

At a word of command from the new thug two of the other men pounced on Yeo-Thomas and dragged him out of the chair: one stood in front of him with his arms on his shoulders and the other, going behind him, began to unfasten his handcuffs. The moment he had been waiting for seemed to have arrived. But just as his handcuffs were removed the big man noticed the ring. '*Dummkopf,*' he roared at the assistant, himself grabbed Tommy's hand, removed the ring and slipped it into his pocket. Yeo-Thomas was ordered to put on his clothes again. He dressed slowly and painfully, angry and frightened because he had been prevented from escaping from the very much more unpleasant attentions which he knew were in store for him.

As he dressed he made quick calculations: he had been arrested at five minutes past eleven; it must now be about three o'clock. Maud, with whom he had had an appointment at one o'clock, would now be aware that something was wrong. When he also failed to turn up at the Avenue Victor Hugo for his emergency rendezvous at six o'clock she would know for certain that he had been arrested. Within twelve hours all his letter-boxes would have been closed down, his meeting places changed and his contacts warned not to keep their appointments. In the meantime, to protect his network, he must, as was the rule for captured agents, hold out for at least forty-eight hours: to do this meant postponing unbearable pain by telling the Gestapo plausible lies and setting them hunting on a false scent.

As soon as he was dressed the big man made a sign to his companions and sat down behind a desk. Tommy was dragged from the chair into which he had deliberately slumped, propelled to the desk and dumped down again in the chair which had been brought up behind him. On the desk were laid out the objects which had been removed from his pockets and from his person: from them his gold fountain pen, his wrist-watch and banknotes of high denomination were already missing; but his pistol was still there, with the barrel pointing towards him and nearer to him than to his inquisitor. Intending to shoot the big man and then himself, he lifted his manacled hands and laid them on the edge of the desk. Nobody seemed to notice this gesture.

'*Vous avez joué et vous avez perdu,*' the big man began. 'You've had your flutter and you've lost. But nothing will happen to you if you're reasonable and listen to sense. But if you don't . . .'

Tommy did not answer; it was always a few seconds gained.

'Well, are you going to talk?'

Once again he did not answer.

'*Ordure,*' the big man shouted as one of his assistants slapped Yeo-Thomas across his puffed and bleeding face. 'Are you going to speak. Yes or no?'

Again Yeo-Thomas did not reply.

The big man sprang up and crashed his fist on to Tommy's mouth. '*Salaud, crapule, saboteur, espion, tu parleras!* I'll make you speak all right.' With the help of his two assistants he started hitting the prisoner again. They did not desist until, his mouth full of blood, his eyes so swollen that he could scarcely see, Yeo-Thomas crumpled up under their onslaught. The big man went back behind his desk and rang a bell.

Pretending not to have completely recovered consciousness, Tommy leaned forward in his chair and slowly slid his hand across the desk towards the pistol: but the big man saw the gesture, laughed, picked up the pistol and put it in a drawer.

'So you thought you'd use it, *cochon?*' was all that he said.

A young, fair, good-looking German with blue eyes and a pink complexion answered the bell. The big man, ordering him to go out and bring back a typewriter, called him 'Ernst', and the young man called the big man 'Rudi'. Tommy made a mental note of the names. When Ernst had fetched a typewriter he sat down at a corner of the desk, inserted a form, a carbon and a blank sheet into the machine and waited in silence.

'Name?' Rudi rapped at Yeo-Thomas.

'Shelley.' That at least it was no good denying.

'Fool. Your real name.'

'Kenneth Dodkin.' This answer seemed to be accepted, for Rudi went on to ask:

'Your serial number?'

'47,685.'

'Rank?'

'Squadron Leader.'

'Branch of the Service?'

'Royal Air Force.'

'Address?'

'I do not require to reply to that question.'

'You will reply all the same.'

'I shall not.' If he was to convince the Gestapo that he was indeed Kenneth Dodkin it seemed to him essential that he should not protest too much by giving them even false information on points about which they were not entitled to ask questions.

Rudi got up, walked round the desk, and using both his hands, began to slap Tommy's face from one side to the other, cutting the already bruised cheeks with his heavy signet ring. His ears crushed, dizzy with pain, Yeo-Thomas swayed in his chair: the two assistants propped him up so that Rudi could go on hitting him.

At last Rudi stopped and sat down behind the desk again.

'Listen,' he said, suddenly changing to a friendly tone. 'It's no good being obstinate. You've had your flutter and you've lost.' Tommy wondered to how many others Rudi had used this phrase which seemed to come so readily to his lips. 'We know all about you, but we'll treat you as an officer if only you'll be sensible. You're a prisoner; you've done your duty; nobody can say a thing against you. Now I'm going to ask you a few questions; all you've got to do is to answer and it'll be all finished with. I say, what about a cigarette?' He took a cigarette from a gold case, stuck it between Tommy's bruised lips, lit it with a gold lighter. 'That's better, isn't it?' he said as he watched Yeo-Thomas take a couple of puffs. 'You see, we're not such brutes after all. If you're reasonable you've got nothing to fear. And when you've answered we'll give you some food and something nice to drink.'

Tommy did not reply, nor did he make any sign; he went on puffing at his cigarette. Ernst sat expectantly at his typewriter.

'I may as well tell you that it's no use telling us any lies,' Rudi went on. 'Your agent-de-liaison has made a clean breast of everything. We know all you've been doing here since the beginning of the year. We know that you know all about the arms dumps. You've only got to tell us where they are and we'll leave you alone'.

Behind his sore face Yeo-Thomas almost smiled. Rudi had been too clever; if Rudi had been as well informed as he pretended to be he would have known that his prisoner had not been in France at the beginning of the year; and Antonin, who had been working for Tommy only for a week, could not have given him much information. Rudi was bluffing; to gain time Yeo-Thomas decided to bluff too.

'Then he's talked?' he asked.

'Naturally.'

Tommy pretended to be shocked and distressed.

'So you know about my appointments?'

'Of course. You see it's no use your making a martyr of yourself. You've had your flutter and you've lost.'

'Did he tell you I had an appointment for this afternoon?'

'We know everything, I tell you.'

'In that case it won't do much good my talking, will it?'

This unexpected piece of logic made Rudi's face harder again.

'This is no time for joking,' he said. 'We know that you have an appointment this afternoon. All I want to know is with whom and where.'

'What time is it now?' Tommy asked.

'Half-past four.'

'In that case it's too late because my appointment is for a quarter to five.'

'Where?'

'At the Porte Maillot.'

'Whereabouts exactly?'

'In front of the *ceinture* railway station.'

'With whom?'

'With a woman who's bringing me a message.'

Rudi picked up the telephone and ordered a car to stand by immediately. One of the guards was sent to fetch another two thugs in civilian clothes, to whom instructions were given by Rudi in German too rapid for Yeo-Thomas to understand. '*Heil Hitler!*' said the thugs and ran from the room; removing Tommy's revolver from the drawer and pocketing it, Rudi prepared to follow them.

'What's this woman like?' Rudi asked.

Yeo-Thomas gave him a fantastic description of an imaginary woman who, he said, would be carrying a bouquet of flowers in one hand and a newspaper in the other.

'If you're lying you'll pay for it,' Rudi shouted as he rushed after the other two men.

Yeo-Thomas knew only too well that he would soon pay dearly for having sent Rudi on a wild-goose chase; but he had gained time, and so far he had not talked. Although his whole head was aching he tried to think out how when Rudi came back again he might gain still more time. His two guards watched him stolidly out of their square, unimaginative, unpitying faces. Ernst moved from his typewriter to Rudi's chair and began examining the property which had been removed from Tommy's person.

'Whose telephone number is this?' Ernst suddenly asked, peering closely at a banknote.

'What telephone number? I don't understand.'

'The telephone number you've written on this banknote.'

'I've written no telephone number on any banknote.'

'Liar!'

'I am not a liar.'

'Yes you are; look at this.' Ernst came over and showed him a ten-franc note on which a telephone number had been scrawled in pencil.

'I didn't write it,' Yeo-Thomas said. 'It must have been there when I got the note.'

This was true, but Ernst didn't believe him and showed his scepticism by punching him heavily in the face.

'Now will you tell me whose number this is?'

'I don't know, I tell you.'

'Well, we shall soon find out.' Picking up the telephone, Ernst gave an order, of which the only part Tommy understood was the repetition in German of the numbers on the ten-franc note. 'You'd have done much better to tell me straight away, *salaud*,' Ernst said, as he laid down the receiver.

Within a few minutes the telephone rang. Ernst listened eagerly. '*Danke*,' he said, asked for an internal number and gave elaborate instructions. 'I now know the name of your friend and his address; you'll be seeing him soon,' he told Tommy. 'The German police are very powerful, you know, and you're very foolish to try to pull the wool over our eyes.' After some insulting epithets he continued his examination of the objects on the desk. 'What's inside this?' he asked, holding up the little brown canvas sachet.

'I haven't the faintest idea.'

'Liar, *pourriture, Scheisskerl*.' With a string of filthy words Ernst unconsciously proved Talleyrand's contention that swearing is the means by which the inarticulate give themselves the impression of eloquence. 'It's no good your coming the innocent with us: we're not bloody fools.'

Taking out a penknife, Ernst slit open the sachet; inside was a small slip of paper, folded in two and covered with small Russian characters. It was the first time Yeo-Thomas had seen this document, which Ernst examined with a scowl.

'Ha, ha,' Ernst said. 'So you work for the Russians, do you? It's your code, isn't it, *Scheisskerl?*'

'I tell you I don't know what it is.'

'You're a liar.'

'I am not.'

'*Scheisskerl!*' Once again Ernst came round from behind the desk and began to beat up his victim. Tommy went limp; it was his only protection. Tiring at length of his sport, Ernst left off and went back to continue his examination of the objects on the desk.

Through the slits which were all he now had for eyes Tommy tried to examine his possessions too. There was only one, he thought, which was really dangerous: the bunch of keys, of which one belonged to the flat in the rue de la Tourelle, the address on his identity card. Of his use of this flat only two people knew: Brossolette, who was in prison, and Maud, who, when he failed to turn up for his six o'clock appointment, would give the place a wide berth. He must avoid answering any questions about the keys until after six o'clock, when, if the persistence of his tormentors became too painful, he would tell them which was the key of the flat in the rue de la Tourelle. The Germans would then rush round to the flat, and, when they found nobody there, bait a trap which would immobilize a couple of their men for a few days. About the keys of the other flats he would have to lie continuously if their owners were not to get into serious trouble. He was still thinking all this out when Rudi burst into the room, livid with rage.

As Rudi had promised, Yeo-Thomas paid for having lied: battered again on his puffed and swollen face, he was knocked down on the floor, picked up and knocked down again. He ached all over; his head throbbed; all his teeth felt loose; his nose was squashed and his lips were split; his jacket and his shirt were soaked with blood. Eventually he was picked up for the last time and thrown back on to his chair; Rudi resumed his seat at the desk.

'You've made me lose my time, *salaud*.'

'I told you you'd be late,' Tommy said. 'She can't have waited. It's not my fault.'

'Liar.'

'It's not my fault if you won't believe me.'

Rudi glared at him; he glared ever more fiercely when Ernst had shown him the folded slip of paper.

'Russian? So you're a Communist as well?'

'It may be Russian; I don't know. But I am not a Communist.'

'You never know anything, do you, you dirty liar? But I'll show you. I'll have this paper examined by our experts. They'll decipher it all right and then you'll see how much you'll pay for your lying.' He telephoned, handed the slip of paper to a small, rat-faced man with gold-rimmed spectacles who came in answer to his summons, and then turned to Yeo-Thomas again. 'Where are the arms dumps you know of?'

'I know of none.'

'Are you going to talk: yes, or no?'

'I don't know anything, I tell you.'

'We'll see if you know nothing.' Rudi signed to the two guards, who grabbed Tommy's arms and jerked him to his feet. Taking from a drawer a long chain and an ox-gut whip with a flexible steel rod inside it, Rudi swished the latter threateningly in the air. Tommy was propelled out of the room, up steps and along a narrow passage lined on one side with small circular windows which looked like portholes; he guessed that he was being taken to a torture chamber.

He had a rough journey: every time he stumbled from weakness he was jerked up by the handcuffs, which bit deeply into his flesh. At the end of the passage a door opened and he was flung on to the tiled floor of a bathroom, through the open window of which blew in a freezing draught. He was dragged to his feet and two men pulled off his trousers and underpants; his hands were unmanacled while his jacket and shirt were torn off and then handcuffed again behind his back. While Rudi bent and twisted the chain tightly round his ankles Ernst opened the cold-water tap and filled the bath. At an order from Rudi one of the guards left the room and came back accompanied by a crowd of German girls in uniform, who crammed the doorway and laughed and mocked at Yeo-Thomas as he stood naked and shivering in the icy draught.

'Where are the arms dumps?' Rudi asked.

'I don't know.'

The ox-gut whip came slashing down on Tommy's chest, searing it and raising a weal; Yeo-Thomas gritted his teeth.

'So you're going to be pig-headed, are you?'

Aching in every joint, Tommy remained silent. He was forced to sit on the edge of the bath. Rudi bent down again, caught hold of the chain around his ankle and gave it a twist and a tug: drawn into the bath on to his feet, Yeo-Thomas stood in the freezing water, facing the grinning, jeering girls. One of the men scooped water up in the palm of his hand and splashed him with it.

'Where are the arms dumps?' Rudi asked again.

'I don't know.'

Rudi crashed his big fist into Tommy's jaw and, as he staggered, pushed him headlong into the bath, so that his face was under the water while his legs stuck up in the air. With his hands manacled behind his back Yeo-Thomas was helpless. Panicking, he tried to kick, but his legs were caught and held in a powerful grip. His eyes were open and he could see faces distorted by the water wavering above him. His mouth came open and he swallowed water. His lungs felt as though they were bursting. He made another attempt to kick himself out of the bath, but the vice-like grip still held him. He tried to lift himself up with his handcuffed arms and failed. Swallowing more water, he became limp; the strength went out of him and he began to lose consciousness; he was drowning and he knew it.

He came to feeling an agonizing pain in his chest. Water was gushing out of his mouth and there was a big wavering black shadow in front of his eyes. The shadow slowly dissolved into lighter filmy circles which shimmered like hot air on a summer's day. As the circles became faces Tommy realized that he was lying on the tiled floor of the bathroom and looking up into Rudi's sadistic eyes. The German girls were crowding round the door, chattering and laughing. Feeling half dead, weak and sick, he closed his eyes so as not to see them. He could breathe only in gasps and his heart, in his own phrase, 'was thumping like bellows in a forge'. He had been pulled out of the water just as he had been about to drown and given artificial respiration.

He was lifted to his feet.

'Where are the arms dumps?'

'I . . . don't . . . know.'

Thrown brutally back into the bath, his head hit the edge. Once more the water engulfed him. Once more he tried in vain to kick and to push himself up with his handcuffed arms. Once more he swallowed water. Once more he felt himself drowning. His mouth opened and the water poured in. There were rushing noises in his ears.

As before he was hauled from the bath just as he was about to drown and was artificially revived. As his consciousness returned he saw the same shimmering visions which slowly took the form of

Rudi, his assistants and the laughing girls. Again he was pulled to his feet, but this time he was so weak that he had to be held up. His ears were still buzzing when he heard a voice coming from far away:

'Where are the arms dumps?'

And he heard another voice, which he presumed to be his own, answering faintly:

'I . . . don't . . . know.'

He was thrown back into the bath several times. Kicking and swallowing water, oblivion succeeding consciousness and consciousness oblivion, he lost count of his torments and soon was unable to trace their sequence. As soon as he saw the distorted faces of Rudi and Ernst he lost sight of them again. The sound of the girls' laughter was absorbed by the pain in his lungs. He no longer had the strength or the desire to kick. He was brought round for the last time by a kick from a heavy boot and knew from the agony that he was still alive. He was lying on the bathroom floor, with walls, bath and faces swirling around his head. Abominably sick and with his stomach as large as a barrel, water came gushing out of his mouth on to his chest. He saw with surprise that the girls were no longer in the doorway. Numb with cold, he was dragged to his feet, on which he could no longer stand, as the chain had stopped the circulation. As he tottered he was struck heavily over the head with a rubber cosh and again collapsed.

When he had recovered from the sickening effects of this blow he was hustled, still naked and dripping with water, along passages and corridors lined with mocking laughing girls in uniform and female secretaries. Back in Rudi's office, the chain was removed from his feet and he was pushed into a chair while his underpants and trousers were slipped on. His handcuffs were loosened, but fastened again as soon as he had been thrust into his shirt and jacket. Once again Rudi sat at his desk facing him.

'Where are the arms dumps?'

'I don't know.'

'Haven't you had enough, *ordure?* Well, we'll see.'

At a sign from Rudi the two guards produced rubber coshes, with which they began to beat him. He was beaten on the head, arms, legs, body and testicles. He did not cry out. Still less did he speak.

'Where are the arms dumps?'

'I don't know.'

Each time that he said this the beating up started all over again. He saw flashes before his eyes; the furniture and Rudi's face began to float in circles. In the end he lost consciousness.

When he came to lying on the floor he pretended that he was still unconscious by keeping his eyes closed; this was not difficult because his eyelids were now so swollen that he could scarcely see out of them. He felt sore and bruised all over. He says to-day that he 'did not know that it was possible to have so many pains in so many places at the same time'.

It was then that the devil took him up into an high mountain and showed him the blessed cities of the plain in which men were not tortured: '*Haec omnia tibi dabo si cadens adoraveris me.*' His sufferings, he knew, would cease immediately if he talked. He rejected the temptation with surprisingly little effort. 'Do you really think, Master, that the Stoics or Epicureans were right in saying that a good man might be happy on the rack?' an undergraduate once asked Dr. Jowett. 'Well, perhaps a very good man on a very bad rack,' the Master of Balliol answered. Yeo-Thomas would have been the last to describe himself as a very good man and even more certainly the last to deny that the rack upon which he was stretched was good; but he knew that he would have been even unhappier in the knowledge that he had betrayed his friends. 'They were wonderful, but sometimes it seemed as though they were wonderful by mistake,' Geoffrey Cotterell makes Tarrant think of certain R.A.F. officers in *Strait and Narrow*; Yeo-Thomas was not wonderful by mistake.

When his tormentors saw that he had recovered consciousness he was picked up and dumped in his chair again. The handcuffs were cutting into his wrists and making them ache. He was beginning to feel hungry too, having had only a cup of coffee for breakfast and nothing since.

Rudi faced him with a malevolent grin, holding up the bunch of keys.

'What keys are these?'

'They are keys.' The question which he had feared had come. The keys had been found in his possession and he could not disown them. However, the lights in the room were already on and through the window he could see that it was dark outside: it must therefore be after six o'clock. Maud would know by now that he had been arrested and would take care not to go near the flat in the rue de la Tourelle. But in order to protect the owners of the flats to which the other three keys belonged he must not yield even harmless information easily.

'For what doors?'

'For no doors. The keys are cover. A man looks suspicious if he doesn't carry keys, so to be in the swim I had some made.'

'I warn you once again not to take me for a fool. I want to know what doors they open.'

'I tell you they open none.'

'Where did you sleep last night?'

'I don't remember.'

'In that case I shall force you to remember.'

Rudi rose from his seat and, with the key-ring hooked round one of his fingers, approached Yeo-Thomas; using the keys as a flail, he lashed his face with them until the blood began to flow.

'Now are you going to tell me, *salaud?*'

With his face pouring with blood, his eyes streaming and his nose feeling as though it were on fire, it was not difficult for Tommy to let his head fall on his chest as though he were in such agony he could not speak. He allowed Rudi to go on scourging his face with the keys for a little longer and then he deliberately flopped.

'There's only one that works,' he said at length. 'It's the big one.'

'Where does it work?'

'33 rue de la Tourelle, Porte de St. Cloud.'

'Couldn't you have said so sooner, *ordure?* Making me waste my time like this. If you've been lying again you'll pay for it.'

After giving some instructions over the telephone Rudi took the keys and walked out of the room. Ernst was about to continue the interrogation when a man came in and whispered a few words in his ear.

'We've found your friend,' Ernst said to Yeo-Thomas.

'What friend?'

'Your telephone number friend.'

The door opened again and two burly Sicherheitsdienst men

came in, dragging with them a limp and terrified wretch. The new prisoner was a weak-looking man with long hair. His face was swollen from the beating up which his guards had obviously already administered to him. When he caught sight of Tommy's battered, bleeding face he cringed and lowered his startled eyes. But on a sign from Ernst he was roughly pushed into a chair facing Yeo-Thomas and slapped by one of his guards until he looked at him.

Ernst glared at them both.

'A pleasant surprise for you both to meet like this, isn't it?' He turned to Yeo-Thomas. 'You see, it's no use your telling any more lies. You may as well talk now.'

'I've never seen this man before,' Tommy said. 'He's totally unknown to me.'

'You're a bloody liar. Don't think I didn't see you tremble when he was brought in.' Ernst threateningly addressed the new captive: 'Even if he's not going to talk I hope you'll be a little more intelligent. You've only got to be sensible and tell us all you know and we'll let you go. But I warn you that it won't be pleasant for you if you tell us any lies.'

The innocent man, caught up in a turmoil of which he had not the slightest understanding, cowered in his chair.

'But Monsieur, I swear to you that I don't know this gentleman,' he pleaded. 'I swear to you that I haven't had anything to do with the Resistance. I am a musician. I earn my living playing in a night club. I've a wife and two children. Why should I lie to you?'

'That's enough of the funny stuff, *crapule*. I'll make you talk all right. If you don't, my men here will put you through your paces. You've got exactly one minute to make up your mind.'

The miserable little man looked in bewilderment at his captors as he pleaded for mercy.

'Don't hurt me, please, Monsieur. I swear to you on the head of my wife that I don't know this gentleman.'

'So you're going on lying, are you?'

'I am not lying, Monsieur. I cannot say that I know this gentleman opposite me when I have never seen him before.'

The Sicherheitsdienst men got to work as soon as Ernst gave them the sign. One of them plunged his heavy fist into the little man's face, drawing blood from his nose and mouth and making

123

his victim shriek. Then the other man joined in and together they beat up the unfortunate creature while he howled with pain and screamed protestations of innocence. Ernst looked on with a satisfied smirk on his cruel face.

The spectacle was too much for Tommy.

'Cowards!' he roared at them. 'I tell you the poor chap doesn't know me. You're hurting him for nothing. Can't you see he's in terrible pain? If a windy chap like him were guilty he'd tell you all he knew. Bloody fools and brutes.'

'You'll get another dose too for that,' Ernst shouted back.

The two guards beat Yeo-Thomas again with their coshes. When he fell off his chair they kicked him in the ribs with their boots. He fainted again.

When he came round he heard the musician whimpering. Before he could protest again he was picked up and dragged from the room and across the landing. A padlocked door on the same floor was opened and he was thrown into a cell about three feet wide, five feet long and ten feet high; on one side was an opening about a foot square with an iron bar across it. Jerked to his feet he was flung on to a chair, over the back of which his handcuffed hands were slipped. One of the guards gave him a parting blow on the jaw; then they both left, slamming and padlocking the door behind them. Not a ray of light came from the aperture which he had seen when the door had been open; he was in complete darkness.

For the first time since his arrest he was alone. He was all aches and pains. The clotted blood on his face was beginning to draw the skin. His head was buzzing and his nose felt as big as a pumpkin. His jaw hurt terribly and all his teeth were loose. His mouth was full of the salt taste of blood, his eyes burned and the handcuffs were cutting into his wrists. Worn out, he sagged on his chair and the handcuffs bit more deeply into his flesh. As he stiffened he heard a shriek of agony coming across the passage.

The shriek was followed by others more piercing: in the room opposite the Sicherheitsdienst men were beating up the little musician whose only crime had been to have given his telephone number to a friend who had inscribed it on a ten-franc note. The shrieks and groans grew louder and louder and soon were accompanied by even more terrible sounds: there was the thump of a human body being battered against walls; there was the crash of falling furniture; there were sickening thuds and flops. Yeo-Thomas began to roar blasphemies and dirty words at the top of his voice, hurling insults at the perpetrators of this brutal injustice. But the shrieks and groans of the victim were louder and drowned his fiery protests, and Tommy gave up. After half an hour the groans became weaker and weaker and finally there was an appalling silence.

Very tired, Tommy tried to sleep, but every time his head fell forward his handcuffs jabbed him back to agonizing wakefulness. He did not know the time, but guessed that it was already past mid-night. His bladder, surcharged by the water he had swallowed in the bath, felt like bursting, but he could not get up nor could he use his hands. He began to shout; nobody came. Once he heard foot-steps but they died away again. Once the padlock outside was rattled and somebody yelled: '*Englisches Schwein.*'

When at length he was taken back to the interrogation room Ernst was still sitting at the desk, and Rudi, who obviously con-sidered that he had been sent on a second wild-goose chase, was standing menacingly beside him. In a corner a crumpled body lay huddled, shivering pathetically from time to time and emitting low, shuddering moans. It was clear that the torturers now realized they had been barking up the wrong tree; it was equally clear that they felt no remorse for having battered into insensibility and perhaps maimed for life an innocent man.

Rudi glared at Yeo-Thomas.

'You've made me lose my time again. You haven't been in that flat for months. Where did you sleep last night?'

'I don't know. I slept with a whore. I always do that: whores don't talk.'

'Liar! I'll get the truth out of you.'

At a sign from Rudi the two Sicherheitsdienst men went over and hoisted up the moaning, whimpering mass in the corner. Hanging limp and bleeding between the thugs' arms, his head wobbling from side to side, the miserable little man was dragged roughly out of the room. Yeo-Thomas never saw him again and does not know whether he was released or, in order to conceal the mistake which had been made, transported to Germany and liquidated in a con-centration camp.

The pain in Tommy's bladder was now becoming unbearable.

'I need very badly to relieve my feelings,' he said.

'*Crapule!* Do it in your trousers like the dirty dog you are.'

A soldier came in and laid on the desk a tray on which were food and a bottle of wine. Rudi and Ernst, fortunately too tired to go on asking awkward questions about the other keys, sat down and began to eat and drink. They did not speak as they ate, although they kept glancing at their prisoner from time to time. Tommy sat watching them munch, forgetting his own hunger in his desire to urinate: his patriotism was now reduced to the pathetic loyalty of not wetting his trousers in the presence of the enemy. Every minute his bladder seemed to get larger and larger and his penis began to burn and ache. He pressed his legs together, knowing that he could not hold out much longer. At last Rudi and Ernst finished eating and ordered the guards to take him back to the tiny cell on the other side of the landing.

'Look here,' he said to the guards as they were about to lock him in, 'if you won't let me pee it'll all come flooding out under the door.'

The guards, after solemn consultation, led him to a lavatory and allowed him to pass water, cursing him for the time he took. Conducted back to the cell, he was thrust on to the chair as before, with his hands slipped over the back, and left in pitch blackness.

Congratulating himself on having won the very essential first victory of having given his contacts time to disperse themselves, Tommy tried to rest in order to gain strength for the trials which he knew still awaited him. Unable to sleep with his arms fastened behind the chair, he attempted to free them. But each movement he made was agony, and when he attempted to rise to his feet his legs and his shoulders were so stiff that all that happened was that the chair slid back until it reached the wall. Finally he fell forward, the chair tipped, his forehead struck the wall in front of him and his arms were free. With difficulty setting the chair upright again, he sat on it and, although more comfortable, found that he had less room than before, as his handcuffed arms now intervened between his body and the back of the chair. He then shuffled the chair into a corner of the cell and leaned his head against the wall. With pain racking him from head to foot and wanting desperately to blow his nose, he eventually dozed.

He was awakened by the noise of the bar outside being lifted and of the padlock being opened, and by a shout of '*Raus!*' Luckily the guards did not notice that he had freed his arms from the back of the chair. Yanked out of the cell, he was pushed back into the now familiar room where two new interrogators awaited him. Smaller than Rudi and Ernst, the new inquisitors were clean-shaven and bull-necked and had glistening, beady eyes. Both began firing questions at him at once, starting not where Rudi and Ernst had left off but, in the evident desire of trapping him in a contradiction, where they had begun. Tired and sleepy, it was fortunate that Yeo-Thomas knew his story by heart.

'Name?'

'Kenneth Dodkin.'

'Number?'

'47,865.'

'Rank?'

'Squadron Leader.'

'Branch of the Service?'

'Royal Air Force.'

'Address?'

'I do not require to reply to that question.'

'Where are the arms dumps?'

'I don't know.'

As previously, the interrogation was punctuated with punches, slaps and insults. He was knocked off his chair and kicked as he lay helpless on the floor. After about an hour he was taken back to the bathroom, undressed and the all-but-drowning process began again, this time without the horrible young women. He had now, however, elaborated a new technique: as soon as his head went under water he kicked vigorously and then, just as he felt himself about to lose consciousness, let himself go limp. As before, he swallowed a lot of water and underwent what he euphemistically terms discomfort, but the icy cold dispelled his torpor and he was brave enough to derive consolation from the thought that he was still gaining time. He was alternately half-drowned and artificially revived for about another hour until he deliberately collapsed and took his own time to recover. Dragged back to the interrogation room he was forced to sit and watch his tormentors eat their breakfast of hot coffee and croissants. Then he was beaten up again until he was almost insensible.

Nearly past caring what happened to him, he was left to recover from the blows. Day was beginning to break, and the screams of prisoners being tortured in other rooms showed that the Geheime Staatspolizei [1] had already opened shop. Tommy began to try to think up a means of escape.

But he was not left alone for long. Rudi and Ernst soon turned up again and started in as soon as they arrived:

'Where are the arms dumps?'

'I don't know.'

Although the keys weren't mentioned again Rudi made his prisoner pay for having sent him on two useless errands and prevented him from exploiting his capture: his questions were accompanied by mighty beatings-up, and another visit was paid to the bathroom, where the half-drowning treatment was again vainly employed.

In the afternoon a new master and a new technique were tried. Put into a car and accompanied by two Sicherheitsdienst men, Yeo-Thomas was driven to No. 84 Avenue Foch, where an armed escort awaited him. He was led into a small office, where a small studious-looking man, whose spectacles increased his appearance of benignity, sat at a typewriter; beside him stood a giant of about six-foot-five, dressed in SS uniform with skull and crossbones on the collar. The giant, lifting Tommy almost with one hand, placed him on a chair in front of his new inquisitor, who for quite five minutes examined him with dispassionate, silent curiosity. Then, when he had filled his typewriter with foolscap and carbon, he leaned back in his swivel chair and joined his hands professorially on his chin.

'I am not like the others,' he said, speaking in the customary correct Gestapo French. 'I shall not hurt you. If you are sensible we shall be good friends. Come now, you will do yourself no good by obstinacy. You've had your flutter and you've lost. Now all you've got to do is to answer my questions.'

Yeo-Thomas did not answer; although the repetition of the flutter phrase amused him, he was very much on his guard.

'Your name?'

'Kenneth Dodkin.'

[1] Gestapo.

Wing Commander Yeo-Thomas, G.C., M.C. and Bar, Légion d'Honneur, Croix de Guerre, Polish Gold Cross of Merit. Portrait taken eight hours before he parachuted into France for the second time in September, 1943

Pierre Brossolette

Actual message written (on page torn out of a fellow-prisoner's diary, with the lead out of a pencil) by Tommy while wearing handcuffs and travelling in a lorry. This message was thrown out into a street in the outskirts of Paris. Tommy saw two bicyclists pick the message up and it eventually arrived on Barbara's desk in London

The certificate of demobilisation, bearing the false identity of
François Thierry, manufactured in London during the war

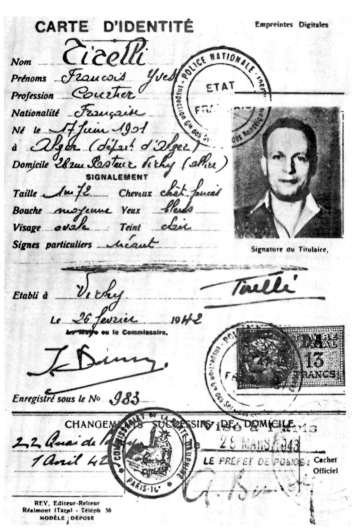

CARTE D'IDENTITÉ

Empreintes Digitales

Nom _Tirelli_

Prénoms _François Yves_

Profession _Courtier_

Nationalité _Française_

Né le _17 juin 1901_

à _Alger (départ d'Alger)_

Domicile _28 rue Pasteur Vichy (Allier)_

SIGNALEMENT

Taille _1m72_   Cheveux _chât foncés_

Bouche _moyenne_   Yeux _bleus_

Visage _ovale_   Teint _clair_

Signes particuliers _néant_

Signature du Titulaire,

Etabli à _Vichy_   _Tirelli_

Le _26 février_ 1942

Le Maire ou le Commissaire.

Enregistré sous le Nº _983_

CHANGEMENTS SUCCESSIFS DE DOMICILE

22 Quai de la

1 Avril 42

28 MARS 1943

LE PRÉFET DE POLICE   Cachet Officiel

REY, Editeur-Relieur
Réalmont (Tarn) - Téléph 56
MODÈLE DÉPOSE

The identity card, also manufactured in London, for François Yves Tirelli, another of the identities assumed by Wing Commander Yeo-Thomas

'Your number?'

'47,865.'

'Your rank?'

'Squadron Leader.'

'Your Branch of the Service?'

'Royal Air Force.'

'Your address?'

'I do not require to answer that question.'

'Where are the arms dumps?'

'I don't know.'

Unlike Rudi and Ernst and their second strings, the little man did not swear or threaten: he just typed down Tommy's answers.

'You know Cadillac?' ('Cadillac' was one of Bingen's code names.)

'Cadillac? I know nobody of that name. It's the trade name of an American car, isn't it?'

An ominous look came into the little man's eyes.

'It would be as well if you were to refrain from playing the fool. I happen to know that you know Cadillac.'

'You are making a mistake.'

The little man shook his head sorrowfully.

'My friend, you are going to force me to resort to methods I don't like very much.'

Yeo-Thomas did not answer; he found this detached manner of examination much more disturbing than Rudi's brutal onslaughts.

'Where is Cadillac?'

'I tell you I don't know Cadillac.'

'What a very great pity! You are forcing my hand, you know. Listen. We not only know who you are; we also know a great deal about you, much more than you imagine. So it's no use your telling us lies and making us lose our time. Although we're kind-hearted we don't like being treated like fools. All you've got to do is to answer our questions; we'll know when you are telling the truth.'

'I can't very well tell you that I know Cadillac when I don't know him.'

'And Pic? Do you know him?' (Pic was one of Pichard's code names.)

'Yes, I know Pic.' This time Tommy could not lie, knowing that

Antonin, who had been Pichard's agent-de-liaison, had almost certainly admitted the connection between his normal master and himself.

'What does he look like?'

Almost as much to test his inquisitor's knowledge as to protect his friend, Yeo-Thomas gave a description of Pichard which was the contrary of reality: omitting to mention that Pichard had a mutilated hand, he made him short and plump instead of tall and thin and when asked the colour of the Air Operations Officer's hair, stated that he could not say because Pichard, who in fact was always bareheaded, never took off his hat. To his surprise his bluff succeeded.

'It's just as well you've told us the truth,' the little man said. 'You see, we arrested Pichard yesterday.'

Realizing that his interrogator had lied and did not know as much as he pretended, Tommy tried to stall for time by answering dilatorily the next very insidious questions and by feigning surprise at their nature. But suddenly the little man, employing the now famous Russian technique, asked him once again:

'Where is Cadillac?'

'I don't know Cadillac.'

'You're lying and I know it. You know Cadillac very well. What's more, you knew him in London. He's a Jew.'

'You know more than I do.'

'Dear me! I can see that my method doesn't suit you at all. Well, I have a friend who is not quite so gentle.' The little man picked up the telephone and spoke in German.

Presently a strongly-built bullet-headed man with small, piercing, pig-like eyes came in and, without a word, crashed his heavy fist into Tommy's face. The small inquisitor looked on with an expression of regret and commiseration.

Led out of the office by the giant, Yeo-Thomas was handed over to two Sicherheitsdienst men, who escorted him to a small room on the fourth floor, where they were immmediately joined by the bullet-headed man. The links on his handcuffs were attached to a hook on the end of a long double chain which hung from a pulley on the ceiling; the other end was pulled and, as his heels left the ground, the steel of the handcuffs was forced deeply into his wrists.

Agony shot through his shoulders, a red film obscured his eyes and, unable to restrain himself, he groaned. As he fainted he heard the bullet-headed man laugh. In intermittent spells of consciousness he suffered pain worse than any he had so far endured. Not until it was dark did they loosen him, and at once he crumpled up on the floor.

When he came to he was in atrocious agony; the circulation in his arms had been stopped by his handcuffs, which had been tightened by the pull on them, and his shoulders had been dislocated. He felt that he had reached breaking point and was afraid that if they tortured him again he would speak and tell them all about the arms dumps and the Secret Army and the Maquis. He knew that his tormentors were fully aware of the extent of his knowledge and would recoil before no brutality in order to make him talk.

But there was to be no more torture for him that night: flat out after more than twenty-four hours' almost continuous interrogation and chastisement, he was half-carried to a small cell at the top of the building, from which he was almost at once removed to another room, in which sat the giant and a mean-looking N.C.O. Flopping on a settee, he asked desperately and was allowed to be taken to the water-closet, where, unbuttoned and watched by his guards, he was forced to sit with the door open and clean himself painfully with his manacled hands.

He had to spend the night chained by his arms and legs to the settee. Hungry and thirsty, he was refused food, but was eventually given a mug of water. The only time he managed to sleep was during the short period when his guards were snoring; otherwise as soon as he dozed off he was shaken awake by the mean-looking N.C.O., who roared at him: '*Nicht schlafen.*' He thought of Barbara and longed like a child for the comfort of her arms. He thought of Brossolette and wondered if he would still be rescued. (He did not know that Brossolette, whose identity had been discovered, was already dead: brought from Rennes to Paris for interrogation, Brossolette, who had previously discarded his poison tablet, had either been thrown out of a window by the Germans or had fallen from it while trying to escape, and, with his cranium fractured and his arms and legs broken, had died in the Hôpital de la Pitié).

When dawn came the giant went out and brought back bread

and sausage and a steaming jug of hot coffee for himself and his companion. The sight and the smell of the warm food made Tommy feel hungry and cold and he asked hopefully for a drink: he was given another mug of water.

'*Ich bin kalt*,' he said, but the only answer he was vouchsafed was '*Englisches Schwein*' and he was left to freeze.

Nor was it only with cold that he was freezing; he was freezing also with fear. As the morning grew lighter he knew that the moment was fast approaching when he would again writhe under the torments of his captors. He was at the end of his tether; he felt that if they did anything too painful to him this time he was bound to break down and speak. He wished for death because it was only in death that he could be sure of not speaking. Terror tore through his bowels when his chains were undone and he was pulled to his feet. Behind his swollen lips this modern saint who did not admire sanctity prayed that the cup might pass from him. 'Ah, yes, for there are times when all pray,' his friend and hero Mr. Churchill had said.

But his resolution returned as he thought of Barbara, of his friends who trusted in him, of Dismore, of Thackthwaite, of Johnson, of Whitehead, of Passy and of Brossolette. Brossolette would never have betrayed the cause and he would not be false to Brossolette. In another office on the fourth floor, with lacerated face, swollen eyelids, tousled hair, collarless and in crumpled clothes covered with coagulated blood, and with the giant seated behind him, he faced a new, sinister and menacing interrogator:

'Are you still going to be pig-headed? Or are you going to talk?'

'I have nothing to say.'

'I can see quite clearly that you are a liar. But we have methods of making even liars talk, methods you don't know yet.'

Yeo-Thomas made a quick calculation: already he had held out for almost forty-six hours; in another two hours he would have accomplished the statutory forty-eight, and then perhaps he could afford to let slip a few unimportant details. In the meantime he must still strive to gain time.

'You know Cadillac, I think. His real name is Bingen. He is a Jew.'

This unexpected knowledge relieved Tommy. In view of his rôle in the Resistance he could not deny knowing Bingen; if he had denied knowing him under his code name of Cadillac it had been in order to avoid being forced to admit that, while he was ignorant of his whereabouts, he could get into touch with him when he wanted.

'I didn't know he was called Cadillac,' he said.

The German seemed surprised.

'Do you mean to tell me that you didn't know that Cadillac and Bingen were one and the same person?'

'No. You see, everybody has several names and one can't be expected to know them all.'

'But you know where he is.'

'No.'

'Yes, you know quite well, and what's more you're going to tell us.'

'How can you expect me to tell you where he is when I don't know myself?'

But the new inquisitor seemed to know all the tricks of the trade.

'In that case you must have a permanent rendezvous with him. Where is that rendezvous?'

'I have no permanent rendezvous with him. In any case he must know by now that I have been arrested.' In spite of his pain, hunger and weariness he still had the energy to lie fluently: 'You see, I had an appointment with him yesterday. As I didn't turn up he will know what has happened. So even if I wanted to I couldn't find him.'

'Ha, ha! So you had an appointment with him yesterday? And you won't tell us, *Schweinehund?* That's another thing you've still got to pay for.' The interrogator suddenly abandoned his threats and spoke in honeyed tones. 'Listen. I am certain that you know where to find him. If you will tell us we'll be kind to you. Of that I give you my word as a German officer.'

'I can't tell you anything.'

'Come, come. Don't be obstinate. What would you say if I were to make a bargain with you? I think perhaps we could release you. We'll organize an escape. You see how simple it is? Nobody will ever know that you have talked.'

Battered, caked with blood, trembling in every limb, Yeo-

Thomas looked the German full in the face out of his puffed eye-lids.

'I can't tell you where to find Bingen,' he said. 'And even if I could I wouldn't.'

His defiance made the inquisitor splutter with rage.

'You're the friend of a dirty Jew,' he shouted. 'I'm beginning to think that you must be a Jew yourself.'

'I am not a Jew and I don't know if Bingen is one, and in any case it's none of my business.'

The German came out with one of those seventeenth-hand boring but incendiary lies which contemporary demagogues serve up as political thought to literate barbarians:

'You English are not a pure race like we are. You're infected with Jewish blood and you'll lose the war because you're decadent. You're governed by Jews, you're owned by the Jews and you're the slaves of Jews.'

'Mr. Churchill governs us and he is not a Jew.' Tommy held himself erect in his chair as he thought of the man who had been kind to him and who had helped him to help France.

'Our Führer is the superior of your Churchill, who is only the lackey of international Jewry.'

Realizing that he was gaining time by this absurd political argument, Tommy did his best to prolong it.

'Germany has lost the war,' he said. 'You couldn't invade Britain, but we shall invade France and you'll be beaten.'

The German rose to the bait; another stream of verbal reach-me-downs poured from him: the British Royal Family was tainted with Jewish blood; impoverished English peers had married the wealthy daughters of greasy Levantines and turned the House of Lords into a Sanhedrin; the House of Commons was a synagogue; Wall Street was a ghetto and Roosevelt a rabbi. It was to liberate the world from the slimy machinations of the yellow-livered yid that Hitler was fighting the war.

To this folly Yeo-Thomas made the mistake of answering with almost equal folly:

'And your Führer. He's not a German; he's only an Austrian house-painter gone wrong.'

The remark was stupid, not only because there was no reason

why an Austrian house-painter should not have made a better politician than the suave incompetents brought up in the chancelleries, but also because it put an end to their comparatively polite conversation The inquisitor again became persistent and threatening:

'Where are the arms dumps?'

Seated within three feet of a window, Tommy gathered all his strength for a desperate leap across an intervening table: provided that he got through the window quickly enough there was every chance, as the office was on the fourth floor, that he would kill himself or at least hurt himself so badly that he would not recover; and even if he didn't die the Germans would have to put him in hospital, where they might forget about him and leave him to be freed by the Allies when they arrived in about three months' time.

'Where are the arms dumps? You have suffered, I know, but I promise you that you shall suffer much more if you do not answer my question.'

He sprang and, taking his captors by surprise, jumped clean over the table. His head hit the glass pane and smashed it and his shoulders passed through. But the giant was too quick for him: seizing Tommy by the ankles, he pulled him back into the room and sat him back on his chair, to which he was now securely fastened by chains hurriedly brought by a soldier.

'So you are frightened, are you?' the interrogator said with a leer. 'Well, now's the time to speak. If you don't it'll be very unpleasant for you indeed. We'll use new methods and you'll suffer. Make up your mind and be quick about it because I can't afford to waste my time.'

Tommy did not answer: he knew that if he spoke it would be to beg for mercy. The faces of those whose lives depended upon his silence passed before his blurred vision in a long pleading procession. He could not keep what the militarists and muscular clergymen used to call a stiff upper lip because his upper lip was smashed, but he obstinately held to the only loyalty he knew: he said nothing and by doing so proved himself to be that rarity in a world of mean shifts and compromise: a man of integrity.

'Well, we shall see,' the interrogator said as he rose.

Accompanied by his inquisitor and an escort, Yeo-Thomas was

driven back to the rue des Saussaies, where another glaring and cursing interrogator awaited him in a different room with a long table in it.

'Now you'll speak,' the thug roared at him. 'You're afraid. It's now or never.'

Desperately terrified, Tommy remained silent. He knew that he was protecting the unjust as well as the just and that brick-faced, martini-sozzling company directors sticking their snitches into black-market lobster would never appreciate his sacrifice. But there was Brossolette, with whom he had walked in the nearest thing he could find to the house of God as friends, and Brossolette would never have spoken. He would not speak either; and he didn't.

Five new thugs came in. Thrown on to the table, chains were fastened round his legs and attached to the desk in such a manner that his feet were spread out. Two men held down his arms; with rubber coshes the other three rained thudding blows on his face, legs and body, concentrating on his testicles. He screamed with agony. The thugs slammed away till he fainted.

When he came to he found himself lying on a couch with broken springs in an empty, bare room. Through the only window, barred and high up, he could see that it was already dark outside; it had been morning when they had started beating him up. He was sobbing and the tears were welling out through his inflated eyelids. His penis and his testicles felt as though they had been crushed. The excruciating pain in his lower abdomen made him want to vomit, but each time that he retched nothing came up and the strain sent deep stabbing pains slicing through his entrails. In spite of his nausea and agony he was hungry. His suffering soon sent him back into semi-consciousness, in which his sore body seemed to float away from him like a balloon.

He began to lose track of the sequence of events. He remembers being questioned, but recollects the questions only hazily:

'What is your name?'

'Kenneth Dodkin.'

'Your serial number?'

'47,685.'

'Where are the arms dumps?'

'I don't know.'

136

'Where have you been living for the past few weeks?'

'I have been sleeping with whores. With many whores in various places.'

This last was the dangerous question and he knew it, but his interrogators knew it too, and they came back to it again and again. One inquisitor, a fair, good-looking man of twenty-six or twenty-seven called Ernst[1] was, however, more subtle and less brutal than his colleagues:

'I know where you live. It's no use your trying to gain time.'

'If you know where I live why do you ask me?'

'Because we have several of your addresses and we want to arrest everybody whom we suspect of helping people like you.'

'When you talk like that it's quite clear to me you don't know where I live.'

'I'll prove it to you that I do. All you've got to do is to show me on the map the district of Paris you live in.'

'That won't help you much.'

A map was brought and on it, with a temporarily freed hand, Yeo-Thomas drew a large circle taking in at least a quarter of Paris. To his surprise Ernst laughed.

'You think you're clever, don't you? But I'll show you that I'm even cleverer. You live at 11 rue Claude Chahu.'

'What makes you think that?'

'I don't think; I know. And, what's more, I know that you weren't the only person to use this address.'

Flabbergasted, Tommy did not reply.

'Had you firearms hidden in this house?'

'What on earth should I be wanting with firearms?' But it was of the identity discs stamped in the name of Kenneth Dodkin and hidden between the floorboards of Suni Sandöe's flat that Yeo-Thomas was thinking: if the Gestapo discovered these they might realize that such compromising possessions could have been brought by an agent to France only in order to conceal his true identity.

'What about that pistol you were carrying? That's a firearm, isn't it? Look here, if you tell me the names of the persons who sheltered you I promise you that no harm will come to them.'

Tommy did not answer.

---

[1] Not the same as the 'Ernst' mentioned previously.

'I give you my word of honour as a German officer.'

'I do not believe in the word of honour of a German officer.'

'You're wrong, and I'll show you. There's an English prisoner here who'll tell you that we keep our word.' A shortish man with a toothbrush moustache was brought in. 'This is the English officer. Ask him if German officers keep their word of honour.'

Yeo-Thomas turned to the newcomer.

'What is all this about?' he asked in English. 'Are you British?'

'Yes.'

'How do they treat you?'

'Not too badly.'

'Do they keep their word?'

'Yes,' the British officer replied with studied carelessness, giving Tommy a look which was almost a wink.

'So you see,' Ernst said when the British officer had been led out again. 'Now what about giving us that name? Not that it matters really. Our men are there already and they'll soon find out from the concierge.'

Tommy knew that whether the Gestapo men were or were not at 11 rue Claude Chahu they could soon force the concierge to tell them that a stranger called Gaonach had stayed from time to time in Suni Sandöe's flat on the ground floor. Whatever he did or did not say, Suni Sandöe was now blown. If she had already been arrested she would be beaten up until she admitted that she knew him and they would ultimately be confronted; there was, however, every chance that, warned by his failure to return for his suitcase in the evening of his planned departure for Rennes, she had gone into hiding. The only thing that he could now do to help her was to represent her as ignorant of the nature of his activities. This he did and Ernst said that he could now go back to the rue des Saussaies, from which, in his fuddled state, he did not recollect having been removed.

Rudi slapped him on the face when he got back and had him flung once more into the tiny cell opposite his office. Still handcuffed and sore, Tommy sat on the chair and waited until he was taken to be interrogated by a sallow-faced, dark-haired, black-jowled man with bad teeth, who asked him in a rough voice questions about sabotage. Yeo-Thomas sagged on his seat and ignored his questions. He was then conducted again to the bathroom, stripped and, as far as he can remember, half-drowned and artificially revived six times.

He did not know whether it was night or day when he was taken to his next interrogation, which was conducted on entirely different lines, by a man of about fifty and by a slim young man with horn-rimmed glasses.

'They've been rather unkind to you, I see,' the young man said. 'It's unfortunate, but that's war for you. I expect you're rather hungry.'

Almost immediately a soldier carried in a tray on which was a jug of hot soup, a cup and a plate of sausage sandwiches.

'It's not much, but at four o'clock in the morning Maxim's is shut,' the young man said. He came round, undid Tommy's hand-cuffs and fastened his sore, stiff arms in front of his body, and with the handcuffs looser than before. 'I'm afraid I'll have to put them back again afterwards. And you mustn't say I've done this, because I'm not supposed to be humane.'

While the young man poured out the soup for him Yeo-Thomas saw his hands for the first time since he had been tortured on the chain: the handcuffs were rusty with blood, the flesh around his badly cut wrists was purple and his left arm was swollen up to the elbow. However, when he had eaten the sandwiches and drunk a cup of soup he was able to pour himself out a second cup. Then the older man stuck a cigarette in his mouth and lighted it for him. Warmed by the food, Tommy felt his strength returning. Knowing that this clemency was part of a technique, he waited warily for the first question.

He was shown a photograph of Clo, who had been Air Operations Officer for the Bordeaux area and whom he knew to be dead.

'Do you know who this is?'

'I think so.'

'I think that you know very well indeed who it is, but unfortunately he is dead.'

Tommy pretended to be surprised.

'I didn't know that; poor chap.'

Many more questions followed, but they were kindly and not too persistently put, and showed a vast superficial knowledge of Resist-ance plans and as vast an ignorance of the details. Yeo-Thomas was, therefore, able to appear co-operative by restricting the truth of his replies to what his interrogators already knew and by giving them false information about what they obviously didn't. He was shown a faulty chart of the B.C.R.A. apparently compiled from similar interrogations and purporting to give the names of all the component officers and their duties; pretending to be impressed by its accuracy, he increased the war establishment by giving the names of non-existent officers to whom he ascribed almost fantastic duties; this information was gravely inscribed on the chart and he was given two more cigarettes as a reward.

At noon he was collected by two guards from Rudi's section and on his way downstairs was horrified to meet Suni Sandöe, also under the escort of guards. Surprisingly he was allowed to say a few words to her and tried to convey to her that she must pretend to have been ignorant of his activities and deny having seen any arms in her flat. He learned later that, having neglected to go into hiding, she had been arrested in her flat in the rue Claude Chahu.

Later that day, which he was astonished to discover was only Friday, he was again interrogated by Rudi, who seemed very pleased with himself and was unexpectedly benign. When this interview ended at dusk he was made to enter a large room in which, seated on chairs evenly spaced but staggered so that no two were side by side, were assembled Commandant Palaud, second-in-command of the Paris area, Doyen, the younger brother of Commandant Manuel of the B.C.R.A., Anne-Marie, Yvonne and Georges of Pichard's secretariat and circuit, Chaland, saboteur and executioner of traitors, and others. Palaud's face was puffed and swollen, his clothes were torn and his hands smeared with blood. Anne-Marie's hair was dripping with water and lay in wet strands down her pale face; and most of the others looked tired and worn. Yeo-Thomas now understood the reason for Rudi's good humour: the catch was certainly a good one.

Made to sit in the chair next to Palaud, but with his back towards him, Tommy turned to warn his old friend not to say that he knew him and was immediately slapped on the face by one of the three guards stationed behind the row of chairs. Determined to prevent the Gestapo from discovering contradictions between Palaud's story and his own, he began to hum the tune of *Madame la Mar-*

quise. When he saw that the guards took no notice he hummed a little louder. Then he sang the words: *'Tout va très bien, Madame la Marquis-e'.* When he saw the guards were still paying no attention he substituted words of his own: *'Je ne connais pas Artilleur.* ('Artilleur' was Palaud's code name.) *Je ne l'ai jamais vu. Il m'est inconnu ainsi que Chaland. J'ai été pris mardi; et vous?*[1] Then he lapsed into humming again, and Palaud joined in, chanting in his turn information as to when he himself had been arrested and what he had and had not told his captors.

About two hours later, when it was dark, there were shouts of *''Raus! Los! Schnell!'.* Accompanied by guards armed with submachine-guns, the prisoners were marched downstairs into a hallway, where Rudi and Ernst checked their names off on a list. 'Dodkin' seemed to be the first name on this list, for it was Tommy who was made to lead the way into the prison van waiting outside; inside the van he was propelled along a narrow passage lined with steel doors and locked into a dark cell with only a vent to give him air. Other doors slammed and they were off. As the van bumped off the pavement on to the causeway Tommy saw through the vent the toes of a pair of German jackboots, but it was with his mind rather than with his eyes that he was able to follow the beloved streets along which they bowled: the Avenue Marigny, the Champs Elysées, the Boulevard St. Germain, the Boulevard Raspail were familiar decades in his rosary of the city, and they lingered in his thoughts even when the van was out in the country, lurching over the cobbles towards Fresnes.

[1] 'I don't know Artilleur. I've never seen him. I don't know Chaland either. I was caught on Tuesday. When were you caught?'

CHAPTER XI

FRESNES

ON their arrival in the courtyard of the famous prison they were greeted with the same brutal shouts of small men giving themselves the illusion of greatness: *''Raus! Schnell!'* Yeo-Thomas was helped to be quick: yanked from his cell, he was almost flung out among the others and found Chaland seated on the cobbles, so badly injured that he could not walk. It was a case of the halt having to help the halt, but, luckily, the halt were not also dumb: as they carried Chaland into the prison Tommy and Palaud told him that so far his name had not been mentioned in their interrogations, and Chaland informed them that theirs had not been mentioned in his and that the Germans had fortunately not discovered his identity as chief executioner of traitors. They agreed that they would try to keep together in prison and, if possible, occupy the same cell.

This, however, was not to be. After a preliminary roll call in the prison hall, the prisoners were marched down a subterranean passage, Tommy and Palaud again carrying Chaland. They were halted in a larger hall, around which gangways and galleries, lined with doors running right up to the roof, resounded with the heavy tread of sentries. Here a second roll call took place, to which Yeo-Thomas again answered in the name of Dodkin. At a shout of *'Troisième Division'*, Palaud, who had spent the previous night in the prison, moved off down another subterranean passage: Chaland, unable to walk, could not follow, and Yeo-Thomas, who tagged on behind Palaud hopefully, was fetched back with a blow from a rifle butt when his absence from the prisoners allocated to the *Deuxième Division* had been discovered.

Angry at having been kept waiting, an N.C.O. in Wehrmacht uniform slapped him, spat several times in his face and kicked him all the way to a darkened cell, into which he sent him careering with a snarl and a parting kick; unable to mitigate his fall, with his hands manacled behind his back, Tommy's head hit a stone wall and he fell full length.

When he was able to stand on his unsteady legs he began, gingerly and in complete blackness, to explore his new dwelling-place: a few steps forward brought him to a wall, another few steps to the right to a corner, and another few steps again to the right to what felt like a flap table; skirting this table he came to a w.c. pan and finally bumped into an iron bed with a palliasse, upon which he sank exhausted.

He could, however, lie only on his right side, because of the position of his hands and the shooting pains in his left wrist. He dozed off, but almost immediately the screams of a prisoner being beaten up awoke him, and after that, as he had no blankets or overcoat, the cold kept him awake for the rest of the night.

In the dismal grey light of dawn he was able to make out the form and furniture of the cell: the sight of a tap over the w.c. pan and a mug on the flat table increased his thirst. But even with his back towards the table his handcuffed arms could not stretch far enough to reach the mug, and he had to give up without having tried the very much more difficult feat of simultaneously holding the mug under, and pressing the button on, the water tap. In misery he began to pace the cell: it was four paces wide and eight paces long.

Soon he heard a noise with which he was to become familiar: the sound of steel trucks on rails. The food trolleys were beginning their rounds. A little later a key grated in the lock and a man in rags, obviously a French prisoner employed as an orderly, stood holding out a steaming ladle.

'*Amène ta gamelle.* Bring your mug. And look slippy about it or the Fritz will start shouting.'

The Fritz started shouting almost before Yeo-Thomas had time to explain why he could not bring his mug.

'*Schnell, schnell, Schweinehund,*' he roared as he came rushing in from the corridor; but when he saw Tommy's plight he filled his mug for him and placed it on the edge of the table.

To drink the hot liquid, which turned out to be a very dubious ersatz coffee, Yeo-Thomas had to kneel on the floor and suck it up the side of the mug. More than once he had to use his head to prevent the mug capsizing and rolling off the table; the last few drops of coffee poured down his chin when the mug finally toppled over.

Another prisoner-orderly came and flung a dirty blanket on his bed and handed him two minute squares of toilet paper cut from a newspaper.

'You must clean up your own cell or Fritz will start creating,' he said.

'How do you expect me to clean up my cell when I can't even go to the water-closet?' Tommy was explaining to the orderly his very urgent need when the N.C.O. who had bullied him the previous evening came in and slogged the orderly on the jaw. When Yeo-Thomas tried to illustrate his requirements by turning his back and waggling his hands he was cursed and given a kick which sent him sprawling to the floor, where he was given another kick for calling the N.C.O. a coward.

Shortly after this visit he heard knocks on the other side of the wall and, although he guessed that a neighbour was trying to communicate with him, he was unable to reply because of the fetters on his hands. Then, from somewhere in the prison, a voice shouted gaily: '*Patrice vous dit bonjour à tous: courage et confiance!*' [1] Almost immediately another voice cried: '*Laurence dit bonjour à Patrice et à tous ses amis: on les aura!*' [2] More shouts followed. Antoine greeted Lecocq and Lecocq hailed Lucien. There was a storm of abuse from the German guards, who rushed about trying to quell the noise, but as they ran to where the shouting seemed to come from the cries broke out somewhere else. Encouraged by this demonstration, Yeo-Thomas went to the door of his cell and contributed to the rebellion by bawling at the top of his voice: 'JE VEUX ALLER AU CABINET! JE VEUX ALLER AU CABINET! JE VEUX ALLER AU CABINET!' [3]

A German soldier came bursting in almost at once.

'*Ruhe, Schwein!*' he ordered.

Once again Tommy explained his need, but the soldier did not possess enough French to understand either the euphemisms of the Boulevard St. Germain or the exactitude of Ménilmontant, and Tommy was obliged to give a pantomimic display on the pan of the w.c.

[1] 'Patrice wishes everybody good morning. Don't lose heart.'
[2] 'Laurence wishes all her friends good morning. We'll get them yet.'
[3] 'I want to go to the closet! I want to go to the closet! I want to go to the closet!'

'Ach, scheissen!'

'Oui, mon vieux.'

'Ich werde den Unteroffizier holen.' [1]

But the Unteroffizier when he came could not do much about it because he hadn't the keys to the handcuffs, for which he said he would have to telephone to the Tribunal.

'And,' he said, 'when a German soldier comes into your cell you must stand to attention.'

Tommy looked the man full in the face, noticing that he wore the Iron Cross and two campaign medals and that he had a kindly expression; but his reply to him was the same as it would have been to the N.C.O. who had kicked him:

'A British officer stands to attention only in the presence of his superiors.'

The Unteroffizier, as he had half-expected, grinned.

'In that case stand well to the rear of the cell or you'll have trouble with my colleagues,' he said as he unbuttoned him and then handed him, in return for a pledge of secrecy, a sheaf of toilet paper of more than the exiguous regulation size.

Late that evening the professorial-looking interrogator from the Avenue Foch arrived and, fawned upon by the bullying N.C.O., removed Tommy's handcuffs and slipped them in his pocket.

'I'm afraid we'll have to put them on again when you go for interrogation,' he said. 'In the meantime that wrist of yours doesn't look very pretty and we'd better put some disinfectant on it.' He gave a sharp command to the orderly, of which Yeo-Thomas understood only the word *'Sanitäter'*.

The Sanitäter, a drunken little runt with a wild alcoholic gleam in his squinting eyes, turned out to be anything but sanitary. Spraying spittle on a foul-smelling breath into his patient's face, he poured ether on a piece of dirty cotton-wool with which he removed the pus from the deep, long, wide cut on Tommy's wrist. 'It's a waste of time treating swine that are going to die anyway,' he snarled. He then held a bottle of iodine upside down over the wound and leered in expectation of the protest which did not come. Smearing a black ointment on another piece of dirty cotton-wool with even filthier hands, he bound it with a crêpe paper

[1] 'I'll fetch the Unteroffizier.'

145

bandage round the wrist and, after swallowing the remains of the ether in the first bottle, staggered out of the cell with a parting *'Schweinehund!'*

Yeo-Thomas slept better that night because his arms were now free and he had a blanket. In the morning there was more knocking on the wall of his cell, but as it was not Morse he could not interpret it. Anxious to make contact with his fellow-prisoners and at the same time to avoid communicating with black marketeers, delinquent collaborators and stool pigeons, he began to whistle loudly the tune of a French Protestant hymn which he thought only the right sort of wrongdoer would know: *'Jusqu'à la mort nous te serons fidèles.'* [1]

Almost immediately a voice shouted:

'Je demande à savoir qui vient de siffler.' [2]

'A newcomer,' Tommy shouted back. 'A British officer.'

'You're a Protestant, aren't you? What chapel do you belong to?'

'The Protestant chapel at Dieppe.'

'Careful. Here comes the Barker.'

The Barker was the bullying N.C.O., and he came roaring along the passage, trying to find out who had been whistling. When he had gone away Tommy's new friend began again:

'Ecoute, Dieppois. I'm going to call you Tartarin. My name is Lecocq. When did you come here?'

'The day before yesterday.'

'You're the man with his hands handcuffed behind his back?'

'Yes.'

'Then you're in the cell next to me.'

He heard knocking on the side of the wall behind the lavatory pan, to which he tapped back. On further instructions he unscrewed the press button of his tap and listened: he heard a scraping noise and then the voice of Lecocq:

'You can communicate with me and the boys above this way, but you must be careful not to be caught. The guards are on the job the whole time and the Barker comes sneaking up to doors in carpet slippers. So you say you're a British officer?'

---

[1] 'We'll be true to Thee till death.'
[2] 'I want to know who's just been whistling.'

This was fun; this was glorious: he no longer felt lonely and abandoned; already he could see himself organizing a revolt among the prisoners.

'I'm a British officer serving on General de Gaulle's staff,' he said into the tap.

'I'm on de Gaulle's staff, too.'

'What circuit?'

'Pic's circuit.'

This sounded too good to be true and, fearful that Lecocq might turn out to be a stool pigeon, he asked for proof of his membership; but Lecocq showed that he knew that Pichard had a mutilated hand and was fully conversant with the history of the circuit.

'How long have you been here, then?' he asked.

'Three months, and it's not funny, especially when they take you for questioning.'

'How often does that happen?'

'Fairly often at the beginning, and after that it all depends.'

Tommy thought that he could guess upon what it all depended. But there was something even more important than finding out how much more he was likely to be beaten up, and that was to let his friends in Paris and London, and above all Barbara, know that he was still alive.

'Can you get a message through to the outside for me?' he asked.

'I think so.'

'Say that Shelley's well.'

'I rather think I know that name. Listen, Shelley: speak to me in the morning after breakfast and in the evening one hour after supper. Careful. Here comes the Barker.'

Convinced that the Barker had guessed from the remark about the handcuffs who had been shouting, Tommy was afraid when the N.C.O. came swaggering into his cell. But the bully had come only to transfer him to another floor, and apparently not because of the shouting but because he was more amiable than usual. Korrel, however, the six-foot-four guard to whom he was handed over and who marched him up two flights of steel stairs and along a gangway to cell number 293, was, to begin with, anything but benign; pushing Yeo-Thomas roughly into his new abode he roared:

'Stand to attention. *Schweinehund!*'

'To hell with you; I am an officer.'

'Stand to attention, I tell you!'

'I am a British officer and I refuse.'

Korrel took Tommy in his powerful arms and shook him.

'Stand to attention!' he bawled.

'I tell you I'm a British officer.'

The N.C.O.'s rage vanished as inexplicably as it had begun; he was suddenly simultaneously ingratiating and suspicious, in the manner of Continental doorkeepers anxious to be promoted from the house of the Lord into the tents of ungodliness.

'So you're a British officer, are you? You speak French well for a British officer.'

'So do you,' said Tommy, not wanting to make an enemy of the man now that his principles no longer seemed to be involved.

His flattery succeeded, and the man became friendly. Korrel told him that he came from Mainz and had learned French when he had been a prisoner during the 1914–1918 war.

'But the French were beasts to us,' he said. 'I'd much rather have been taken by the British.'

'The French couldn't very well have been worse to you than the Gestapo have been to me.'

'Those fellows aren't soldiers,' Korrel said.

'That's quite obvious. Soldiers like you and me would never behave like that.'

Korrel was delighted at the compliment.

'It's easy to see you're an officer,' he said as he went out. 'Well, I'll be seeing you.'

Glad that he had apparently established amicable relations with yet another gaoler, Yeo-Thomas set about examining his new abode. The cell was lighter and cleaner than the one he had just left, the palliasse was thicker and the blanket not so dirty. One of the lower panes in the window had very little putty round it and, when he had scraped the putty with his fingernails, he was able to remove and replace the pane at will: with the pane out perhaps he would be able to shout a message to Lecocq, from whom he had been so abruptly and regrettably separated.

He paced the cell, thinking of Barbara and wondering if she were thinking of him. He had nobody to talk to, nothing to do, nothing to read; the solitude which lay in front of him was likely to end only in death, when they took him away, tied him to a post and shot him as a spy. So as not to think about these gloomy things he counted his steps as he paced the cell: four steps one way and eight the other. This small world could be conquered only by escaping from it.

Removing the pane of glass, he made a preliminary reconnaissance. Opposite was the massive Third Division building with rows of heavily barred windows and crowned by a gangway running round the roof. Below, a low construction connected the Third Division with the Second Division in which he still was, two floors above and about twenty-five windows to the left of his previous cell. On either side of this connecting passage was a series of pens enclosed by twelve-foot walls which stopped short before they reached the roof propped over them like a canopy. Along the walls there was a gallery from which guards were watching the pens, in some of which prisoners were beating blankets. More guards were walking on the gangways and on the wide alley of meagre grass between the pens. Birds flying across the sky symbolized in beauty the liberty so hard to attain.

Replacing the glass, he sat down on the bed and tried to think. People had escaped from prison before, and what others had done he could do. As both Lecocq and the professorial-looking interrogator had hinted, he was almost certain to be taken back to Paris for questioning. He must study the habits of the guards on such occasions: perhaps during transfer or while arriving at or leaving the Avenue Foch or the rue des Saussaies what seemed out of the question here in Fresnes would not be impossible.

But to escape he must keep fit. He must do physical exercises every day. Whatever the temptation he must not get slack, lazy or careless. And somehow, without soap, tooth-paste, towel or change of linen he must keep clean. He began to inspect his body and his clothes with the same thoroughness as he had examined the layout of the prison, and the result was almost as discouraging: when, with difficulty because of the pain in his left arm, he had removed his gory jacket and trousers he found his shirt and underclothes too rusted with blood for him to wash them without soap in the w.c. pan; and his body was covered with cuts and bruises, and his testicles were swollen and discoloured. He dressed gloomily and, to cheer himself up, removed the pane of glass and looked out again at the sweet blue promise of the sky. The pens were now empty and there were no guards in sight.

He heard footsteps approaching and had just time to slip the glass into his pocket before the swivel cover on the outside of the door was lifted. Standing in front of the window and trying to look unconcerned, he saw an eye watching through the spy-hole; but even when the cover was lowered again he did not replace the pane of glass and allowed a little of the freedom of the outside world to go on pouring into his cell.

Suddenly, to his joy, he heard a voice shouting in English from the building opposite and another, more muffled, replying. He waited until the conversation had finished and then he bawled with all his might through the hole in the window:

'Who is that speaking English?'

'R.A.F. Warrant Officer. Who are you?' the first voice asked at once.

'An R.A.F. officer.'

'Where were you shot down?'

'I wasn't shot down; I came down on purpose.'

'What the hell do you mean?'

'I came down with an umbrella.'

'Cave.' There was a pause. 'Hello, R.A.F. What is your name? Over to you.'

'Call me Tommy. What is your name? Over to you.'

'Jim. Just where are you? Over to you.'

'Opposite you, I think. Second floor. There's a broken pane. Look for a bandaged arm.'

'Target sighted. Are you alone?'

'Yes. And you?'

'There's a Yank with me and there's an Aussie. I'll call you again later. Cheerio.'

Heartened by this exchange of messages and the ordinarily meaningless valediction, Yeo-Thomas began to pace his cell again, counting the boards on the floor instead of his steps. Between two planks he noticed a nail, which he picked up and pocketed as a weapon for his armoury. Then he read the inscriptions pencilled and scratched on the walls of the cell. Apart from crude pictorial manifestations of concupiscence and threats of death to Jews, fascists, clergymen and cabinet ministers, the pre-war tenants of the cell had not been communicative: Julot de la Bastille had merely noted that he had still forty days to do ('*Quarante au jus*'), and Totor de la Villette had restrained the expression of his antipathies to a run-of-the-bistro 'MORT AUX VACHES'.[1] Recent occupants had been more dignified in their legacies, and some of them had even chiselled out prayers on the plaster: surmounted by a cross between two tricolor flags was this particularly moving message inscribed by a man whose name Tommy has unfortunately forgotten:

'... CONDAMNE A MORT PAR LES BOCHES ET DEVANT ETRE FUSILLE DANS LES 24 HEURES, DIT COURAGE ET CONFIANCE A CEUX QUI LE SUIV-RONT DANS CETTE CELLULE. NOUS VAINCRONS. VIVE LA FRANCE!'[2]

Humbly Yeo-Thomas scratched in a corner with the point of his newly-found nail his own contribution to this fresco of arrogance, lechery, pride and petition: a calendar on which the first date was 21st March, 1944.

Before he went to bed that night he had to reply to quite a number of greetings:

'*Lecocq demande des nouvelles de Tartarin.*'

'*Tartarin va bien, merci.*' This message was relayed by somebody opposite.

'Tommy, Jim calling. Good night from Texas and me.'

'Good night, Jim and Texas. Good night, Aussie.'

'Good night, Tommy.'

'*Ruhe.*'

He had barely replaced the pane of glass when he heard the cover of the spy-hole move. Pretending to be absorbed, he did not look up. The cover dropped. He still did not move. The cover opened again, dropped again. When he had made the pane secure with a substitute putty obtained from his lunch slice of bread he tucked

[1] 'Death to the swine.'
[2] '... sentenced to death by the Boches and due to be shot within 24 hours bids those who follow him to be brave. We shall conquer. Long live France!'

himself up in his blanket and went to sleep with the shadow of a shade of happiness in his slightly less lonely heart.

Next morning a knock at his door and a shout of '*Tribunal!*' warned him to prepare for interrogation. He was marched by Korrel down into the main hall, where other prisoners were already waiting under the surveillance of a dozen guards armed with sub-machine-guns. The Barker called the roll, and as Tommy answered his name he was handcuffed. With the others he marched down the subterranean passage and was locked up alone in a compartment of the prison van.

The second Ernst, in uniform but without badges of rank, was waiting for him at the Avenue Foch. He was bland, genial and insidious. Remarking on the bandage on Tommy's swollen wrist, he undid the left cuff and fastened it to the chair. He then gave him a cigarette and lighted it for him.

'You've been telling us quite a few lies, Shelley, haven't you?' he began. 'There's not much use your denying it. After all, it's your duty to tell us lies, isn't it? But now I think that you can talk without feeling guilty. You see, we know everything now.'

'In that case why bother to ask me questions?'

'Routine, that's all.' The falsely smiling eyes never left Tommy's face. 'We want to know what arms dumps you visited in January.'

'I visited no arms dumps in January; in January I wasn't in France.'

'It's no use your lying, Shelley: we have proof.'

'That's quite impossible. Well, show me your proof.'

'You're surely not going to deny that you know Horace?' (Horace was the young man whom Yeo-Thomas had engaged as agent-de-liaison on the recommendation of José Dupuis and a priest and whom he had dismissed for unpunctuality and false-hood.)

'Of course I know Horace.' His suspicion that Horace, while working for him, had simultaneously been in the pay of the Gestapo seemed now to be confirmed. 'Do you mean to say that he told you that nonsense?'

'It's not nonsense. Horace is one of our best agents.'

'Horace is a traitor and a thief and a liar.'

'Then why did you keep him in your employ?'

'I didn't keep him in my employ after I had found out what he was. I ought to have killed him last year and I'd kill him now if I could get my hands on him.'

'I forbid you to insult him. He's a good Frenchman who serves his own country and Germany. It's through him I know what you've been doing this year and that you've been visiting arms dumps all over France. You saw Horace as well and you told him everything.'

'That's not true.'

'Be careful now. I can confront you with him and prove it.'

'Confront away. That's just what I should like you to do. And what's more I.ll make a bet with you: I'll prove to you that Horace is a traitor, a thief and a liar. And I'll show you that he's unpunctual as well.' The vehemence of Tommy's anger ought to have convinced Ernst of his sincerity.

'I warn you. You'll be exposing yourself to terrible consequences.'

'I am not afraid of them. Do you hear me? I demand to be confronted with Horace.'

'Then your blood be on your own head. I shall arrange a confrontation for some morning next week at ten o'clock.'

'He'll be late and if he knows whom he's going to meet he won't turn up.'

'He will not know whom he is going to meet.'

'I bet you he'll still be late.'

Ernst passed to other questions, to which Yeo-Thomas replied within the limits of what he believed to be his interrogator's knowledge. Rudi, however, by whom he was questioned later the same day in the rue des Saussaies, came back at once to the starting point:

'Where are the arms dumps?'

'I don't know.'

And, as before, he beat up his victim, although, with unaccountable clemency, he did not throw him in the bath.

Next morning when he awoke Tommy was bitterly cold; stone walls might not a prison make, but they certainly kept out warmth. His arm too was hurting him badly. Depressed, he lay listening to the measured tread of the guards, telling time like a clock. Soon there was the quick patter of feet running from one cell to another and cries of '*Tribunal*', '*Tribunal*'. But to-day there was no warning for him, which he felt was just as well, because Rudi's bludgeoning of yesterday had made him feel frightened again. 'Am I letting down the Service of which I have the great honour to be a member?' he asked himself; the doubt was as pathetic as Jean-Marie Vianney's fear that God would send him to hell for having been a bad priest.

But the question strengthened his resolution: he would not give in. Warmed by the bitter coffee, he walked up and down his cell until the orderly came to present him with his meagre daily ration of toilet paper; one of the two small squares had been cut from the *Pariser Zeitung* of 22nd March and provided him with the mental exercise of trying to reconstitute the amputated sentences. When he had successfully failed to divine them he set about cleaning his cell with a rusty and perforated dustpan and an almost hairless brush, but, because ersatz coffee, mangel-wurzel soup and magma bread were as unproductive of crumbs as the mutilated newspaper article was barren of subject and predicate, his task was soon finished. For exercise he polished the wooden floor with the handle of the brush, deciding to shine two laths a day. Then he did physical exercises, limiting himself because of his sore arms to flexing his legs and trying to ignore the throbbing in his testicles.

But the relief he obtained from these occupations did not last for long. Hearing the key turn in the lock he retreated to the window, where he stood legs apart, determined not to come to attention for anybody. His visitor was a burly Wehrmacht Feldwebel with pig-like eyes, a long upper lip and a short nose: striding across the cell in heavy jackboots he stood in front of Tommy and glared at him. 'Pritish officer?' the Feldwebel said. 'Vee will kill you slowly.' He then smashed one of his fists on Tommy's nose and mouth, crashed the other on his chin, kicked him in the groin and laughed bestially. Dazed and bleeding Yeo-Thomas staggered against the wall. 'Thank you,' he said, but the irony was lost on the N.C.O., who laughed again as he went out.

He was back in the depths of despair again when a gay voice came from the building opposite:

'Good morning to Tommy from Texas and Jim. How are you?'
He rushed to the window and removed the pane.

'Good morning, Jim. I have just been beaten up by a bastard.' The complaint was made almost joyfully now that he was again talking to a friend. 'Jim, can you get a message back to Blighty for me?' The very sound of the old 1914–1918 name made the cliffs of Dover seem nearer, and near they had to seem if he wasn't going to lose heart at the thought that he might be taken out any moment and shot.

'Not from here. But when I get to a P.O.W. camp I'll be able to write.'

'All you've got to do is to send a postcard and say that you've seen Tommy and that he's well. I'll give you the name and address.'

Making sure that no guard was approaching and under the cover of the other messages that were then being shouted across the yard he spelled out in Able Baker Charlie Dog his own true name and number and Barbara's sweet name and address. His message was simple and telegraphic: 'I AM QUITE WELL KEEP CHIN UP I LOVE YOU TOMMY.' This short salute eventually reached 5 Queen Court, Guilford Street, London, and after the war Yeo-Thomas met Warrant-Officer Jim Gillman in England and thanked him for sending it.

Korrel was so delighted when he came in and found the cell looking clean and tidy that, after showing Tommy photographs of his wife and children and giving him a cigarette, he went out and brought back a cake of grey gritty soap and a tooth-brush with dubious bristles. Undressing, Tommy washed first his body and then his blood-soaked underclothes, using the w.c. flush as a basin; the operation wasn't very successful and his vest and pants still looked dirty when he laid them out on the table to dry.

About five o'clock the evening messages began:

'Good night to Tommy from Jim and Texas.'

'Good night to Tommy from Aussie.'

'Lecocq demande des nouvelles de Tartarin.'

But tonight there was also a new one:

'Brigitte demande des nouvelles du grand poète.'

Brigitte was Clouet des Pesruches' agent-de-liaison, to whom Tommy had been about to pass instructions through Antonin when he was arrested. Suspecting that the desire for news of the great poet might come from the Gestapo, he replied with a reference to a small Pluto which Brigitte had recently given him.

'*Pour Brigitte: j'ai perdu mon chien.*'

But the reply came without hesitation and so was obviously authentic:

'*Brigitte regrette beaucoup que le grand poète ait perdu son chien mais elle est heureuse d'avoir des nouvelles. Elle tâchera de les transmettre au dehors.*'[1]

It was thus that he gathered that Brigitte, like himself, had been arrested when she went to keep her rendezvous with Antonin on 21st March. This realization depressed him in spite of her hint that she was still able to communicate with their friends outside.

After his third day his life in prison began to settle down into a routine. In the morning there was coffee. When he had finished doing his physical exercises and cleaning his cell the Feldwebel with the long upper lip came in to say 'Pritish officer, vee will kill you slowly,' punch him, kick him in the groin and laugh when he said 'Thank you'. Then there was the daily attempt to decipher the bowdlerized and fragmentary news on the toilet paper. For lunch there was mangel-wurzel soup with a slice of magma bread and for supper there was neither soup nor bread. And at all times there were messages from his good and loyal friends and families, Jim, Texas, Aussie, Lecocq and Brigitte.

This routine was, however, broken by frequent visits for interrogation to the Avenue Foch and the rue des Saussaies. Much as he disliked being beaten up by Rudi and his associates Tommy welcomed these journeys because they afforded him an opportunity of studying the route taken by the prison van and the habits of the guards. After four trips he had prepared his plan of escape.

The prison van was always followed at a distance of about ten yards by an open car in which were four Gestapo men armed with sub-machine-guns. In the van itself were two guards with Sten guns, of whom one sat beside the driver and the other stood inside the rear door of the van watching the central passage. This central passage was always crowded with black marketeers and lesser delinquents for whom there was no room in the cubicles, reserved for

[1] 'Brigitte is very sorry that the great poet has lost his dog, but is pleased to have news of him. She'll try to pass it on to those outside.'

terrorists and those under sentence of death. From conversations with those strap-hanging prisoners through the air vents in his cubicle Yeo-Thomas learned that when, as frequently happened, the guards were Italian, the guard at the door of the van, with the incorrigible laxity of the Latin, sat down on a small folding seat and propped his Sten gun against the opposite corner. By leaning heavily with his shoulder against the door when he was shut into his cubicle at the rue des Saussaies, Tommy thought that he could prevent the top lock from closing; with the aid of a friendly prisoner from outside he hoped to be able to open the lower catch, which was the common model found on railway carriage doors. Then, when at the end of Boulevard Raspail the van turned into the Avenue d'Orléans, he would leave his cell and, under cover of the prisoners standing in the passage, approach the back of the van and grab the Sten gun while the others overpowered the guard. Through the grille in the rear door he would fire the contents of the Sten gun into the windscreen of the following car: the men in it would either be killed or wounded or the vehicle itself would run off the road and pile up. Then, followed by the other prisoners, he would hop out of the car and, concealing his fettered hands under a scarf already obtained from an obliging woman prisoner, vanish in the confusion, making his way to the nearby rue d'Alésia; there, in an artist's studio, he had hidden away a set of false papers, money, a change of underclothes and a pistol. He could arrange later for a friend to come and remove his handcuffs.

He put this plan into execution one evening at the beginning of April when the prison van was late in leaving the rue des Saussaies and it was already dark. When the guard, who was an Italian, shoved him into his cubicle, Tommy pressed with his shoulder against the door and, as he had foreseen, prevented the top lock from closing. Speaking through the air vent to one of the prisoners standing in the passage, he told him that he was stifling and persuaded him to open the lower catch with a penknife, which, as the man was only a minor offender, had not been removed from his person. At the customary stop at the Cherche-Midi prison this prisoner got out, unaware, because Tommy had not yet moved, of the true purpose for which his help had been asked. When the van reached the junction of the Boulevard Raspail and the Avenue d'Orléans, Yeo-Thomas left his cell and, edging his way along through the standing prisoners, observed that the guard had indeed propped his Sten gun against the corner and was sitting on the folding seat with his eyes shut. Creeping up until he was within two feet of the guard, he saw through the grille of the door the car following behind. As they passed the Alésia métro station he acted: grabbing the Sten gun, he shouted to the prisoner next the guard: 'Prends le garde et tiens-le pendant que je liquide les gars de derrière.'[1] Unfortunately the man was scared and refused to co-operate, and when Tommy raised his one good arm to slog the guard with the Sten gun another two prisoners prevented him. The struggle aroused the guard, who gave Yeo-Thomas a smashing blow on the jaw, disarmed him and led him, railing at the faint-hearted, back to the cubicle. For some hours after his return to Fresnes Tommy trembled in fear of terrible reprisals; but next morning when Korrel presented him with a tin basin he gathered that the Italian guard had been too frightened of being reprimanded for carelessness to report him.

It was not long before he made a second attempt. One evening the van was late in arriving to collect the prisoners at the rue des Saussaies, and Yeo-Thomas managed to hide behind a bale of straw while they were waiting in the hall. When the van arrived and the guards moved forward to herd the prisoners into it he was left outside the cordon. While the guards were counting their passengers he dodged round the van and, crouching, crossed the courtyard in the shadow of the building, dashed past the two sentries at the gate and out into the street. Intending to hide somewhere in the maze of surrounding alleys, he sprinted along the pavement and might have escaped had not a German soldier emerging from a doorway noticed his handcuffs and tripped him up. The guards from the van, who had noticed that they were a man short, came tearing along, picked him up and dragged him back to the van, where they beat him cruelly. He was given another beating when he got back to Fresnes and deprived of his scanty food every alternate day for a fortnight.

After that he was so carefully watched that his only hope was that his discoloured left arm would become so swollen that it would require to be amputated. Once he was in hospital he was ·

[1] 'Look after the guard and hold him while I bump off the chaps behind.'

sure that he would be able to organize a Gestapo-proof means of escape. But the interrogators at the rue des Saussaies, afraid lest their victim should die of blood-poisoning before they had made him speak, gave orders that his arm was to be more carefully attended to in his cell; and although the additional dressings were applied by the same filthy Sanitäter the cure succeeded and his arm slowly healed.

His circle of unseen friends in the prison increased. Besides Jim, Texas, Aussie and Brigitte there were now a badly beaten-up elderly man in the cell next door and Patrice and Laurence, his fiancée, who relayed messages to and from Lecocq. This exchange of messages was not as simple as it sounds because both parties had to calculate the time necessary for the approach of a guard and make sure that no spies were lurking in the courtyard. The use of names became dangerous, as the guards beat severely those whom they suspected of shouting or being shouted to, and a call sign, consisting of a masturbatory moan from one of the more revolting American dance songs, was substituted. In this way Tommy was able to instruct Brigitte how to corroborate in her replies to her inquisitors the answers he had already given to his.

In addition to the private messages there was the news bulletin to circulate. Every week-day as hundreds of cyclists passed alongside the prison walls on their way to work they shouted snatches from the Allied official communiqué and extracts from the B.B.C. news. These were memorized by the prisoners in the cells at the end of each block of buildings and relayed diagonally across the courtyards. Because of his powerful voice Tommy became one of the chief relayers.

He used this powerful voice to broadcast rebellion as well. When the pathetic little calendar which he had scratched on the wall told him that it was the twenty-third of April he celebrated St. George's day by singing 'God Save the King' at the top of his voice. The hymn was taken up by the whole prison, and as the subsequent cries of '*Vive l'Angleterre*' died away, Tommy added his own personal defiance. '*L'Allemagne a perdu la guerre*,' he bawled. '*Deutschland kaputt*.' On other occasions he organized the communal singing of the *Marseillaise* and *Madelon* and on others the simultaneous banging by the prisoners on the doors of their cells. To all these demonstrations the guards reacted violently, rushing along the corridors in a roaring and vain search for the offenders, who temporarily ceased singing or banging when they heard the crash of their feet.

One morning towards the end of April Ernst gave him a cigarette when he arrived at half-past nine at the Avenue Foch for interrogation.

'I shall be confronting you with your old friend Horace at ten o'clock,' Ernst said.

'I'm ready,' Tommy said. 'But if he turns up at all I'll bet he'll be late.'

'Once and for all I forbid you to talk like that. Horace doesn't know whom he's going to meet and you'll be proved a liar.'

Tommy smiled.

'On the contrary, it is I who shall prove to you that Horace is a liar. I shall also prove that he is unpunctual, a thief and a traitor.'

At ten minutes past ten there was still no sign of Horace.

'What did I tell you?' Tommy said.

At ten-thirty Horace was ushered in. At first he did not see Yeo-Thomas, who was seated to the side of the door through which he entered. After rebuking Horace for being late, Ernst made him sit beside him at the desk, facing Tommy.

'Do you recognize this gentleman?' Ernst asked.

Horace, looking hard at Tommy's bearded face and tangled, uncut hair, seemed genuinely puzzled.

'I don't think so,' he said. 'Let me think.'

'You're going to have a good deal of thinking to do before I'm through with you, you dirty traitor,' Tommy spat out.

Horace began to look uneasy.

'Why, of course, it's Shelley,' he said.

'So you recognize him now?' Ernst said.

'Yes, yes. But you see it's the first time I've seen him with a moustache and a beard.'

'Well, Shelley,' Ernst asked. 'And what have you got to say?'

'Nothing. As it is Horace who is doing the accusing it's up to him to say on what grounds.'

'All right. You've asked for it. He's going to put you in an awkward spot and it won't be much use your lying.'

Tommy's face took on the stubborn expression with which he was accustomed to confront bullying bank managers and ivory-from-the-navel-up air commodores.

'We'll see about the lying when the time comes,' he said.

Horace, now obviously frightened, fidgeted as he said to Ernst:

'It's Shelley all right, but as I've already told you all about him there's not much good my going over the whole story again.'

'On the contrary, I insist upon hearing it,' Yeo-Thomas said. 'You're a liar, a thief, a traitor and a miserable mercenary and I'll prove it.'

Ernst interrupted impatiently.

'I forbid you to talk like that. Come on, Horace. It's your turn now.'

With trembling hands Horace pulled out a small diary and nervously flicked over the pages. He began by saying that he had had a meeting with Yeo-Thomas on the evening of the 17th November, 1943.

'You're quite sure of the date?' Tommy asked at once. 'You're certain that it was the 17th November?'

'Of course,' Horace answered unhappily. 'It's all written down. And I see here that I spoke to the Herr about it the very next day.'

'I remember perfectly,' Ernst said. 'The date is exact. He told me and I made a note of it.'

Tommy said nothing. He let Horace stumble on and, still consulting his diary, speak of other meetings with himself alleged to have taken place in December, 1943, and January, 1944.

'How much do you pay this scoundrel?' he asked Ernst when Horace had finished.

'Fifteen thousand francs a month, but I don't see that it's any business of yours.'

Tommy smiled. It was quite clear now what Horace had been doing. Pretending that he was still employed by himself, Horace had invented a lot of meetings with the important Shelley, and, to conceal the falsity of this and the majority of his other information, had denounced a few agents of minor importance. In this way he must have, at the current rate of exchange, earned about £430 in five months.

'In that case he has swindled you out of seventy-five thousand francs,' Tommy said.

'Don't talk nonsense,' Ernst said. 'And take that silly grin off your face. This is no laughing matter. And for once you'll not be able to lie yourself out of it.'

'Please bear with me a little longer,' Tommy said. 'I have already proved to you that Horace is unpunctual. I shall now keep my word to you completely and prove to you that he is a liar, a thief and a traitor as well. Tell me. I presume you keep a record of all the B.B.C. messages?'

'We do.'

'Then it may interest you to learn this. Every time I returned to England from France I sent this message: "*Le petit lapin blanc est rentré au clapier.*" This was done for three consecutive nights, beginning with the night immediately following my return. The first time I returned to England was on 16th April last year; therefore your records ought to show this message as having been sent on 17th, 18th and 19th April, 1943. The second time I returned to England was on 16th November, 1943, and that's why I say that it was quite impossible for me to have met Horace on the 17th. Once again your records ought to show that my message was sent on 17th, 18th and 19th November. Furthermore, as I was in England during the whole of December and January, Horace couldn't have had any contact with me during those months. I came back to France on 24th February of this year, landing in the early morning of the 25th. A few days before I left I sent the phrase "*De Tommy à Hélène*" to warn my friends of my arrival.'

Ernst immediately gave an order for the register to be brought to him. But any doubts which he may still have had must have been dispelled by Horace's green guilty face, spasmodically shaking jaw and trembling body. It was quite clear that Horace was terrified.

The register was brought in; it did not take Ernst long to confirm the truth of Tommy's statement.

'*Pourriture, infecte crapule,*' he roared at the quaking Horace.

'I think that I have now done what I said I would,' Tommy said. 'I have proved Horace to be unpunctual, a liar, a thief and a traitor.'

Ernst stood up.

'I apologize for having preferred the word of a traitor to that of a British officer,' he said in a rather theatrical manner.

The catechizing of Horace which followed was also theatrical and cruel as well. Chained to a chair outside the room in which it took place, with one of Ernst's cigars stuck in his mouth and with two silent guards on either side of him, Tommy heard it all through the door. The story was one of those sordid treacheries which have become a commonplace of war since the essentially below-the-belt weapons of machine-guns and bombs have outmoded the comparative chivalry of the sabre. Caught stealing a few months previously in a German office, Horace had been allowed to go unpunished upon his promise to act as an indicator for the Gestapo. On the instructions of the Germans he went in the company of another young *agent provocateur* to St. Mars, where the local curate was a well-known recruiting agent for the Maquis. Professing a desire to join a Resistance Group, they won the confidence of this brave priest, who had recommended them and the loyal Josseaume to his good friend José Dupuis when she had asked him to find her reliable go-betweens for herself, Yeo-Thomas and Brossolette.

Horace, as was to be expected, did not face the punches and the kicks with heroism. He squealed and shrieked and cringed and begged for mercy.

'I told you about Josseaume and the only reason you didn't catch him was because you were too slow,' he pleaded. 'I told you about Madame Bosc, who was Shelley's letter-box.'

'Why did you lie to me about Shelley?' Ernst asked.

'I was frightened. Shelley had threatened to bump me off on the slightest provocation. Shelley's a hard nut. He'd bump me off now if he got the chance.'

Horace went on to reproach the Gestapo for not having arrested the curate of St. Mars. Ernst said that the priest was much more valuable to them free than as a prisoner. Whereupon Horace begged to be allowed to prove his devotion to the German cause by going back to St. Mars and obtaining from the abbé, who still trusted him, the names and hiding-places of the leading men in the Maquis. But there were depths to which even the Gestapo could not sink.

When the interrogation was over Yeo-Thomas was given his

first decent meal since his arrest: a bowl of warm soup, bread, sausage and cheese, a bottle of red wine and another of Ernst's cigars to wind up with. And that evening Horace, handcuffed, accompanied him in the van on his journey back to Fresnes Although Tommy is not the sort to kick a man when he is down, for traitors he had no mercy. Through the air vents in the door of his cubicle he communicated to the others the nature of Horace's defection, and Horace, standing miserably among the black market-eers in the corridor, was reviled both by them and the locked-up terrorists. And that night, knowing that Horace would stoop to any treachery in order to curry favour with the guards, Tommy broadcast a warning message round the prison: '*Tartarin prévient tout le monde qu'un mouton est arrivé aujourd'hui à Fresnes. Il se nomme Horace. Il a vendu ses camarades à la Gestapo.*'[1] The cruel words must have chilled even Horace as he heard them, cowering in his cell. Horace had backed the wrong horse: after the war he was rearrested by the French and sentenced to hard labour for life.

Tommy's confounding of Horace must have earned him a new reputation for veracity, for at his now almost daily interrogations his inquisitors seemed to swallow every lie he told them. Their absorption in typing out those untruths for his signature was such that one day he managed to steal a pencil from under their noses. Because he was still constantly searched he removed the casing and kept only the lead, with which he inscribed his code name and dates of interrogations on the wall of the small cell in the rue des Saus-saies in which he was so frequently locked. José Dupuis, moving heaven and earth to find and deliver him, discovered this austere little memento after the liberation of Paris. '*C'était si simple et si tragique,*' she says. '*Mes jambes tremblaient. J'aurais tant aimé être seule et pouvoir un peu pleurer.*'[2]

He now found it easier to ward off his interrogators than his con-stantly recurring fits of loneliness and depression. Korrel brought him a Bible, which he read from cover to cover, pacing his cell like

[1] 'Tartarin warns everybody that a stool pigeon has arrived in Fresnes today. His name is Horace. He betrayed his friends to the Gestapo.'
[2] 'It was so simple and tragic. My legs almost gave way under me. If only I could have been alone and wept.'

a Trappist reciting his breviary. Some of his other diversions were less monastic. On 1st May he looked out through his window and saw a formation of R.A.F. fighter bombers flying across the sky towards the airfield at Orly. There was a noise of concentrated ack-ack as the aircraft dived to bomb. Removing the pane of glass, Yeo-Thomas began to broadcast a description of the event, hopping with excitement and yelling '*L'Allemagne est foutue!*' Immediately singing, cheering and banging of doors broke out all over the prison, and shouts of '*A bas Adolphe*,' '*A mort Hitler*' and '*Vivent les Alliés*' almost drowned the clatter of the boots as the guards rushed down the steel stairs for shelter and the noise of the exploding bombs.

But there were not air raids every day, and when his friends Jim, Texas and Aussie were transferred to a P.O.W. camp Tommy's depression deepened. Characteristically he sought to forget his own misery by trying to banish the very real despair of those who had been in Fresnes for much longer than himself, some of them for two or three years. He launched a series of slogans which, relayed by Laurence and by Brigitte, went reverberating through the prison with the threatening thunder of revolution: '*Tartarin salue tout le monde. Ayez du courage.*' '*Tartarin dit bien le bonjour à tous ses amis et leur annonce qu' Hitler commence déjà à faire pipi dans sa culotte.*'

Naturally the guards set about trying to discover the identity of this Tartarin who alleged that the Führer was piddling his trousers, and on 17th May the bullying Feldwebel unmasked him, reading the Bible in his cell: 'Vell, Tartarin; how are you, Tartarin? You are surprised, English swine, that I know that you are Tartarin? You think that you are clever, Tartarin. You cause a lot of trouble, Tartarin. Now vee will punish you, Tartarin.' But perhaps Tartarin's worst punishment was to learn that it was a newcomer to the next-door cell who had betrayed him, in return for a promise of increased rations.

His official chastisement, however, was anything but benign. After having been thoroughly beaten up, he was deprived of his socks and handkerchief and, barefooted in his shoes and clad only in his shirt, trousers and jacket (his underclothes, which he had just washed, were drying), was taken downstairs and thrown into a damp subterranean punishment cell.

Shut up in complete darkness, he felt his way round the dungeon. The floor was spongy and covered with fungus. The walls were clammy with moisture. Where the bed should have been there were only two iron clamps jutting out from the wall. There was no table. There was a w.c. pan but no tap.

Even when his eyes had become accustomed to the darkness he still could not see. The blackness was so black that he knew that it would be impossible for him to distinguish day from night. Cold and shivering, he leaned against the wall near the door, hoping against hope for an improbable delivery. In the silence he could hear the click-cluck of drops of water as they dripped with dreary rhythm from the invisible roof. Panicking at the thought that he might be left here to die, he began to walk up and down: the dungeon, like the cell he had just left, was eight paces long and four paces wide. When he began to feel sleepy he guessed that it must be night, and squatting on his heels he let his head fall between his knees. But it was so cold and damp that he could doze only fitfully. In misery he rose and began once more his restricted perambulation, varying his route as best he could. Crossing the cell diagonally instead of laterally, he unexpectedly stumbled on a broken chair, with a back leg missing. By propping it in a corner by the door he found that he could sit on it, but did not dare to take his ease for long in case a guard might come and confiscate this possibly unintended mitigation of his discomfort.

It was only, he calculated, when he had been incarcerated for thirty-six hours that the Feldwebel with the campaign medals arrived to give him a mug of cold water: from this still kindly N.C.O. he learned that the Commandant of the prison had sentenced him to three weeks' solitary confinement in the dungeon, with food once every three days.

The prospect was terrifying, and Yeo-Thomas decided that he must keep active if he were to avoid tuberculosis, pneumonia or lunacy. As soon as the Feldwebel had left he began violent physical exercises, marking time, jumping up and down and swinging his arms. When a hint of warmth had been restored to his frigid body he walked up and down the dungeon until he felt drowsy, but at first he was afraid to doze off for fear of becoming cold again. Eventually, after a sip of water, he gave in and, sitting on his rickety

166

chair with his hands stuffed up his sleeves, fell asleep. When he awoke his body was frozen, his jacket was soaking, moisture from the wall was oozing down the back of his neck and his teeth were chattering. Long and vigorous exercise was required to accelerate his circulation. Then, so as not entirely to lose heart, he started on a campaign of annoyance.

He began by singing all the songs he knew, bawling them out at the top of his voice: the mahogany patriotism of *God Save the King* was succeeded by the now almost reactionary respectability of the *Marseillaise*, the wink to *Madelon* mingled with the curtsey to *Annie Laurie*; *Tipperary, The Yanks Are Coming, We'll Hang Out Our Washing on the Siegfried Line, Roll Out the Barrel, There'll Always be an England* were roared out in a tremendous thunder in which the old confidence lost its anachronism in the shining actuality of the new. From song he turned to brief, but loud insults in English and in French: 'To hell with Hitler', '*J'emmerde Adolphe*', 'F—— Germany' and '*L'Allemagne est foutue*', punctuated by lusty kicks at the door of the cell at last drew a '*Ruhe*' from a nearby guard. 'Yew called me babee doll a year ago-oh'. The preposterous plaint of the 1916 flapper did the trick. The door was opened and, in a blaze of light, a guard stepped in and caught the singer a heavy blow with the butt of a rifle. Even so Tommy did not stop, perhaps because even a painful break in the monotony was a relief. As soon as the door closed he began again, dancing and hopping round his cell, singing and shouting until his throat was sore and he tired himself into sleep.

After three days they brought him some macaroni soup, which he had to drink out of the can, as he had no spoon. The soup warmed him, and, leaving some in the tin to be drunk later, he pranced gaily round the dungeon, bawling and singing even more loudly than before. Then, while he paused for breath, he heard voices talking above him in the darkness, in the blessed accents of Belleville:

'*Il y a un Anglais au cachot. Il gueule comme un âne.*'

'*Il doit s'emmerder, le pauvre type.*'

The second speaker was right. The Englishman that bellowed like a bull was so bored that he immediately propped his three-legged chair in a corner and climbed up in a risky attempt to reach the air vent in the ceiling down which he guessed that the sound of the voices must have come. Standing unsteadily on the back of the chair and fumbling over the ceiling until he got his fingers in the grille, he pulled himself up until his lips were level with the opening.

'It's the Englishman who bellows like a bull,' he said. 'What day of the month is it and what's the time?'

'It's the 20th May and it's ten o'clock,' the reply came.

'Ten o'clock in the morning or ten o'clock at night?'

'Ten o'clock at night.'

'Thanks. I can't hang on any longer, but I'll come up every day for the news.'

The chair toppled as his legs returned his weight to it and he fell sprawling on the floor. But he was happier when he went to sleep because now he would be able to count the days by the number of news bulletins he received from his new friends upstairs. He was awakened by rats scurrying over his face in search of the remains of his cold and soggy soup, but even then he did not finish it, knowing that it would be almost three days before he got another ration.

There were four men in the cell above, and he communicated with them regularly. In return for the consolation of the daily communiqué he tried to encourage them by promising that it would not be long before the Allies invaded and set them free. Then one day, when he was feeling too weak from lack of nourishment to be able to pull himself up to the air vent, a voice came shouting down to him:

'Our comrade Louis has just been taken away to be executed. *Vive la France!*'

With difficulty Tommy climbed on his chair and pulled himself up to the air vent.

'*Vive la France et bon courage!*' he said simply.

When he had been silent for a little he sang for poor Louis his own private requiem: it consisted of *God Save the King*, the *Marseillaise*, *Madelon* and *Auprès de ma Blonde*. I think that Louis would have liked it, and it's quite on the cards that God liked it too.

That night he had a dream. In his dream he saw a monster calendar whose leaves kept slowly flicking until they stopped at June 5. It was prophetic. He was sure that that was the day on which the invasion would take place.

'*Dis donc, l'Anglais, et le fameux débarquement?*' one of the men upstairs asked next day through the air vent. 'If your invasion doesn't take place this year we'll all be dead.'

The man's doubts convinced him that the dream had been sent to him as an augury with which to hearten the despondent.

'The invasion will take place at the beginning of next week,' he said and, deciding that it would be imprudent too definitely to commit General Eisenhower, added: 'On Monday or on Tuesday.'

'How do you know?'

'Don't ask me. I know. That's all.'

He could hear the man discussing the news with his companions.

'The English officer says that the invasion will take place at the beginning of next week.'

'*Il se fout de nous.*'

'No, he's sure. Pass it on to the chaps next door.'

He knew that if the invasion did not take place as he had predicted he would have done great harm to the morale of his fellow prisoners. When on the evening of 5th June there was still no news of the invasion he sang more loudly than ever in order to buoy himself up. But he wasn't alone in his doubts; through the air vent came the question.

'Twenty-four hours to go. You're still sure?'

'Yes, I'm still sure.'

He dreamed that night, not of calendars, but of the sun shining on the green and golden fields of France. The contrast of his freezing cell when he awoke was terrible. Hopping and dancing to get warm, he heard a shout from the air vent:

'*Allo, le camarade anglais.* Your comrades have landed. *Vive la France!*'

In the depths of his dungeon he could hear the other prisoners singing the *Marseillaise*; to him it was like the heavenly choir. With tears pouring down his bearded, battered face, in his clammy rags he stood to attention and added his own paean of *God Save the King*. If it was anybody's victory it was his. If anybody had worked for French Resistance it was he. There was still every chance that he would be shot before he saw the full results of his labour, but he knew that the Germans would now feel the full weight of French Resistance, properly equipped at long last thanks to the help of Winston Churchill who had listened to him in his moments of despair. The hope that had come to him at the Pointe-de-Grave in 1940 had been fulfilled; Pierre Brossolette had not died in vain. In those moments he experienced the joy of Péguy's chair-maker, who took care that the unseen straws should be as carefully plaited as the seen. He sang *Tipperary* as his *Te Deum* and then knelt and scratched with his nails on the damp walls of the cell an-other record of his witness which José Dupuis discovered also when she passed that way to look for him: S/L. K. DODKIN, R.A.F., 17-5-44; the date of his departure was added before he left the dungeon.

His friends in the cell above, who shared his jubilation, kept him informed of all that was happening in the prison and of how the guards were unable to quell the riot; he heard his prescience cele-brated in a message shouted to the cell two storeys above his own:

'*Il avait raison, le camarade anglais. Maintenant il est heureux comme un poisson dans l'eau, mais il a froid et faim ; si seulement on pouvait lui faire passer quelque chose.*' [1]

But the Englishman as happy as a fish in water was much too excited to be cold or hungry. For the next three days, in spite of Oberkommando der Wehrmacht reports that the Allies would be thrown back into the sea, he hopped and jumped and shouted and sang.

On 9th June his sentence was up. He was removed from the dungeon and, after a brief visit to his old cell to collect his soap, toothbrush, underclothes (still damp) and overcoat, he was trans-ferred to cell number 30 on the ground floor. This cell was colder and less well lighted than that which he had previously inhabited. It was one of the cells ordinarily used for the beating up of pris-oners, and the walls, floor, blanket and palliasse were stained with congealed blood.

His first visitor was his old enemy the Feldwebel, who struck him, knocked him to the ground and kicked him as he lay prone.

'Pritish officer, vee will kill you slowly.'

'Thank you. Thank you so very much.'

'Pritish officer, vy do you say "thank you"?'

---

[1] 'Our English friend was right. Now he's as happy as a fish in water, but he's cold and hungry; if only we could give him something.'

'You would not understand, but in England we are always polite, even to our enemies.'

The Feldwebel glared and went out, but he never struck Yeo-Thomas again.

He was lonelier now than he had been on the second floor. Korrel no longer came to see him and, instead of a Bible, he had only the generally senseless snatches of news on his daily ration of toilet paper to read. To pass the time he counted the two hundred odd fleas he caught in his palliasse and killed each day and, imitating the psalmist, longed for the wings of a bird that he might fly away and be at rest. This desire became almost a conviction that, with the exercise of will power, he could transform himself into a sparrow and fly through the window, one of whose panes, inadequately secured with unhardened tar, he had quickly succeeded in removing. But a sparrow, he realized, might very well fall victim to a cat and so he decided that he had better change himself into a crow as soon as he had flown out of the window. A crow, however, might be shot by a farmer anxious to protect his crops and so, perhaps, he might as well change himself into a snail right away and see what he could do by slithering.

As he could not read toilet paper, count dead fleas and trans-migrate his soul all day long he began shouting messages again, through the hole in the window out of which he hesitated to fly as a bird. This time he called himself 'Edouard' and to allay the suspicions of the guards he shouted '*Edouard demande des nouvelles de Tartarin.*' Some hours later the reply came. 'For Edouard: Tartarin has been put in the dungeon. Since then we have had no news of him.'

One day the N.C.O. with the Iron Cross came in with a news-paper in his hand.

'The war will soon be over,' he said. 'You'll be able to go home.' Although he knew that the invasion had been a success, Yeo-Thomas was surprised and excited by the news.

'So Hitler's going to throw up the sponge?' he asked.

'Of course not.' The N.C.O. was shocked. 'It's the Allies who are beaten. The Führer is using the secret weapon. London is in flames, the Government has left for the north of England and the population has fled.' He unfolded the *Pariser Zeitung*, on which under tremendous headlines, there was a photograph of a V1 falling through clouds of smoke on a burning city. 'You see, it's true. London has been destroyed. The war will be over in a few days.'

Tommy's first thought was for Barbara. Had she perished among the flames? Then, although he could not read the headlines, he saw that the photograph was faked. The morning after his arrival in France in February he had read in the *Pariser Zeitung* that London had been half wiped out by a small tip-and-run raid which he, himself, had experienced two nights previously.

'Listen,' he said. 'When you and Korrel are prisoners of war I shan't forget you, as you two have always been decent to me.'

Nor did the German authorities appear to share the N.C.O.s' confidence in the nearness of their victory. Aware that the Allies were approaching Paris, they prepared to evacuate compromising prisoners from Fresnes. On 10th July, Yeo-Thomas was medically examined and passed as fit for forced labour in Germany. The night of 16th July he spent in a larger cell with eleven other prisoners, among whom were the two brothers Simon who had helped him to plan Brossolette's escape from Rennes prison; from them he learned the sad news of Abeille's death. Apart from them and two others called Luquet and Deschamps most of the rest were black marketeers, thiefs and ponces. When one of these tried to steal food from the Simons, too weakened by torture to resist, Tommy laid him out with a punch in the solar plexus. He was getting his hand in.

CHAPTER XII

THIS SIDE UP . . .

THE bullying Feldwebel seemed to be getting his hand in too, wishing for war but preparing for peace.

'Sorry, Sir,' he said to Yeo-Thomas next morning as he slipped a pair of handcuffs round his wrists.

A roll call was held in the big cell by the Feldwebel, in the presence of armed guards. As each prisoner answered his name he was required to file out. Tommy's was the last name to be called. 'After you, please, Sir,' the Feldwebel said, stepping respectfully aside. Tommy was dumbfounded: it sounded just like his favourite Itma.

Perhaps the Feldwebel knew more than Yeo-Thomas: perhaps he knew that Tommy was being transported to Germany only as a minor offender. But he could not have known how this had come about. While in Fresnes, and without being informed, Tommy had been sentenced to death, and his execution had been fixed for 18th May, the day when he had begun to bellow in the dungeon. José Dupuis had, however, with great difficulty succeeded in tracing him to Fresnes and, through an intermediary, had approached the Gestapo officer in charge of the case; in return for a bribe of four million francs cash specially parachuted by H.M. Government this official had agreed to lose Tommy's file. (Further negotiations to facilitate his escape had fallen through because the Gestapo officer in question had been killed while making an arrest.) This was possibly the reason why the Feldwebel was attempting to make unto himself friends of the mammon of the coming unrighteousness.

Yeo-Thomas, of course, at the time knew nothing of this, and when with the other prisoners he was made to climb into an uncovered lorry he began to watch anxiously for an opportunity to escape. But four armed guards sat on a bench at the back of the lorry, which travelled quickly, and all he could do was to drop to a group of cycling workmen a message to José Dupuis scribbled with his uncased lead on paper provided by one of his companions. In this message, which, like others, was ultimately delivered, he told her that, as the guards had informed him, he was being transferred to Compiègne, whence he would shortly leave for Germany.

The camp to which they were taken was an old Army barracks situated not at Compiègne itself, but at the neighbouring Le Royal Lieu. It consisted of about eight low one-storied buildings separated from one another by alleys and situated in a compound surrounded by Miradors. On the high covered platforms of each Mirador were a searchlight and a machine-gun manned by SS troopers.

Yeo-Thomas, Deschamps, Luquet and the brothers Simon managed to get into the same room in block 'B'. This room was a long dormitory lined with two tiers of a double row of bunks placed head to foot, and with a long table in the middle. Outside there were washing troughs, daytime latrines next the cookhouse and a library for the use of prisoners. Although the mattresses were infested with bugs and at night-time latrine buckets overflowed their nauseous and dysentery-charged contents on to the floor it was, in comparison with Fresnes, Claridges.

The daily routine of the camp began with a morning roll call. The inmates of each block lined up under the supervision of their block chief, a privileged prisoner, who counted them and reported to the German duty N.C.O. in charge of the parade. Apart from such chores as cleaning out their dormitories and peeling potatoes, the prisoners were free until the evening, when another roll call was held. After seven o'clock they were confined to their blocks and forbidden as much as to put their heads out of a window. This discipline was enforced by two armed soldier thugs, each with a good score of would-be escapees to his credit, who paraded the camp with police dogs.

In spite of their leisure, escape during the day turned out to be as impracticable as escape during the night. As soon as the five friends approached the Miradors the SS men shouted and trained their machine-guns on them. They studied the habits of the working parties that left the camp, but found their category of prisoner had been forbidden such employment. They discovered a large sewer which ran behind one of the blocks and out of sight of the Miradors towards a corner of the barbed-wire enclosure; but on lifting the cover of the manhole they found that after a few yards the concrete passage became too narrow for them to crawl through it, and they had no tools with which to enlarge it.

A solo reconnaissance by Yeo-Thomas revealed that the enclosure in which they had been searched on their arrival in the camp was poorly guarded. If only he could hide somewhere near he thought he might be able to creep out under the barbed wire at night. But the hiding-place, he realized, would have to be especially secure, as a search would be made as soon as he was missed at evening roll call. A hut in the enclosure storing straw for palliasses seemed to afford just such a refuge. One day, assuring himself that he was unobserved, he made his way stealthily towards this hut, but just as he reached it a German N.C.O. opened the door and came out. Fortunately the N.C.O. was a notorious homosexualist and had his own reasons for concealing his visit to the straw, and all he said was: 'I know that it is your duty as an officer to try to escape. Perhaps you will have better luck next time.' Marching Yeo-Thomas back to the camp as though he were a work fatigue, the N.C.O. dismissed him with a twinkle in his eye. From that time on, although he was not reported, Tommy was carefully watched.

He fell back on a variation of the plan which he had evolved to rescue Brossolette from Rennes. A wealthy French resistant in the camp called Roberty had managed by bribing two of the guards to get into touch with his friends outside. With him Tommy hatched a plot for German-speaking accomplices wearing German uniform to drive up in a car carrying a German military number and present the camp authorities with forged instructions for the transfer of Roberty and himself to the bearers.

But while the preliminary negotiations were taking place another group of 150 prisoners arrived to overflow the camp, and to relieve the congestion the immediate departure of a convoy to Germany was announced. In order to avoid this inconvenient departure Yeo-Thomas arranged, with the connivance of the camp dentist, Marty, to be given an injection producing a high temperature. When the parade for medical inspection took place he was lying tossing with fever in his bunk, and, because the Germans feared any disease which might cause an epidemic in their homeland, he was not sent on the convoy. Unfortunately, the Simon brothers, Luquet and Deschamps were selected, and none of them returned.

Fearing another convoy, Yeo-Thomas prolonged his convalescence, reporting daily to the infirmary for pills which he never took. Then about a hundred priest prisoners arrived: Oblates of Mary Immaculate, they were deprived of their cassocks and forbidden to say Mass or to pray together. Almost immediately afterwards several hundred more prisoners were crammed into the already overcrowded camp. It was obvious that the next convoy would be a big one, and morale in the camp sank low. Depressed himself, Yeo-Thomas went about preaching his solemn, platitudinous but, coming from him, always effective little sermon of never-say-die: Britons had held out in 1940 and they had won through; therefore if Frenchmen held out in 1944 they too would win through. His sincerity was so evident that if there was an undistributed middle in his argument his congregation didn't notice it.

Through the agency of the Block Leader of Block 'B', a character called Michel, one of the prisoners who was a wealthy brothel owner had received food parcels from outside; and, as the only Briton in the camp, Yeo-Thomas was invited to a feast at which the wages of sin confounded the theologians by appearing as cold lobster, smoked salmon, sausages, hefty hams, chocolate, cigarettes, coffee, vintage wines, brandy and a case of champagne. Fuddled as he became with this hospitality, Tommy was, nevertheless, able to notice the excellent terms on which Michel was with the German guards, who kept dropping in and partaking of a portion of the pimp's bounty.

Anxious to have an alternative means of escape to that in preparation with Roberty, Yeo-Thomas asked Marty the dentist to approach Michel with the offer of a bribe. After much haggling and argument about procedure, it was ultimately arranged that for the sum of two million francs the Sonderführer of the camp would allow Tommy to escape: five hundred thousand francs were to be handed over as soon as the prisoner was through the barbed wire and the remaining fifteen hundred thousand when he was safely in hiding; to avoid all possibility of double-crossing, Tommy was to be allowed to arrange for the money to be sent directly to himself from his friends outside who, he was confident, would help him; and the Sonderführer was to accompany the escapee and surrender to the Allies under his protection.

While Tommy was trying to get into touch with José Dupuis a second convoy to Germany took place which another massive injection enabled him to avoid. Then, just as his plan to escape with Roberty was about to be carried out successfully, disaster overtook him.

On 8th August his name was called out on parade and he was informed that he was to leave at once for an unknown destination. Handcuffed by an N.C.O., he was marched between two armed guards to the gate of the camp and, after farewell gifts of food from his comrades had been confiscated by a corporal in charge of the sentries, pushed into a waiting Paris motor bus. There he was chained by an additional pair of handcuffs to one of the guards who sat on either side of him. Two more guards sat behind him and yet another two stood on the rear platform.

Discovery of the loss of his file had caused an investigation which had revealed that his classification had been altered. Consequently, from a one-star minor offender he had been promoted once more to his former three-star rank of *Nacht und Nebel, Rückkehr Ungewünscht*—dangerous terrorist, to be exterminated.

CHAPTER XIII

... MURDER WITH CARE

To make the threat quite plain a Gestapo official in civilian clothes accompanied them. When after a little the bus broke down this official stormed at the French driver, who seemed to be taking his time about getting it going again. Perhaps he suspected that the engine trouble was not accidental, as the area in which it had occurred was thickly tenanted by groups of armed partisans. At any rate he was running no risks. Transferring Yeo-Thomas, the guards and himself to a passing coach carrying armed German soldiers to Paris, he ordered the driver to take them to the Gare de l'Est. There, surrounded by his imposing escort, Tommy was marched along the platform to a waiting train, in a wagon of which were two special compartments with windows covered with grilles. When his handcuffs had been removed he was pushed into one of these compartments.

There were already eighteen other prisoners in this compartment, constructed to accommodate eight, but from which the seats had been removed. They were handcuffed together in nine Siamese pairs, and among them, as the Resistance world was small, Tommy was not surprised to find a French officer, Lieutenant Hessel, whom he had known in London and who spoke German. Another Frenchman was Robert Benoist, the pre-war world champion racing motorist. Among the British were Squadron Leader Southgate and two Canadians, Captain Pickersgill and Lieutenant McAlister. From Hessel Tommy learned that they were being deported to Germany.

His privilege of being the only unhandcuffed and separate prisoner did not last for long. A quarter of an hour later a six-foot-four, leather-faced Wehrmacht N.C.O. in charge of the guard came along to inspect the new prisoner. Finding Yeo-Thomas unmanacled, he grabbed him with an enormous hand and, thrusting a Lüger automatic into the pit of his stomach, threatened to shoot him. Shaking with rage and still covering Tommy with the pistol, he ordered one of the guards to search him; the discovery of a small clasp knife acquired at Compiègne and concealed under the lining of the prisoner's waistcoat roused the ranting N.C.O. to roaring but illogical fury. Confiscating the knife, he gave orders for Yeo-Thomas to be handcuffed to two other men, of whom one was a Belgian called Rechenmann. Rechenmann, although he had been searched before, was then unhandcuffed, made to strip and stand naked while his garments and his person were examined minutely. When this search was over and he had dressed again Rechenmann was handcuffed to another two prisoners, and Yeo-Thomas, whose misdemeanour had caused the trouble, was left handcuffed in comparative comfort to only one prisoner. There were now eight pairs in the compartment and one group of three.

When the train eventually started, Yeo-Thomas, as senior ranking officer, assumed command and, with the assistance of Squadron Leader Southgate and a French major called Frager, organized the group. As space was too restricted for all to sit on the floor at once, they arranged to take it in turns to rest and to stand up. The two days' food which the guards had given them was then split up equally. Selfishness, however, is not exclusively confined to civilians: when those fortunate enough to possess Red Cross parcels were asked to pool the contents two of them refused, and it was only under pressure that they finally consented to contribute a portion of their privilege. Yeo-Thomas was unfortunate enough to be handcuffed to one of these recalcitrants.

At first the guards refused to allow them to use the toilet, but in the end Hessel, appointed interpreter, persuaded the now more reasonable N.C.O. to allow them to go in staggered groups, provided that they were accompanied by a guard and that the lavatory door remained open. In any case it was an awkward and embarrassing procedure, especially for the group of three. When his turn came Yeo-Thomas noticed on his way along the corridor a compartment without a grille in which were huddled a number of women prisoners; among them, although he did not know it at the time, was the renowned and indomitable Miss Violette Szabo.

The Resistance world turned out to be smaller than even Yeo-Thomas had imagined: as the occupants of the other compartment with a grille passed along the corridor on their way to the toilet he recognized in the sorry procession Captain Barrett, who had been a sergeant of his at the beginning of the war, and Captain Desmond Hubble, whom he himself had recruited for the Jedburghs and who had served under him in 'R.F.' Section. He managed to speak to them, impressing upon them that his name was now Kenneth Dodkin and no longer Forest Frederick Edward Yeo-Thomas.

The roster for sleeping that night was even more complicated to arrange than the shifts for resting. As only four men could lie on the floor simultaneously and as the three handcuffed together had to count as four, each group had only two hours of sleep and the last on the roster had to wait eight hours for its turn.

Those not sleeping had to stand and, while not dozing, occupied their time with discussing possibilities of escape, which were slender. There were two factions: those who wanted to make the attempt at any risk and those who preferred to play for safety. It was to one of the prudent that Yeo-Thomas was handcuffed, and with him he had acrimonious argument. The ratchet attachment on their handcuffs caused further disputes: when a prisoner moved without warning his twin, the handcuff on the latter's wrist tightened and caused him pain, and Yeo-Thomas, Major Frager and Robert Benoist spent half the night patching up the consequent quarrels. A Frenchman called Yves Loison helped to restore harmony by attempting, even although vainly, to unfasten his handcuffs with a hairpin which he had found in his pocket. The remarkable fortitude of the two Canadians, Pickersgill and McAlister, weaker than the rest because of a recent and heavy beating up from the Gestapo, also increased morale. To strengthen them Tommy gave the Canadians a cardboard box of malt syrup which was the only parting gift from his fellow prisoners at Compiègne that the sentry at the gate had allowed him to retain. They were both very grateful and Pickersgill put the box in his pocket.

Next morning they were again allowed to go to the toilet, but were not permitted to wash. As the August sun beat down upon the roof of the carriage the heat in the compartment became unbearable, but it was only after an eloquent appeal by Hessel that the guards allowed them a tumblerful of water each. Their discomfort increased when Pickersgill, searching for the syrup out of his pocket, found that he had crushed the carton in his sleep: when he withdrew his hand it was covered with a gooey, sticky mess which soon smothered not only his own clothes, but those of McAlister and his immediate neighbours as well. Trying to lick his hand clean Pickersgill succeeded only in smearing syrup all over his face, and all the time more syrup was oozing from his pocket. McAlister, attempting to help, spread the stickiness further. And when the guards refused Hessel's request that the two Canadians be allowed to go to the lavatory and clean themselves the surly members of the party became vituperative.

As the day drew on the heat became more intense, and the prisoners, refused more water by the guards, grew thirstier and thirstier. The train crawled along, with an occasional alarm when aeroplanes were heard above. In the middle of the afternoon the guards appeared nervous and the N.C.O. kept looking anxiously out of the window in the corridor.

Suddenly there was the roar of fast aircraft flying low and the noise of 20 m.m. cannon. British fighters were coming in to attack the train with that slap-happy administration of vengeance which so often punishes the just more heavily than the unjust. As the guards cowered in the corridor there was a thundering explosion and the train stopped. But the German N.C.O. kept his head: rapping out an order to the guards to follow him after they had locked the prisoners in the carriage, he ran alongside the train carrying a light machine-gun. Standing next the grille, Tommy could see him mount the gun and start firing at the aircraft which were still circling round the train. Amid the roar of engines and the blast of cannon civilians rushed terrified across the fields. As he saw the shells bursting against the train Yeo-Thomas prayed that an incendiary might not hit their carriage, in which case they would all be burned to death. His fear seemed to communicate itself to his companions for he felt a painful wrench at his wrist as he was jerked forward by his twin on top of a mass of bodies seeking cover from the shells and the machine-gun bullets. They were all rather ashamed of their panic when, a few minutes later, Violet Szabo and another girl came crawling along the corridor to bring them water.

The raid was successful: either the engine or the track must have been damaged, for the train did not move on again when it was over. Eventually two motor trucks arrived to collect the prisoners, who were warned by the N.C.O. that all of them would be shot out of hand if any single man or woman attempted to escape. The women were piled into one truck and the men into the other, and both were heavily guarded.

The men from both compartments were now together, and Tommy met for the first time new friends who were going to be his constant companions in distress: the British section now consisted of Yeo-Thomas, Squadron Leader Southgate, Captains Kane, Mayer, Wilkinson, Peulevé, Hubble, Barrett, Steele, Pickersgill; Lieutenants McAlister and McKenzie; and the French and Belgian section of Commandants Frager, Robert Benoist, Allard, Defendini, Detal, Leccia, Garel, Garry, Geelen, Rechenmann, Corbusier, Chaignot, Gerard, Loison, Mulsant, de Seguier, Vellaud, Culioli, Guillot, Evesque, Avallard, Rambaud, Hessel and two others. In all there were thirty-seven of them.

Their first stop was at Châlons-sur-Marne, at Gestapo Headquarters, where the Sicherheitsdienst officer accompanying them dropped off for instructions. While the guards were keeping the local population at a distance some of the prisoners managed to scribble messages to their friends which they let fall later on the road in the hope that sympathizers would find them and send them on. Then in the courtyard of another building they were allowed to wash at a fountain, a privilege especially appreciated by the two sticky Canadians. Here the men were able to exchange a few words with the women prisoners, whose fortitude was inspiring: although they had been insulted, beaten and tortured, these women had remained undefeated.

Late that night they were driven into Verdun. The town was blacked out and the streets rang with the tramp of jackboots and the harsh staccato singing of invisible German troops. 'The impression created in the dark,' Yeo-Thomas says, 'was one of brute strength and impersonal discipline.' For the underground fighters in the trucks this sound of organized troops symbolized the merciless strength of the enemy whom they had seldom met face to face, and whom they now only heard without seeing. For Yeo-Thomas, who had done more than any other Briton to organize French Resistance, the experience was especially galling: the Allied Armies were advancing across France and the partisans were now coming into open conflict with the Germans. Because he had not fought with the irregulars he had raised he felt that he had kept only half the oath which he had sworn at the Pointe-de-Grave and he was beginning to be afraid that he might not live to see the liberated France for which he had worked. Listening to the trudge of the heavy boots, he experienced the bitter pride of the poet who knows that he will get good reviews in *The Times Literary Supplement* when he is dead, but would have liked to spend just one night at the Waldorf-Astoria when he was alive.

They slept that night in the stables of Verdun barracks, six to eight men in each stall on the right of the centre alley and the women similarly apportioned in the stalls on the left. A long string was fixed along the alley to separate the men from the women and the Sicherheitsdienst officer ordered the guards to shoot anyone attempting to cross from one side to the other. Because of the dim lights, however, several of the men and some of the women were able to crawl near enough to the string to exchange stories and to warn one another what to say and what not to say when they were next interrogated. They did not know that there were to be no more interrogations for any of them and that they had all been condemned to death.

Next morning they were not only allowed to wash, but their handcuffs were also temporarily removed in order that they might clean themselves properly. Yeo-Thomas took advantage of this privilege, which they owed to the fact that they had a Wehrmacht and not an SS escort, to lose his grumbling partner and be handcuffed instead to Hubble, upon whose co-operation he knew he could count if an opportunity to escape presented itself. After a cup of ersatz coffee they were loaded into the trucks again.

It was a lovely day, with the sun shining in a cloudless blue sky. Liberty seemed both far and near: far when they looked at their guards and their manacles, and near when they beheld the green and gold leaves of the trees, with here and there a shine of silver in the refracted magic of the sun. Liberty seemed near too when, at long last, Loison managed to open his handcuffs, but for the present his success was kept a secret between himself, Yeo-Thomas, Southgate and Frager in case a careless word might warn the guards. And liberty seemed nearer still when they saw the expectancy on the faces of the inhabitants of the town and villages through which they passed, and the glares of hatred directed at their guards. Their hearts rose high when some of those men and women hesitatingly returned their greeting of the V sign, and they began to hope their trucks might be attacked by maquisards and themselves set free.

Soon, however, there were no more timorously friendly villagers, and no more villages. Instead, there were rows and rows of concrete blocks. With the sun beating down upon their heads and blistering them with heat and thirst they passed through the Maginot Line, that monument to the folly of those who, putting their confidence neither in the Lord nor in princes, omitted to extend their distrust to the sea. After that they crossed the Siegfried Line, upon which we had so signally failed to hang even our pocket handkerchief. There could be little hope now: they were in Germany, and in front of them loomed the dark grimy town of Saarbrücken.

Hope vanished finally as their truck slowed down at the approaches to barbed-wire enclosures, surrounded at intervals by machine-gun-manned Miradors. The truck turned in between two rows of wire, lurched through a heavily guarded gate and came to a stop in an open space surrounded by low wooden huts. In the middle of the space was a tank of water, filthy with dust from the black gritty soil.

A dozen or more SS men and N.C.O.s with cruel, bestial faces stood waiting for the prisoners to alight when the flap at the back of the lorry was lowered. Yeo-Thomas and Hubble were the first to receive their attentions: as his feet touched the ground Tommy was given a stunning blow on the nose and, when he staggered, a kick in the back which sent him forward to get another smash on the jaw, followed by a kick in the stomach and several slaps on the face. When his eyes cleared and he regained his balance he saw two N.C.O.s standing over him and laughing at him.

Still spitting blood, he had to line up with the others while the SS men passed along the ranks, punching, kicking and slapping the prisoners all over again. Hubble's uniform seemed specially to attract their spite, and he and Tommy were given a more thorough beating up than the rest. While this process, which lasted for half an hour, was going on the women prisoners were driven in in their truck and marched away under an escort of jackbooted SS female plug-uglies flourishing whips; Tommy never saw any of them again and does not know whether they survived.

After being listed in a register the men prisoners were then chained together in groups; in Yeo-Thomas's group there were five. The chains were in the shape of an X, in the centre of which was a ring fitted to a pair of handcuffs which were fixed round Hubble's ankles so as to force him to take short, shuffling steps. At the extremities of the chains were more handcuffs which were fastened to the ankles of the four others in the group. To prevent them from using their hands to keep their balance, the prisoners were no longer attached to one another in pairs by their wrists, but each man's hands were shackled separately. In these cumbersome fetters they were marched across the camp to the distant latrines and, as they tripped and stumbled, were kicked and beaten with truncheons, coshes and fists by the SS men. In the latrines, where fat slimy worms crawled among the overflowing faeces, they were forced to relieve themselves in these chained groups. After this painful, humiliating and awkward procedure they were marched back across the camp under the gaze of scared white faces crowding the dirty windows of the huts round the square. It is not surprising that their hearts were filled with anger and hatred.

For the moment, however, their tormentors had had their fun; the chains were removed from the prisoners' feet and they were again manacled together in pairs, except Yeo-Thomas, who was given a pair of handcuffs to himself. The thirty-seven of them were then locked in a small hut behind the camp kitchen. This hut was nine feet long, eight feet wide and approximately nine feet high and was lighted by one small window about a foot square situated some six feet from the ground. Narrow benches, about eight inches wide, ran along three of the walls. An old oil drum had been placed in a corner near the door to serve as a latrine bucket. With the August sun beating down on the tin roof the heat in this confined space was overpowering.

Once more they were faced with the problem of disposing themselves so that all could rest in turn, and once more the unco-operative grumbled. Yeo-Thomas, Southgate, Kane, Benoist, Frager and Hubble silenced them and worked out a plan. It was found that only twenty-three or twenty-four men could sit on the benches, and that most uncomfortably, while the rest who stood or squatted were even more uncomfortable, and when one moved all had to move. A more satisfactory variation of this pattern was finally adopted: eight men lay on the floor, four with their heads under the benches on one side of the hut and four with their heads under the benches on the opposite side; the twenty-four men sitting on the benches placed their feet on either side of the bodies of those lying on the floor; and the remaining five stood leaning against the door or against the wall on either side of the door. When one man wanted to go to the oil drum the man to whom he was handcuffed had, of course, to accompany him; Yeo-Thomas paid for the privilege of being handcuffed alone by being ninth man on the floor when his turn came and he slept under a bench with less air than he had sitting or standing up. All that evening and night they remained like this, hungry, thirsty and sweating, without food, without drink, in a foetid atmosphere progressively polluted by the stench coming from the oil drum.

In the morning they were ordered out with the customary shouts of '*'Raus*', '*Schnell*', '*Los*', qualified by a vocative '*Schwein*' or two. Lined up outside their hut they were compelled to watch a distressing spectacle which was obviously of daily occurrence. Cringing and yelping under blows from coshes, sticks and rifle butts wielded by SS thugs, hundreds of haggard, gaunt, almost fleshless men in rags and with a hunted, helpless look in their eyes were advancing across the compound towards a narrow railed-off passage leading to the kitchen door. Each miserable man carried a small metal pannikin, and as he entered the gangway, broad enough to admit only a single file of prisoners, he was belaboured and bludgeoned by SS guards armed with truncheons who stood on either side and whose blows he could not avoid if he was to eat. As soon as a prisoner was given his ration he rushed back across the compound, gobbling his food as he went, so as to have finished before the guard posted at the door of his hut beat him and knocked the pannikin from his hand as he entered. None of the thirty-seven watching prisoners was maltreated by their guards, who laughed uproariously at the spectacle and kept running into the crowd to administer extra kicks and punches to the milling skeletons.

Sick and horrified and wondering what might be in store for themselves, the thirty-seven were marched to the latrines, where they emptied their oil drum. After that they were allowed to wash in the grimy water of the pool in the middle of the compound; this turned out to be merely a relative clemency because the water came up to within only four feet of the top of the tank on the sloping edges of which the prisoners could not get a grip, and each man had to slide down to the level of the water and, hanging by his handcuffs to his partner's wrists, wash himself as best he could. Occasionally the guards would push a prisoner down into the water and stand laughing while his companion struggled to pull him back.

Then they in their turn visited the kitchen and each was given a pannikin of boiled water with pieces of mangel-wurzel floating in it, a slice of bread which appeared to be made of dark flour and sand, and a tumbler of cold water. Instead of being lashed by the guards while they were eating their meal they were treated to a second spectacle. SS men with coshes and sticks lined up outside the doors of each hut on the square in the middle of which stood an N.C.O. who shouted '*'Raus, 'raus, los, schnell!*' As the prisoners came running out the guards slogged at them and beat them and when the wretches were ordered back to the huts they beat them again. As soon as the last prisoner had regained his hut the N.C.O. shouted '*'Raus*' again and the performance was repeated.

Although quite a few among the thirty-seven guessed that this demonstration had been staged as a warning to break their morale, more managed to believe that the fact that they themselves had been exempted from this brutality proved that they were on their way to an Oflag, where they would be treated with the consideration due to their rank. And as they sweltered once more in their tiny hut they argued and hoped and despaired. One school of thought maintained that for them this was only a transit camp through which they were passing to better things, and the other, the minority, that, although here indeed they had no lasting habitation, it was to very much worse things that they were passing.

It seemed at first that the majority was right: three days later they were paraded outside their hut and formally handed over by the Sicherheitsdienst officer who had accompanied them from Paris to a kindly-looking Feldgendarmerie officer and about a dozen comparatively unferocious Feldgendarmerie guards. They were then locked in pairs into the cubicles of proper prison vans into which the pathetic bundles of those who possessed them were also loaded. Hubble was especially pleased by this latter attention: in his bundle were two shirts, a pipe and a portable chess set which his mother had given him.

They were driven to the station in Saarbrücken which they could see had been badly bombed; but even the sight of the scared and underfed civilians who gaped at them as they were escorted along the platform failed to move Yeo-Thomas to pity.

The train in which they were to travel was a Germany-bound troop carrier and was already crammed with jubilant janizaries. Two trucks had, however, been rescued for the prisoners: one for their bundles and bags and for the guards when they were resting; and a goods wagon for themselves in which there was room for them to recline at ease. Immediately in front of this goods wagon was an anti-aircraft wagon armed with a 20 mm. Oerlikon-type gun manned by Luftwaffe soldiers. Only three guards were left to watch over the prisoners and when the train moved off a door on the side of the wagon was left open. The presumption seemed to be that handcuffed prisoners were helpless and could make no attempt to escape.

The presumption was wrong, or very nearly wrong. With the

aid of a small piece of tin, recently acquired, Loison unfastened his handcuffs and those of his companions. Under cover of the noise of the train and keeping in small groups so as not to attract the attention of the guards, the prisoners discussed the possibility of escaping when night fell. The faint-hearted opposed the scheme, arguing that even if only a few attempted all would be shot summarily and that it would be foolish to exchange the almost certain comfort of an Oflag for so unpleasant a death. In the end the decision was left to Yeo-Thomas as senior officer and he naturally opted for escape. Roles were assigned to each man. As soon as it was dark the guards were to be strangled or killed with their own weapons. The prisoners would then jump out of the train in small groups of three or four and, taking care to keep out of the beams of the Oerlikon searchlight which would probably be sweeping the countryside, would, still in their small teams, make their way back to France. This plan had, however, to be abandoned when the dissidents informed Yeo-Thomas that they would warn the guards if he persisted in carrying it out. Forced to fasten their handcuffs again and await another opportunity, it was only fear of compromising the loyal which restrained Tommy and Robert Benoist from taking violent action against these men.

In any case the train stopped at a station before it was dark and the prisoners were transferred to another train. And at first it seemed that the unco-operative had been justified in their prudence: accompanied by all their guards and by the Feldgendarmerie officer the thirty-seven now sat in a real railway carriage with rows of unpartitioned seats in which they reclined at ease. The Feldgendarmerie officer who sat in one of the bays with Tommy, Hubble and a guard was so friendly that, after explaining the difference between the Intelligence Corps and the Intelligence Service, Hubble unpicked one of his Intelligence Corps flashes from his battle-dress and gave it to him as a souvenir. And when it turned out that the officer knew the vineyard owner, Julius Kayser, with whose family Hubble was distantly related, Yeo-Thomas was emboldened to ask if it was indeed to an Oflag that they were being transported.

No, said the Feldgendarmerie officer, they were not being taken to an Oflag, but to a very special kind of concentration camp where they would be treated as officers. There would be amusements, very little work, a band to cheer them with martial music and, who knew? perhaps a not too *farouche* girl friend or two. The name of this holiday camp was, so the Feldgendarmerie officer said, Buchenwald.

CHAPTER XIV

BUCHENWALD

ABOUT midnight their carriage was detached from the train and shunted along a side-line bordered by barbed-wire fences. On the platform of a station also surrounded by barbed wire an SS officer and SS guards were awaiting them. The Feldgendarmerie officer handed over to the SS officer a brief-case containing their documents and the latter took over command.

Under their new escort the prisoners were marched off through an unreal, pale, moonlit world. The ground crunched under their feet and occasionally there were weird howls from unseen dogs, but otherwise the night was silent and eerie. If the prisoners whispered among themselves the guards cursed them loudly and the night was silent again except for the gravelly sound made by their feet and the sinister moaning of the dogs. Faint lights appeared in the silver grey darkness and gradually grew brighter than the twinkling of the stars: they came from Miradors set up all round the camp in case any of the prisoners might be tempted to escape from the military bands or the girl friends.

The darkness of a square building with a tower was thrown up into the sky against the lesser darkness of the night, and the prisoners were halted in front of an iron gateway bathed in a pale mean light. Guttural words were exchanged between the N.C.O. in charge of their escort and an unseen guard behind the ghostly gate. Then the gate was opened and they were marched into a large compound surrounded by low huts lying in darkness against a shimmer-

189

ing curtain of moonlight. Here was awaiting them another escort, clad in what appeared to be a variant of the old Keystone comedy striped convict garb.

Handed over to these geometric gaolers, the prisoners were marched over rough ground past rows and rows of darkened huts sepulchral in their share of moon. Again the night was silent save for the occasional whine of a dog crying its antiphon of loneliness to the loneliness of the stars. The world was empty, empty, empty, but everywhere there was a feeling of hidden purgatorial hosts. In spite of the warmness of the summer night air Yeo-Thomas was chilled to the bone.

Light in this plain of macabre shadow came upon them with blinding suddenness, from electric bulbs hanging from the roof of a huge hall into which they were pushed by their warders, whose grotesque clothing they now saw clearly for the first time: clad in blue and white vertically striped suits and dark berets, these tough and expressionless officials wore black armbands on which was lettered in white 'LAGERSCHUTZE'; but, to make it quite plain that they, too, were men under authority, on their jackets and on their trousers were red triangles with numbers on white tapes sewn on below the triangles.

For the present, however, these Lagerschutze were the vicars of their vicious masters and exercising their portion of power. On an order from their leader, another expressionless ghoul with 'KAPO' on his armlet, the prisoners were led into a long room, made to lay their belongings on a long table and lie down on the cold tiled floor to sleep. No sooner had they done so than they were ordered to stand up again, undress and fold their clothing and pile it neatly on the table. When they had stood naked in line for about half an hour they were commanded to dress and lie down and sleep again. They had barely dropped off when the order came for them to strip once more. When Hessel protested at this senseless procedure the Kapo replied, looking at him out of glazed unlighted eyes which seemed to have seen so much sorrow that they could no longer reflect either joy or misery:

'Just obey orders, my friend. Don't ask any questions, my friend. This is a very dangerous place and the less that you will talk the better it will be for you. There are stool pigeons everywhere.

Here you have no friends, my friend. Beware, my friend; continually beware.'

But this time the process was not without purpose. As soon as they had undressed they were marched into a large room fitted with shower baths, beneath which they washed themselves with a gritty, latherless soap. When they had dried themselves with rags they were moved on into another room, from whose ceiling a number of electric clippers hung on long wire. Under each clipper was a stool and behind each stool stood a striped barber, himself completely shorn except for a long tuft of hair running from his brow to the back of his head. Soon the prisoners were shorn too; from their heads to their feet the clippers were ploughed, removing every particle of hair on their bodies. From unshaven bandits with monster beards and moustaches they were transformed into meek-looking, egg-headed tonsured monks. Their bellies and their genitals were then painted white with an astringent liquid which stung their testicles for several days afterwards.

Looking more like savages now in their phosphorescent woad, they were taken to the quartermaster's store, where they were issued with their prison uniforms, multiform in their incongruity: Tommy received a pair of blue and white striped underpants with long lacing legs, a pair of old grey trousers tailored for a man six foot tall and weighing twenty stone, a faded blue mechanic's jacket with sleeves which came down to his elbows and a back which barely reached his waist, a striped forage cap, a pair of wooden clogs and a white nightshirt trimmed with red round the neck; Hubble got a too-short jacket and pair of trousers which made him resemble Larry Semon; and the rest were attired in other varieties of ill-fitting reach-me-downs. The only similar item in their outfit was their wooden clogs. As they made fun of one another's weird appearance the Lagerschutze looked on in silence, with unamused spectral faces.

A fellow Briton had also been watching their mirth with no trace of amusement on his face: he was Perkins, one of Colonel Buckmaster's officers, and he warned the prisoners in much the same terms as the Kapo.

'You have little to laugh about,' he told them. 'This is one of the worst concentration camps in Germany. I just can't tell you how

191

bad it is, but you'll soon find out for yourselves. The treatment is terrible and deaths can't be counted any more. For heaven's sake watch your step.' And he added another admonition: 'And don't let on that you are officers. And if any of you held any executive position in peacetime keep it to yourselves. The internal administration of the camp is in the hands of Communists, and they don't like either officers or capitalists.'

An opportunity for practising this reticence occurred almost at once, when they were paraded in front of a middle-aged and shifty-eyed Schreiber who filled out their identity forms in accordance with their answers to his questions. But Yeo-Thomas, Hubble, Southgate, Kane, Frager, Hessel, and a few others made no attempt to conceal their rank from the scrivener, who was manifestly disgusted by their admission. When he had noted their particulars this registrar issued them with number tapes and red triangles to sew on their jackets and trousers; Yeo-Thomas was given the number 14,624.

It was broad daylight by the time these processes were accomplished. As they were marched across the camp the prisoners had their first glimpse of their fellow inmates, and it was anything but reassuring. The compound was filled with emaciated, hairless wretches shuffling wearily round and round in heavy wooden clogs. The eyes of those listless sub-human creatures were mean with terror. On the faces of many of them a sticky stream of yellow rot oozed from purulent sores set in the middle of purple weals. Others were so weak that they staggered as they walked. Even when their clothes were too short for them they were too wide because of the thinness of the frail bodies which they covered. The same grim question occurred simultaneously to all the thirty-seven as they beheld this gruesome spectacle: 'how long is it going to be before we look like them?'

The new prisoners, too, had difficulty in walking, because they were not used to their loose-fitting clogs, and they stumbled and staggered across the rough stony ground. They were glad when they were halted before and then marched into a hut surrounded by barbed wire. On the outside of the hut was the number 17.

This hut was really not so much a hut as a block with wings. At the entrance was a small corridor, with a washing-room with troughs and a circular basin on one side and a lavatory with urinals and latrine pans on the other. The room in which the Block-ältester took their names and numbers had also the appearances of public-school comfort: fitted with rows of lockers and furnished with a number of trestle tables, it had a partitioned-off cubicle—for the Blockältester. But their own dormitory, which was situated in another wing of the block, was much less luxurious and consisted of three tiers of long rows of bunks set two by two. Two men were to sleep in each bunk. The palliasses were only half-filled with straw and the blankets, of which there was only one to each bunk, were dirty and long enough to cover only half a man.

But even in this filthy flop-house they were not allowed to linger: during the day they had to remain outside the block. Within a minute of their exit they were surrounded by a mob of other prisoners, talking every man in a different tongue, in Russian, Polish, German, Rumanian, Spanish, Italian, Czech and French. The questions asked in the languages which they didn't understand were obviously the same as those asked in that which they did: who were they and why had they come to Buchenwald? When the newcomers replied that they were parachutists who had been captured by the Gestapo the impression created was tremendous, and the news of their heroism spread rapidly round the camp. From distant alleys thin bony creatures came tottering to gaze with watery-eyed admiration at those who had dared to strike a blow at the tyranny which was responsible for their own distress. Better-fed prisoners, in the striped livery of their privilege and with KAPO, VORARBEITER or LAGERSCHUTZ on their armlets, also called to pay their respects to the intrepid, and some of them even added the tribute of cigarettes, which the newcomers shared, four men to a cigarette, taking it in turns to have a puff.

Unlike the Lagerschutze who had supervised their initiation the night before, all these prisoners did not wear red triangles: some wore black or green or yellow or pink or violet, and those who wore red often wore also a qualifying F., R., T., P. or S. A Frenchman called Guignard explained the meanings of these markings: the red triangles without letters were worn by Germans and those with F., R., T., P. or S. by Frenchmen, Russians, Czechs, Poles or Spaniards; the black and green triangles denoted criminals condemned for common law offences, the yellow Jews, the pink homosexualists and the violet Jehovah's Witnesses, whose common misery had been brought about by very different misdemeanours.

Guignard also corroborated what Perkins had already told them, adding dismal details of his own. They were, he told them, in the worst camp in Germany. Their chances of survival were practically nil: if they did not starve to death they would be worked to death; and if they were not worked to death they would be executed. Every single day more than three hundred prisoners died from starvation or from being beaten by their guards while working in Kommandos. Each Kommando consisted of hundreds of prisoners quarrying stone, dragging logs or cleaning out latrines under the supervision of Kapos and Vorarbeiter. But the SS guards were also there and so were their Alsatian hounds, and when enough amusement couldn't be derived from bludgeoning a man's brains out there was always the alternative of setting the dogs upon him to tear out his throat.

They soon saw for themselves that these reports were not exaggerated. Walking up and down in the sunlight behind their barbed wire and conversing in makeshift esperanto with the other inmates of the Block, they remarked groups of SS men wandering about the camp. They noticed, too, that the prisoners tried to avoid them and that when they couldn't they politely removed their forage caps. But this salute did not prevent the guards beating up any prisoner whose appearance attracted their displeasure; and their new companions informed the thirty-seven that anyone attempting to resist this attention was punished either by death by shooting or strangulation or, if he were lucky, by twenty-five strokes on the small of the back with the handle of a pickaxe.

A squat black chimney just beyond the Block was pointed out to them. 'That's the crematorium,' they were told. 'It's the surest of all escape routes; most of us will only get out of this camp by coming through that chimney as smoke.'

Their predicament was indeed grave and Yeo-Thomas held a council of the thirty-seven to discuss the possibility of escape. In spite of the protests of the few who were still able to believe that wine, women and song or at least their austerity ersatz of beer, bitches and broadcasting lay just round the corner, a committee to direct the activities of three escape groups was formed: Yeo-Thomas took charge of one group, Southgate of another, and Frager and Benoist of the third. The committee undertook the time-honoured ritual of studying the lay-out of the camp and the measures of control operated by the guards. The findings of an immediate topographical reconnaissance, necessarily restricted to their own compound, which they were not allowed to leave, were pathetic: their Block was in a space between two other Blocks, the back of one of which overlooked the space; the other Block was on a slightly higher level, from which they concluded that the camp was built on a slope; the space itself was bordered at either end by barbed-wire fences; running alongside their own Block were two forlorn flower-beds filled with wilting daisies, most of whose petals had been removed by prisoners who smoked them.

They spent the whole of that day without food, the distribution of which they had missed while being disinfected and clothed. In the late afternoon they received a visit from Perkins and Burney, another 'F.' Section officer, from whom they learned that it was not only the SS whose habits they must study if they wished to escape from the camp. Among the prisoners, their visitors told them, there were all sorts of dissensions and intrigues, the adherents to one faction asking for nothing better than an opportunity to betray to their German masters the adherents to another. The chief civil strife was between the common law offenders and the political prisoners, each of which bodies was anxious to secure for itself the valuable prerogative of controlling the internal administration of the camp. This struggle was incessant, but for the present the Communists had prevailed over the cut-throats, and from the former they, as officers, could expect no help.

Perkins and Burney left before the Appell or evening roll call. For this the 380-odd prisoners in Block 17 were paraded behind their private barbed wire while the Blockältester went through the laborious process of counting them. They were then stood at ease, until an SS man in uniform and jackboots came swaggering into their compound. '*Mützen ab!*' [1] the Blockältester shouted, clicking his clogs and saluting the perky little representative of authority. As the prisoners stood capless before him the SS man passed along

[1] 'Caps off!'

the front rank checking the Blockältester's count and punching the face of any prisoner whose appearance displeased him. As they watched this process the thirty-seven understood why their companions had seemed so eager to remain in the rear ranks; it was, on a larger scale, like the competition in the hoary old war to fall in second-from-the-left, but the advantages of success were greater than that of never forming fours. When the SS man had finished his inspection the Blockältester shouted 'Mützen auf!'[1] and the prisoners put on their caps again, and the parade was dismissed. After that delegates were allowed to visit the kitchen, just in case any food might be going.

Because Block 17 was considered a convalescence and isolation hut the thirty-seven had been exempted from the larger and much grimmer Appell which had taken place simultaneously on the main square of the camp. This, too, was a count and not an answering to the calling over of a nominal roll; as there were some 80,000 prisoners to be counted by SS guards with shaky arithmetic, it sometimes took as long as four hours, during which the prisoners were required to stand to attention, mützen ab, no matter what the weather. Moreover, so as not to tax the brainless tellers with a reconciliation of the camp state, it was a roll call for the dead as well as for the living. Stiff and cold, the corpses of those who that day had died of exhaustion or been murdered by their guards had to be held up by their feeble comrades who would soon be relying upon others to help themselves to answer the same ghastly 'Adsum'.

More visitors came that evening to visit the parachutists. Among them was Colonel Manhès, a fire-eating French regular who had been arrested at the beginning of Tommy's first mission in 1943 and who, when he addressed his old friend by his right name, had to be informed that Yeo-Thomas was NOT repeat NOT Yeo-Thomas but DODKIN repeat DODKIN. Similar warnings had to be given to Commandant Julitte and Péry, whom Tommy had known in London and who were also surprised to find him among the terrorists on whom they too had called to leave their cards.

Before they went to bed that night the thirty-seven caused another sensation: after undressing with the others at 10 p.m. and piling

[1] 'Caps on!'

196

their neatly folded clothes on the trestle tables in the so-called living-room they washed themselves from head to foot, and even Jehovah's Witnesses marvelled. Then in their shirts they pitter-pattered like little boys to their bunks and tried to make themselves as comfortable as they could in their beds, because there were two of them in each. Tommy and Hubble shared a bunk, and, as both were broad, had to lie on their sides and 'when father said "turn" they all turned'. Their blanket was too skimpy to cover them either sideways or longways, but in spite of their discomfort they were able to fall asleep with a great hope in their hearts: that they would be able to last out until the liberating Allied Armies reached them, when this tyranny would be overpast.

Next morning they discovered that they were again among the privileged, although they did not yet know that their presence among the convalescent and the isolated was merely a precaution that they should not escape the highly unpleasant form of execution already prepared for them. '*Aufstehen*' for the rest of the prisoners, who had to hew stone and cart human dung under the lash of whips and the baying of wild dogs, was at 4 a.m.; for Block 17 there was no shouting until 6 a.m., when the thirty-seven once more astonished the devout and the devious by the thoroughness and the complexity of their ablutions. And even among the privileged the new contingent was privileged: their clothing was so worn and tattered that none of their new friends attempted to steal it.

Once more as they walked again in a new day behind their private barbed wire the daring discussed means of escape. Guignard called again, and Perkins and Burney came with a burly Dutch Naval officer called Peter Cool, who brought bread, which was divided out among all the members of the group. All these visitors considerably compromised their own safety by these visits, because the thirty-seven had already been officially proscribed as terrorists, untouchable even by the normally courageous Communists.

Later in the day, those who had brought bundles were allowed to visit the Effectenkammer and withdrew a few articles for their personal use. Although they naturally found that many of their possessions had already been stolen, Robert Benoist retrieved his razor and a few blades, and Hubble shaving soap, a pullover, a khaki shirt, which he gave to Yeo-Thomas, handkerchiefs, which he shared out among his friends, a pocket knife and his all-important pocket chess set.

To the further astonishment of the companions the thirty-seven celebrated this windfall by shaving in a body, taking it in turns to use Benoist's razor and Hubble's soap. Nor was this all. If cleanliness was next to godliness, a martial bearing, their committee decided, was next to cleanliness. Henceforth, the leaders ruled, when the group moved as a body, they would march in step and in column of fours; they would do, *gloria Monty*, physical exercises every morning and would always act in such a way as to maintain and improve the morale of those with whom they came in contact. All but the usual few dissenters accepted this decision, and soon the Block-ältester, a Communist, was holding up the capitalists as an example to proletarian delinquents.

To prevent themselves from brooding, they began a chess tournament in which Tommy started out a likely winner. For those who could not play chess there was bridge, played, as cards were forbidden in the camp, with painted pieces of cardboard, of which they manufactured four packs; this diversion, however, could be indulged in only during the two hours after their scrappy lunch when they were allowed to use their dormitory, on the top bunks and with a couple of men keeping watch.

Close friendships were naturally formed among different members of the group. Hubble, Kane and Yeo-Thomas became almost inseparable and soon knew all about one another: Hubble spoke of his wife and children, Kane of his father, and Tommy, of course, of Barbara. Yeo-Thomas also grew to like very much Pickersgill and McAlister, whose lack of French was such that he had at first concluded that they had been left behind after the Dieppe raid, captured while trying to escape in civilian clothes and treated as spies; he found to his horror that the two Canadians had indeed been parachuted into France as agents in spite of their almost total ignorance of the language.

Thanks to the collusion of Perkins, Burney and Cool, the thirty-seven later, but only occasionally, were all to visit the rest of the camp. Yeo-Thomas, Hubble and Kane eagerly used the first of these opportunities to extend their abortive preliminary reconnaissance. The results were even more depressing: not only was the barbed wire by which the camp was surrounded electrified, but the outside of the enclosure was constantly patrolled; and the Miradors all had machine-guns trained on the camp and powerful searchlights. There appeared to be no hope at all of getting out under the wire; a ruse for smuggling arms into the camp and fighting their way out seemed the only possibility of escape. And escape they must if they were not to become like the skinny, fleshless sub-men they kept meeting, shambling along and gazing at them sideways out of terror-stricken eyes.

The more they examined the camp, the more they realized the urgency of their plight. They saw the Revier (hospital), from which few ever emerged alive. They saw, too, Revier Block 50, where the experimental vaccines were manufactured and the grim appendent Block 46, known as the 'Guinea Pig Block', where, under the supervision of Sturmbannführer (Major) Ding-Schuler and his Kapo, prisoners were inoculated with typhus and other germs and their reactions, almost always ending in death, under the various vaccines studied.

They visited the main square where the gruesome Appell took place, and the adjacent Pathological Block. Facing this Block, on the other side of the square, was the entrance to the camp surmounted by its tower; on either side of the tower was a wing lined with steel shutters inside which were the Bunkers or punishment cells.

There was also a cinema in the camp where German propaganda films were exhibited and, so that even walls might not escape their turn of tears, prisoners beaten up. The brothel, called the Sonderbau, was the only place where pleasure was unadulterated, perhaps because it was brief: there, for the sum of two marks, Kapos, Vorarbeiter and non-class-conscious SS could find fugitive ecstasy in the sweaty embrace of prostitutes or apathetic volunteers seconded from the concentration camp at Ravensbruck. Perhaps it was of this establishment that the Feldgendarmerie officer had been thinking when he had spoken of girl friends. At any rate in one respect he had not lied: there was, indeed, a military band whose musicians, garbed in the gold-braided uniform of the Yugoslav Royal Guard and clogs, tooted out of trumpets *Die Wacht am Rhein* to the greater glory of the thousand-year empire which had only another eight months to run.

Perhaps, because only God could make one, in the whole camp there was only one large tree, called Goethe's tree; the superstitious said that when it fell it would be a sign that Germany was doomed.

But there was an inner circle of misery: if conditions in the main camp were bad those in the lesser camp were worse. In the latter there were no 'permanent' buildings but only long, low, windowless huts and tents. In the huts, instead of bunks, there were three or four tiers of shelves split up into compartments in which three men had to sleep in a space designed, under a norm of cruelty, for one. In the tents there were neither shelves nor floor; and in each of them the space was so cramped that three hundred or more men had to sleep squatting on the ground, which in wet weather was like a quagmire, with their knees drawn up under their chins. Neither in the huts nor in the tents were there enough blankets, and the tenants, who were mostly Jews, were systematically starved: every day hundreds of lean, famished men yelped, squealed and grunted as they kicked and clawed one another in the struggle to get at a few pounds of potato peelings or to scrape the grease from the bottom of a cookhouse canister.

The reconnaissance party was naturally depressed when it returned to Block 17, and fortunately other visitors soon called to cheer them up. The Newton brothers, two Englishmen employed as batmen by their Blockältester, came and, introduced by Commandant Julitte, Professor Balachowski of the Institut Pasteur in Paris, who, with his thick and wavy dark hair, was one of the few unshorn prisoners in Buchenwald. Balachowski owed this privilege to the fact that he worked in Block 50 on the production of anti-typhus vaccines. With him Yeo-Thomas, Kane, Benoist and Hubble became friendly and later, when they had been given the freedom of the camp, were invited by him to Block 50 to partake of rabbit, which tasted none the less delicious for having been previously used in a typhus experiment. Nor was the rabbit the only gift they received from their visitors: an artist came too and drew portraits of Yeo-Thomas and others. And, not to be outdone in courtesy, the three chief internal administrators of the camp called, Lagerältester I and II and the very unoperatic Kapo of the barbers: all were Communists and, from their excessive courtesy, it was quite clear that capitalist officers, who had battened on the misery of sergeants-major and the fatherless, had no help to hope for from them.

Perhaps the Germans knew that none of the thirty-seven could succeed in escaping if Figaro and his colleagues were unfriendly, for soon they were allowed to move about the camp more or less as they liked. When together they marched in step, for this was now the only hymn by which they could honour their calling, but they dispersed at the approach of German soldiers, so as not to be forced to salute them.

From Burney and his friends they obtained thirty-six marks, which they used as a common fund for the purchase of cigarettes and watery beer from the prisoners' canteen. Each cigarette had to be shared among three men and sometimes four, because crafty Ukrainians, under pretext of obtaining a light, often sucked through paper tubes rolled to look like cigarettes a goodly portion of their benefactors' smoke.

But whatever the Germans might think of their chances of escape Yeo-Thomas was determined to explore every possibility. Both the Polish and the Russian prisoners of war, interned in Buchenwald contrary to international convention, had good underground intelligence networks, and with the aid of Kane, who spoke Bulgarian, he got in touch with two Russian colonels: one was a tall, white-haired ex-artillery officer of the Imperial Army and the other a broad, squat rather boorish Mongol from a Tank regiment who, because he was also a Political Commissar, exercised the greater authority. These representatives of the old polite rotten world and the new rude rotten world shared as orderly a slim, handsome young Georgian to whom, as he spoke both French and English, Tommy was able to explain the urgency of their needs. With Kane tackling the high-ups and Yeo-Thomas their lieutenant, they soon managed to elaborate one of those hopeless plans which can be concocted only by the truly desperate. When the Russians agreed that it was not absolutely impossible to have arms smuggled into the camp, Tommy and Kane were convinced that Stens, grenades and sub-machine guns were already in their possession. After two or three meetings, at which the British were invited to share their hosts' more elaborate P.O.W. rations, Saxons and Slavs had agreed to divide up their groups into units of ten which, under the command of an officer or N.C.O., would fight their way out of the camp when the signal was given. In earnest of this pledge the aristocratic Russian colonel presented Yeo-Thomas with an old leather belt so that his too loose trousers might not lend a temporary advantage to the enemy by falling down in public on the day of victory.

From Sasha, the orderly, whom he came to know well, Yeo-Thomas learned of the perhaps not wholly incomprehensible lies current about Britain in Russia.

'You must belong to the nobility and be very wealthy,' Sasha said to him one day.

Tommy, remembering perhaps the days when he had slogged at other people's accounts for fifteen hundred francs a month, laughed.

'What makes you say that?' he asked.

'You are wishing to deceive me. You think that we know nothing in Russia. You are wrong. We know many things in Russia. We know that in England officers must buy their commissions and it is clear, therefore, that you must belong to the privileged classes.'

'That is simply not true,' Tommy said. 'And the proof is that I myself started out in this war as a ranker.'

'I do not wish to be rude to you, but I cannot believe that. That is not what we are told in Russia. And in England the ordinary soldiers are not allowed to walk on the pavements when they pass officers and they must also allow their wives to sleep with the officers if the officers wish.'

And even when Yeo-Thomas had explained all about O.C.T.U.s and second-lieutenants being court-martialled for impropriety when they winked at a private in the A.T.S., Sasha still seemed to prefer to believe the truth which he had learned in Russia.

Poor Sasha, he went to his death shortly afterwards, little shaken, no doubt, in his conviction that the Western democracies were cemented with deceit and privilege instead of riddled with a rather touching stupidity. For this, and not the atom bombs which the Kremlin now possesses, is the strength of Communism: the power to turn decent young men and women into fanatics and martyrs for a wrong cause. And fanatics and martyrs for a wrong cause will never be conquered except by fanatics and martyrs for a right cause, who live not by N.A.A.F.I. and P.X. alone but by the rather uncomfortable words which proceed out of the mouth of God. Fanatics are not made by talking threadbare balderdash about 'the British Way of Life', which means anything from tarts on Piccadilly to the litany on Wednesdays and Fridays via football pools and the erudition of the *New Statesman*; and martyrs are not mustered by a call to defend a Christianity in which leading national ecclesiastics themselves claim to have blown holes. 'I like to think of God as a vast oblong blur,' a more than ordinarily nonsensical American clergyman said in the 1920s. Stalin was clever enough to know that men do not willingly die for blurs.

On the afternoon of 24th August Allied aircraft flew in over Buchenwald on their way to the Gustloff factory opposite the garage of the SS barracks and the Deutsche Rüstungswerke, whose buildings touched the perimeter of the camp. As soon as the air-raid alarm went the prisoners were confined to their Blocks, but the Ältester of Block 17 was indulgent enough to allow the thirty-seven to stand where they could get a good view. Shining like lovely moths in the sunshine, the bombers closed in with an illusory benevolence to drop their deadly load on the factories, which they flattened completely. At first no bombs fell on the camp, but when incendiaries started small fires in several of the Blocks, including Block 17, the SS and the German Lagerschutze panicked and began shouting contradictory commands, now ordering the prisoners to run to the small camp, now ordering them to remain where they were. The thirty-seven, forgetting their own danger, remained where they were, cheering as they saw the bombs fall and the smoke rise in black plumes against the pale blue patience of the waiting sky. Yeo-Thomas, practical even in pleasure, kept a special watch to see if the barbed wire was cut at any point.

The barbed wire was not cut, and the prisoners' jubilation soon changed to sorrow when they saw the dead and wounded among their fellows hoisted on to stretchers, carts and planks. Of the guards about 80 had been killed and 300 wounded, but the prisoners had suffered much more heavily: nearly 400 had been killed and 1,450 wounded, of whom 600 seriously: among the last was Princess Mafalda of Italy, who, there being no women's hospital in the camp, died in the arms of a prostitute in the brothel; her body was then thrown naked on to the stock pile and burned with the others in the crematorium. Once again the just had suffered more than the unjust.

Perhaps the fact that an incendiary had damaged Goethe's tree badly put SS officers and men on edge. 'A British Air Force officer, eh?' the SS Hauptsturmführer with the Totenkopf badges on his sleeves sneered at Yeo-Thomas when he paraded after a medical inspection in the cinema. 'The Luftwaffe sweeps them from the sky.' 'I didn't see anything but flak the other day,' Tommy answered with unwise bravado. The SS men avenged their fright with deeds: one of them, Krautwurst, pushed a particularly frail prisoner into a pit full of faeces from the latrines and, when the poor wretch tried to pull himself out, stamped with his jackboots on his fingers and skull until he drowned.

This savage desire for revenge became more and more evident. The water pipes damaged by the bombardment had scarcely been repaired when more than 170 British and American airmen arrived in Buchenwald and were herded together in the small camp, without food, blankets or shelter. Their senior officer, Squadron Leader Lamason, a New Zealander with the battered-looking nose of a boxer, protested angrily to the Camp Commandant Pister and his assistant Schobert that such treatment was contrary to the rules of war, as they had all been taken in fair fight. But Pister and Schobert would have none of it: the airmen were not airmen but terror-flyers and as such were murderers and liable to summary execution.

These airmen were squatting miserably on the only cobbled space in the small camp when Yeo-Thomas, in search of more allies, called to see them. In spite of having passed a bitterly cold night in the open the newcomers were cheerful. Lamason and Yeo-Thomas hit it off immediately and together they visited the two Russian colonels, who organized among their prisoners-of-war a collection of blankets, clothes and clogs for the airmen.

To Yeo-Thomas the arrival of these new recruits for his army seemed providential. Not only with a potential of more than 200 men at his disposal was he now in a better position to bargain with the Russians, but the fact that the majority were trained flyers appeared little short of miraculous. About twelve miles from Buchenwald, he had recently learned, was a small and poorly guarded airfield called Nohra. Provided they could fight their way out of

Buchenwald, he was soon persuading Lamason, there would be little to prevent their attacking the airfield, seizing the bombers and flying back to the Allied lines. The combined forces of themselves and the Russians would be divided up into units of ten, this time not according to nationality, but with a pilot, navigator, air-gunner, engineer and radio operator in each team. Lamason, as hot-headed as Tommy, readily agreed. There seemed to be only two stumbling-blocks: one was the presence in Lamason's group of a so-called American flyer suspected to have been planted there as a stool pigeon, and who would require to be kept in ignorance of their plans and watched; and the other was the lack of arms. But even the latter was not insuperable: there were, Yeo-Thomas had also discovered, arms in the camp, but only the Communist leaders knew where they were concealed, and so far all his attempts to make them divulge this secret had failed.

Then suddenly, on 9th September, the blow fell. Over the camp loudspeaker came the command: *'Achtung! Achtung! Achtung! Die folgenden Gefangenen von Block 17 müssen sich sofort beim Turm melden:* [1] *Hubble, Kane, Benoist, Allard, Defendini, Detal, Leccia, McAlister, Mayer, McKenzie, Garel, Garry, Geelen, Pickersgill, Rechenmann, Steele. Achtung! Achtung! Achtung! Die folgenden Gefangenen von Block 17 müssen sich sofort beim Turm melden: Hubble, Kane, Benoist. . .'* The sixteen of them were to report to the Tower at once.

At first neither the summoned nor their comrades were greatly alarmed: they thought that it was just some sort of identity check although, in case there might be a search of their persons as well, Hubble left his penknife and his pipe in the care of Yeo-Thomas. The sixteen fell in gaily enough in front of the Block and marched off in column of fours, keeping in step to the greater glory of Great Britain and France, whose very proud sons they were.

When he had watched them right wheel in the direction of the Tower, Yeo-Thomas went back into the living-room. The expression on the Blockältester's face as he sat in his cubicle frightened him and, through Hessel, he asked the man why he thought his comrades had been called to the Tower.

[1] 'Attention! Attention! The following prisoners from Block 17 must report to the Tower immediately . . .'

The Blockältester did not beat about the bush. 'I do not think that you will ever see any of them again,' he said. 'When prisoners are called to the Tower in that way they never come back. They are executed. It is always the same for spies and terrorists. Sooner or later all of you will be called to the Tower that way and none of you will come back. I am sorry that it should be so, because you are good men who have done your duty and I like you.'

After that there was nothing to do but go outside and hope, in the mockery of the lovely summer morning sun, that the Blockältester might be wrong. For the present, as they did not wish to alarm the others, Tommy and Hessel kept the bad news secret, telling only Southgate, Frager and Peulevé and, eventually, Lamason.

Even when the sixteen failed to turn up for Appell in the evening they still went on pretending that there was nothing wrong. That night, even although he had his bunk to himself, Yeo-Thomas could not sleep. He had come to love Hubble and Kane as he had loved Brossolette. Were they too to be taken from him? He prayed that God might be merciful and stay the hand of the enemy and let the sixteen men live.

Next morning there was news: a member of the Polish organization whom Yeo-Thomas contacted in the small camp told him that the sixteen had been thrown into bunkers after being beaten up but were still alive. In the evening the news was slightly better: the sixteen had been seen out for a walk but had been taken back to the bunkers. But the morning after when Yeo-Thomas again met his Polish friend in the small camp the Pole stood to attention and saluted:

'I am sorry to have to tell you that your sixteen comrades were executed last night. There can be no doubt: one of our organization has seen their bodies. They were brave men and we grieve for you.' The Pole then told Tommy of the manner of his friends' death: they had been hung by hooks in the wall of the crematorium and allowed to perish by slow strangulation; their corpses had been burned in the furnaces and the chimney had belched smoke all night.

Tommy could not speak. For a few minutes he stood in silence. Then with tears in his eyes he turned and walked back to his Block. On his way he met a prisoner wearing an old British Army cap; in exchange for his own forage cap and a piece of bread he obtained this symbol and stuck it proudly on his head: when his turn came to die by slow strangulation he would go to his doom wearing at least a part of the uniform he loved so dearly.

Balachowski was waiting for him in Block 17: he had brought Hubble's note-book, which had fallen out of his pocket after he was dead, and he had already told Southgate and Frager the sad news. There could no longer be any doubt: the thirty-seven had now become twenty-one. Yeo-Thomas then summoned the others and told them what had happened, and warned them that a similar end almost certainly awaited them all. 'And because we shall have to die slowly it is all the more important that we die bravely,' he said. When they gasped and choked and struggled on the hook their pain would be not only their own pain, but that of Great Britain and France as well, and they must bear it nobly. For this was his ethic, and about it he never cheated or compromised.

In the evening the belongings of the dead were distributed among the quick: Tommy got Hubble's pipe and insisted on keeping also his chess set, just in case he should still manage to escape and be able to carry it home to Hubble's children.

During the next few days, however, it became more than ever clear that neither he nor any of them would be able to escape. In spite of all his efforts he could not obtain any definite information about the arms which he had heard were concealed in the camp. Julitte warned him that his plans were foolhardy and bound to end in failure, the two Russian colonels were fearful and even the doughty Lamason was hesitant. And on the evening of 14th September came the news through the Dutch organization that further executions were imminent.

Yeo-Thomas knew now that he was going to die, and he wrote farewell letters to Colonel Dismore and Barbara for Balachowski to have smuggled out of the camp. Later, thinking that it was his duty to communicate to his Government the very important information he had found out about Buchenwald and to make one last effort to save them all, he coded one last desperate signal.

It was, perhaps, fitting that a doomed White Rabbit should compose his last official telegram in a cellar lined with hutches in which were other doomed rabbits. For it was in the Pathological Block, in which he and Peulevé had been hidden by Balachowski, that he drafted in his old Seahorse code which would prove the authenticity of his message the following:

INVALUABLE DOCUMENTS CONCERNING LATEST RESEARCH AND DISCOVERIES
BACTERIOLOGICAL WARFARE KEPT HERE AT BUCHENWALD STOP ALL PREPARED
TO SECURE THEM BUT CAN SUCCEED ONLY PROVIDING RAPID ASSISTANCE ARRIVES
JUST BEFORE OR IMMEDIATELY UPON GERMAN CAPITULATION AS CAMP OFFICIALS
WILL TRY TO DESTROY ALL STOP VALUE OF DOCUMENTS WARRANTS EVERY EFFORT
STOP SPEEDY ARRIVAL AIRBORNE OR PARATROOPS ESSENTIAL WILL FIND ORGAN-
IZED ASSISTANCE WITHIN CAMP BUT I HAVE NO ARMS STOP BEARER THIS MESSAGE
TRUSTWORTHY AND KNOWS EVERYTHING WILL FIND ORGANIZED ASSISTANCE
WITHIN CAMP ACKNOWLEDGE BY IODOFORM [1] DU MOINEAU AU LAPIN STOP HAVE
EVERYTHING UNDER CONTROL AND HOPE FOR EARLY VICTORY STOP VINGT CINQ
SEPTEMBRE STOP ALL MY LOVE BARBARA TOMMY STOP CHEERIO DIZZY ASYMPTOTE

Accompanying this cyphered signal was a letter in clear, countersigned by Hessel, to the Intelligence Officers at the Allied Headquarters to which it was hoped both the signal and the letter would be delivered.

Bearer is trusted messenger. We have important and valuable documents of considerable value to Allies. Please transmit urgently to London attached coded message and convey the reply to bearer for onward transmission to me. The matter is of considerable importance and delay may mean disaster to us all as well as to documents.

He had drawn a long bow and, as he knew that he would very likely be dead before the arrow reached its destination, he had made arrangements for a sort of apostolic succession of Allied Resistance to be continued at Buchenwald after his execution. The signal and the letter, bound in the cover of a book, were smuggled out of the camp by a German called Hans Baumeister who had been imprisoned for opposing the Nazi regime; but they did not reach the 'trusted messenger' in Dortmund till December, and he had to await the arrival of the American troops before he could hand them on.

Then, when Tommy's despair was at its blackest, hope suddenly dawned once more, through a cluster of very complicated clouds.

Through the agency of Balachowski a meeting was arranged between Yeo-Thomas and Eugen Kogon, the Austrian Catholic secretary of Himmler's personal friend, Ding-Schuler, the Sturmbannführer of Block 46, where the typhus experiments were conducted.

[1] Message in B.B.C. French Service.

At this meeting Kogon agreed to approach his master with the warning that as an Allied victory was now certain it was time for him to take precautions for his own safety; and to suggest that, in return for a promise from Yeo-Thomas to testify on his behalf at the war crimes trials, he should agree to save the lives of the remaining twenty-one prisoners in Block 17 by substituting their identities for those of other prisoners who died of typhus in the Guinea Pig Block. Before undertaking this mission, however, Kogon pointed out that it might not be possible to save all twenty-one of them, as the substitutions would have to be staggered and orders for further executions were liable to be given at any time. To this possible modification Tommy gave his consent, stipulating only that salvation should be by juniority, with himself as senior officer bringing up the rear.

Once again it was a shot in the dark, but this time it hit bang on the target. Within half an hour Yeo-Thomas learned that Ding-Schuler had accepted and with great glee in his heart he set about drawing up a nominal roll in order of juniority with his own name last on the list. For security reasons, however, he kept the good news to himself and it was fortunate that he did so, because shortly afterwards Balachowski arrived to tell him that Ding-Schuler had had second thoughts and would agree to save only three men of whom Yeo-Thomas must be one. To Yeo-Thomas's reply that he insisted upon the three men being the three most junior Ding-Schuler countered that Yeo-Thomas was not in a position to make conditions and that if he wished any men at all to be saved he himself, who as senior officer could speak most competently in Ding-Schuler's defence, must be of the number. After further argument Yeo-Thomas was forced reluctantly to yield, but even Balachowski's scheme for saving another three officers by securing their admission to the T.B. section of the hospital failed to soothe his sense of guilt.

Ding-Schuler made another condition, and that was that the complicity of the Kapo of the Guinea Pig Block, whom he wished to be kept for the present in ignorance of his own part in the plot, be obtained separately. Once again Hans Baumeister, who was friendly with the Kapo, came to the rescue and succeeded, in return for a promise of testimony from the prisoners on his behalf, in persuading him to help. In spite of the fact that he, like his master, was likely to be called to account on the day of judgment, it was surprising that the Kapo should have been willing to take such a tremendous risk: because of his privileged position in Block 46 the Kapo was untouchable and could, if he refrained from frustrating the designs of the Gestapo, survive unharmed until the Camp was liberated by the Allies from whom, as a prisoner who had always acted under authority, he would have very much less to fear than Ding-Schuler.

Kogon then acquainted Yeo-Thomas with the details of the plan: the three prisoners, taking care that nobody observed them entering or leaving, were to go to the Guinea Pig Block where the Kapo would give them each an injection productive of a high fever; returning to their own Block, they would report sick next morning to the hospital, where they would state their symptoms, making a point of adding that they also suffered from lice, which were the greatest carriers of typhus germs; the Kapo would then arrive as though by chance, diagnose typhus, and have them taken to Block 46, from which nobody would expect to see them emerge alive.

Yeo-Thomas was now faced with the very disagreeable task of choosing who were to be his two companions: Southgate and two others were to be saved by Balachowski's T.B. scheme, which meant that seventeen remained, of whom he had to condemn fifteen to almost certain death. Nor was there any possibility of easing his conscience by drawing lots because on security grounds it was essential that only he himself should know of the plan. With heaviness in his heart he sat in Block 17, looking at his comrades, watching their familiar faces, listening to their familiar voices. From them he had to choose one Briton and one Frenchman, but how could he, knowing the anxieties and the conditions of each one of them, decide who was to be the Briton and who was to be the Frenchman? Which Briton was to see the big red buses running up Regent Street again and which Frenchman change again at the Concorde for the Champs Elysées? And which Britons and which Frenchmen were to twist to death in agony struggling in the noose of a cruelly adjusted rope? Praying that wisdom might be upon him, he began by eliminating the selfish, the grumblers and the unco-operative. Then when those that remained were all of a virtue he played in the silence of his mind a game equivalent to the drawing of lots: and from the invisible twirling wheels the names of Peulevé and Hessel emerged.

Although he intimated this selection to Balachowski, Kogon and Baumeister, for the present he said nothing to the two men concerned for fear that the Kapo might be double-crossing them and he might arouse false hopes. To make sure that the Kapo didn't revenge an approach which he had every right to regard as an impertinence by injecting the three of them with typhus and killing them, he evolved a stratagem by which, without the Kapo suspecting that he was suspected, he himself should be injected alone first and then, if all were well, the others; it was the nearest he could get to being last man to leave the ship.

And when towards the end of September he bared his arm to the Kapo in the Guinea Pig Block he felt that he had been wise to take these precautions. The man's appearance was frightening: his thin lips, kept grimly shut in a straight line, looked as though they had never smiled; his expressionless face tapered down from a broad forehead into a thin, pointed chin; his eyes were grey and cold and hard; and his shaven skull glistened like a paving-stone under the manipulated surgical light. No words were exchanged between them, because the Kapo had no French or English and Yeo-Thomas no German. The needle of a large syringe containing a colourless liquid was plunged into a vein on the inside of Tommy's elbow, the puncture was dabbed with alcohol and the ceremony was complete. When the Kapo had made sure that the coast was clear the patient left the Block and returned to his own quarters.

It was now time to take Peulevé and Hessel partially into his confidence. Calling them aside, Yeo-Thomas told them, under pledge of absolute secrecy, that he had evolved a plan of escape; they must not be surprised when he disappeared the next day and when he sent them back instructions through Balachowski they were to obey without asking any questions.

Two hours later he broke out in a sweat, and all night long he tossed in his bunk with a raging fever. Next morning he reported sick to the Blockältester, who ordered a Czech doctor prisoner to take his temperature; it was 40.7° centigrade. Alarmed, the Czech suggested that he should take Yeo-Thomas over to the hospital for examination, and the Blockältester readily agreed. And, knowing that, whether the Kapo had or had not double-crossed him, he would never come back, Tommy took his possessions with him: among them was Hubble's chess set.

In the hospital everything happened according to plan. When describing his symptoms Tommy said that he also suffered from lice. While he was being examined the Kapo turned up, looked into his eyes and felt his pulse, diagnosed typhus and ordered his immediate transfer to Block 46. The Czech doctor fled in consternation; and Yeo-Thomas, escorted by the Kapo and avoided by all who deduced his malady from his company, walked the two hundred yards which separated the clean from the unclean.

But whatever might be said about the inmates purdah itself was antiseptic, and much more comfortable than the other Blocks. Instead of dormitories with dirty bunks there were beds with clean sheets and pillows and blue and white coverlets, and in the washing room there were baths. What in Block 17 had been the living-room was here a laboratory with a padlocked mortuary chamber opening out of it, so that even death itself seemed tidy.

The nurses, however, were striped and not starched, male and not female, and their badge of efficiency the green triangle of burglars and assassins. Under the care of two of them Yeo-Thomas was undressed and put into a bath in which he wallowed contentedly while his clothes were taken away to be destroyed; it was his first bath for more than six months, and in spite of his high fever he enjoyed it greatly. He enjoyed also the clean bed in an empty ward into which he was made to climb in a long white nightgown; but he enjoyed it less when one of the nurses told him that the ward on the other side of the passage had twenty patients in it, all of whom had been inoculated with typhus germs and all of whom would probably die. With his teeth chattering, his limbs trembling and the ward swimming before his eyes, Tommy began to be very afraid.

Shortly afterwards the Kapo came in, wearing the white linen ephod of a surgeon. He felt Yeo-Thomas's pulse, took his temperature and shook his head gravely. 'Fleckfieber,' he murmured to the two attendant orderlies, who immediately rushed out and returned with an india-rubber sheet and an ordinary sheet soaked in icy-cold water. The rubber sheet was inserted under the patient on the bed, and the soaked one wrapped around him and he was left to shiver. He underwent this treatment several times until in the evening his fever had left him; but when the orderlies had gone for a moment the Kapo came back and gave him another injection and soon his temperature was soaring again.

He knew now that the Kapo was not double-crossing him, but was only making sure that the evidences of his distemper should be real enough to convince the orderlies. And so he was not alarmed when the latter, impressed by his new rise in temperature, ran in agitation to fetch the Kapo, who, examining him with concern, ordered a renewal of the soaked-sheet treatment. This he bore with equanimity, even although it continued all that night and all the next day; and when, on the third day, his temperature again normal, the Kapo brought him a note from Kogon to ask if all was well he scrawled across it with the intermediary's pencil: 'O.K.; the others can come.' Next day Peulevé and Hessel, inoculated in their turn, sweated and shivered beside him in the same ward.

The Kapo then had the two male nurses transferred to other duties in another Block while they were still under the impression that their patients were going to die; in this way he both protected himself and ensured that the bad news would be spread throughout the camp. As soon as the orderlies had gone, Yeo-Thomas, Peulevé and Hessel were smuggled into a large room above the ward. This room, divided into two by a row of cupboards, was used half as an office, half as a bedroom by a Dutchman called Schalker and a Pole called Gadzinski, both of whom worked in the Block and were friends of Kogon and Balachowski; in the bedroom part there were three extra beds, and in these the three fugitives slept.

Here they were kept in close confinement: they could not risk being seen by any of the other inmates of the Block and, in case they might be recognized from outside, had to duck when passing in front of the windows. This last precaution was not without its advantages, for although their room was a room with a view, it was one which would have chilled Mr. E. M. Forster: at the back of the Block was the small camp, where the Jews rotted to death in hunger and cold; and on the other side of their private wire was a long low wooden hut in which more than 1,200 emaciated wretches stood dying on their feet because there was no room for them to die on the ground.

For part of the day they helped Schalker and Gadzinski to plot the progress charts of prisoners who had been inoculated with disease; the switchbacks of those grim graphs almost always ended in a cross, which was the only symbol of mercy accorded to the sufferers. So that they could keep up with the war news Kogon sent them the not always inaccurate communiqué of Oberkommando der Wehrmacht, and for the rest of the time they played games: bridge, crapette, halma, and an extra-liturgical variant of ludo which they baptized 'silly buggers'. The Kapo also brought them French and English books, and occasionally tobacco and cigarettes.

The Kapo was indeed a strange man, a victim of circumstances perhaps, and through Hessel's interpretations they came to know him better and even to like him. He had already been a prisoner for twenty years and it was perhaps his own familiarity with discipline which led him to be so remorseless with others. For he ruled the Guinea Pig Block with a rod as iron as that with which he himself was ruled: when his masters ordered him to inject a prisoner with typhus or poison he did so and he mercilessly and accurately observed their sufferings, making perhaps a vice of necessity. And yet to Yeo-Thomas, Peulevé and Hessel he always kept his word, and to help them he risked more than his life. He was in love with one of the women in the camp and married her after the war.

Sturmbannführer Ding-Schuler, who had now reached an understanding with the Kapo, was a youngish man with a weak chin and mouth, and a round, pink, babyish complexion. He was shining and elegant in his SS uniform when Yeo-Thomas went to meet him in the Kapo's office.

'So you are Dodkin?' he asked in English.

'And your senior in rank,' Tommy said.

Sturmbannführer Ding-Schuler clicked his heels and stood to attention before the prisoner in his striped garb; he was making sure of getting into the new disorder on the ground floor.

'I have risked my life to help you, and I hope that you are grateful,' he said.

Tact has never been Tommy's strong point and, forgetting that he was still at Ding-Schuler's mercy, he talked to him just as though he had been an Air Commodore too cushioned in custom to appreciate the potential of French Resistance.

'You would be risking your life even more certainly if you did not help me,' he said. 'You know as well as I do that nothing can save Germany now. You will be tried for your crimes and hanged. But if you help us we shall testify on your behalf, and then perhaps you will be given a lesser punishment. And it's not only for our own safety that I am asking you. I also want you to promise me to save all important documents and information and hand them over to the Allies: results of research on typhus, bacteriological warfare and poisons; plans of the underground factories, the identities of the men you have killed or who have died, everything.'

Ding-Schuler, because he was Ding-Schuler, promised; and Yeo-Thomas, because he was Yeo-Thomas, was not surprised.

It remained now for Yeo-Thomas, Peulevé and Hessel to exchange their identities for those of three prisoners who had died of typhus. This was not as easy as it had at first appeared. Most of the prisoners inoculated with typhus were Russians or Germans and these were unsatisfactory for two reasons; none of the three could speak Russian and only Hessel could speak German, and the Germans so treated were almost all criminals whose misdeeds, obligatorily kept secret in Buchenwald, might later lead to the scaffold those who assumed their identity.

Fortunately there had recently arrived in the camp a convoy of prisoners who had been working on fortifications in West Germany. Many of them had contracted typhus and were now segregated in a special ward in the Revier. On the pretext of preventing an epidemic the Kapo secured their transfer to Block 46: among them three Frenchmen, Maurice Chouquet, Marcel Seigneur and Michel Boitel, were on the point of death, and with them it was arranged that Yeo-Thomas, Peulevé and Hessel should exchange identities.

But the three Frenchmen put up a good fight for their lives, and the candidates for their names were insistent that everything should be done to save them. And on 4th October, while the struggle was still going on, there came over the camp loudspeaker the long delayed and dreaded announcement:

'*Die folgenden Gefangenen von Block* 17 *müssen sich sofort beim Turm melden: Barrett, Corbusier, Chaignot, Frager, Gerard, Loison, Mulsant, de Seguier, Vellaud, Wilkinson, Peulevé. Die folgenden Gefangenen* . . .'

The situation was alarming: none of the three Frenchmen showed any signs of dying immediately and Ding-Schuler was absent in Weimar. Nor did the pitilessness of the Camp Commandant Oberführer Pister make matters easier: informed that one of the condemned men was ill with typhus in the Guinea Pig Block, Pister ordered that he should be brought immediately to the place of execution and be destroyed with the others. An appeal for clemency on the grounds that the execution would be an unnecessary cruelty practised on an already dying man was refused. And to his horror the Kapo learned that Pister was sending round an SS N.C.O. to take delivery of the sick man on a stretcher. The danger was immediate, and not only to Peulevé: for even the inexpert eyes of the executioners would see that Peulevé was not suffering from typhus, and their plot would be exposed.

The Kapo, however, was a man of resource: on the arrival of the SS N.C.O. at the Block, he contrived to be out and the N.C.O., afraid to enter the plague house, went away. Returning as soon as the N.C.O. had gone, the Kapo gave Peulevé a super-injection which sent him flying into a delirium, and had him carried down to the ward where the real typhus cases lay. When the N.C.O. came back again he refused to hand over Peulevé, on the grounds that he could not do so without an order from Sturmbannführer Ding-Schuler, who alone had authority over Block 46 and who was absent in Weimar. In the meantime Kogon and Baumeister telephoned Ding-Schuler, who came rushing back from Weimar on his motor bicycle to find that Pister had now sent an ambulance to fetch Peulevé.

The interview between Ding-Schuler and Pister was stormy: Ding-Schuler protested that it would be inhuman to execute a dying man with a temperature of 41° centigrade. Pister roared back that neither he nor Ding-Schuler were in Buchenwald to practise benevolence, but to carry out the orders of their superiors; these orders were that Peulevé was to be summarily executed and there was no reason why even a dying man could not be brought to the Tower and despatched with a revolver bullet while he lay on his stretcher. Ding-Schuler protested that there was one very good reason against taking such a course, and that was the risk of spreading typhus throughout the camp, even into the Commandant's quarters. This argument impressed Pister, who cancelled the order to remove Peulevé from Block 46 and commanded instead that he should be killed there by an injection from Ding-Schuler himself. Ding-Schuler protested that such an act was outside his terms of reference and suggested a more suitable deputy, Hauptsturmführer Schidlowski, should be delegated to perform the task. To this proposal Pister, now calmer, eventually agreed.

Much time had now been gained, but more still was required if one of the three Frenchmen were to die of his own death soon enough to save Peulevé. Knowing that Schidlowski had had his fill of executions and feared reprisals from the Allies, he persuaded the Hauptsturmführer that he himself should appoint a delegate, an N.C.O. called Wilhelm, whose reputation for sadism was well known and who could therefore be relied upon to carry out such congenial instructions. Wilhelm, however, had a reputation for drunkenness as well as for cruelty and when he arrived at Block 46 the Kapo had a special meal and a bottle of Schnaps waiting in his office for the executioner. Wilhelm did not require much inviting and when he had finished the whole bottle of Schnaps by himself he was so drunk that he could scarcely stand. The Kapo then led him into the typhus ward, showed him a moribund man whom he alleged to be Peulevé and pointed out that it would be a waste of his own valuable medicines and of Wilhelm's energy to give a lethal injection to so obviously dying a man whose corpse would in any case be delivered to the crematorium next morning. Wilhelm, keeping his balance with difficulty, agreed, staggered out and reported to Schidlowski that he had executed Peulevé.

Once again it was only a temporary respite which they had gained: a corpse had still to be produced, and if one of the three Frenchmen had not died by ten o'clock the next morning Peulevé would still have to be sacrificed.

Late that evening it began to be clear that Seigneur had not more than twenty-four hours to live, but Yeo-Thomas and Hessel were adamant that nothing should be done to hasten his end: they knew that Peulevé would not wish to owe his life to a man who *might*

have been saved. All that night they lay awake in terror and sus-
pense, listening to the groans of the dying man. At one o'clock
they were strong, at two o'clock weaker, at three o'clock stronger
again, and four o'clock weaker once more. At five o'clock the Kapo
wearied and perturbed, appeared and begged with them to be
allowed to give the man a fatal injection. 'It'd be a kindness really,'
he pleaded. 'He can't last much longer but it's still just possible
that he may live till noon.' Once more Yeo-Thomas and Hessel
refused. The dying man's groans became fainter and fainter, and
at half-past seven they ceased: Peulevé had been saved by a margin
of two and a half hours.

Two days later Peulevé had rejoined them in the upper room,
secure under the identity of Marcel Seigneur, No. 76,635. But on
7th October the camp loudspeaker blared again:

'*Die Gefangenen Avallard, Evesque, von Block 17 müssen sich
sofort beim Turm melden.*'

On 9th October it blared again:

'*Der Gefangene Rambaud von Block 17 muss sich sofort beim Turm
melden.*'

There remained now only six of the original thirty-seven, and of
these six Yeo-Thomas and Hessel formed two. Maurice Chouquet
and Michel Boitel were still not quite at death's door and if their
names were called neither Yeo-Thomas nor Hessel could hope to
escape by the same good fortune as Peulevé. There was nothing
that they could do except to watch and listen and pray and play
'silly buggers'.

Peeping out of the windows of their room they could glimpse
the autumn misery of the cold world from which even a painful
death would not have been such an unpleasant escape had there not
been another world of laughter and sunshine to which they longed
to return: in the small camp they could see their friends the Allied
airmen, distinguished by their soldierly bearing in misfortune; they
could see the wretched Jewish prisoners, with the cold wind flapping their rags about their fleshless bodies, shuffling, their heads
sunk into sockets on their rounded shoulders, to work under the
cries and blows of their masters; and in the evening they saw the
same prisoners return carrying their dead with them, sometimes as
many as sixty a day.

They had visitors too, smuggled into the Block by the Kapo: Kogon and Baumeister and, on one occasion, Lamason, whom Yeo-Thomas asked to send back news of them to England when he was transferred to a P.O.W. camp. From Schalker they received both the B.B.C. and the O.K.W. communiqués and, because all play and no work makes Jack an even duller boy, helped him and Gadzinski to plot the charts of those in an even deeper despond than themselves. But neither play nor work nor conversation nor contemplation of the horrors they witnessed from the window could keep them from brooding upon their main preoccupation: were Yeo-Thomas and Hessel also going to be saved? Perhaps it was Peulevé who suffered most.

The days passed and there was still no summons from the loud-speakers. The two sick Frenchmen took a turn for the worse, and on Friday, 13th October, Maurice Chouquet died. Because his height corresponded more to Tommy's than to Hessel's, Yeo-Thomas took his identity and number 81,642, and Chouquet's body was sent to the crematorium as Kenneth Dodkin, No. 14,624. This substitution was made in the nick of time: next day Ding-Schuler informed Tommy that the order for his execution had just arrived. Tommy now lived in the same anxiety as Peulevé: was Hessel going to be saved?

So once again they played 'silly buggers', plotted the expiring breath of the doomed, watched the death march from their window, imagined dinners in Soho, imitated Tommy Handley's saying, 'Shine your lamp, Sam', and kept their ears open for the dreaded order: *'Die folgenden Gefangenen müssen sich sofort beim Turm melden . . .'*

The order did not come: on 18th October Michel Boitel died and his corpse was sent to be burned as Hessel's. Yeo-Thomas, Peulevé and Hessel had ceased to exist; and it was Chouquet, Seigneur and Boitel who, peering through their lattice, saw the whole of the Copenhagen police force, arrested in one fell swoop by the Germans, arrive in the camp and carry trunks for the despots, two men to each trunk, keeping in step like guards, until hunger and cold should have worked their way with them too.

The problem which Chouquet, Seigneur and Boitel now faced was only less acute than that which Yeo-Thomas, Peulevé and

Hessel had confronted; the loudspeaker could no longer blare their names, but they still had to survive until the Allied Armies arrived in triumph to liberate them. They had now to fear their fellow prisoners almost as much as they had formerly feared the Germans: for the Communists, if they learned that officers had managed to cheat the gallows, would certainly denounce them. (M. Michelin, the director of the famous tyre company, whom Tommy had seen on several occasions, could have been saved, but was sent to a certain death because his communist fellow-countrymen refused to help a capitalist.) The only solution was for Kogon and Baumeister to have them transferred from Buchenwald to a work Kommando where there would be little chance of their being recognized; and, to prepare for their new duplicity, Chouquet, Seigneur and Boitel set about learning all there was to be known about Chouquet, Seigneur and Boitel.

Kogon and Baumeister arranged these transfers quickly; at the beginning of November Peulevé and Hessel were sent to fill two vacancies which had occurred in a small Kommando attached to an aircraft factory at Schönbeck: Peulevé, because he was technically qualified, as an electrician, and Hessel, because he spoke German, as a clerk. Yeo-Thomas was not left in solitude for long to mourn their departure. On 8th November the Kapo told him that Kogon had arranged for him to be sent to a small Kommando called Kommando Wille at Gleina, where he was to get into touch with a prisoner called Hummelsheim, who had been warned of his arrival and would do all in his power to aid him.

Because the Kapo had risked his life to help them Yeo-Thomas now risked his life to help the Kapo: he wrote out a detailed statement of all that the Kapo had done on their behalf, which he signed with his real name, rank and number and gave to him. Perhaps the risk was less than Tommy imagined because his signature is almost illegible. At any rate this document, while it may have saved the Kapo's life, did not prevent him from being sentenced to a long term of imprisonment by an Allied Court after the war.

On 9th November, carrying among his chattels Hubble's chess set and food and a pair of hobnailed leather boots which the Kapo had given him, and wearing underneath a ragged striped coat a pair of fairly good trousers and a corduroy jacket which were also the Kapo's gifts, Prisoner No. 81,642 Maurice Chouquet made his way through a blinding snowstorm to the gates of Buchenwald. Although the snow caked his clogs and made walking difficult, he blessed the cold misery which bit into his face, because it gave him every excuse for keeping his face down, and the few who were abroad were too busy covering their own faces to spare a glance for the hurrying figure whom fair weather might have enabled them to recognize as Prisoner No. 14,624 Kenneth Dodkin. At the gate about twenty other prisoners were already waiting: three of them were Dutchmen, and the rest Central European Jews. Their names sounded strange when the SS guards read them out in a roll call, but none sounded stranger than his own, in which he had been made neither a taxpayer nor an inheritor of the kingdom of heaven. The shouts of '*Hinein, schnell*' when the truck drove up were however familiar, as were also the kicks and the blows from the rifle butts. The gates of the prison swung open and they drove out of Buchenwald into the lovely white silence of a snow-covered world.

CHAPTER XV

GLEINA AND REHMSDORF

IT was bitterly cold in the truck, and the red-nosed, peaky-faced prisoners huddled together for warmth, envying the plutocratic comfort of the guards, who wore jackboots, thick greatcoats and fur-lined gloves. Next to Tommy crouched a Jewish boy, Andreas Weiss, who had succeeded in being sent to Gleina to join his father and who spoke a little French. His lack of spirit and oriental fatalism astounded Yeo-Thomas, who was soon exhorting him as he had exhorted so many others. The sermon which he preached was his old homily about never saying die and going down with one's colours flying; if for most of us such phrases have lost their meaning, it is perhaps because they have been so often used by those who never have themselves known danger and have no intention of doing so. With Tommy these words were like Cinderella's slipper: they fitted and because they fitted they shone. Soon he had the Jewish boy full of fight, and the other prisoners singing and humming, making, as the psalmist had counselled their forefathers, a merry noise in Jacob, which seemed all around them, perhaps because it was so very far away. The guards growled but took no violent action to stop them: they knew that the prisoners would not sing for long.

Even Tommy ceased singing when night fell, cloaking in blackness the sweet white earth which had made him hope. The truck lurched over the frozen ruts and the prisoners were bumped against one another, their frightened faces swinging in the darkness like dim lanterns. On and on they went through invisible avenues of uncharted shadow unwound from and wound up again into the greater shadow of the night. At last they entered a village, with its roofs flung up like ranges of mountains against the high indigo of the sky, with here and there chinks of light shining from behind windows, like stars which had somehow come too near. The truck stopped at a gate in the middle of the village. In front of the gate stood an SS sentry, his buckles and buttons looking like holes punctured in the night.

As the gate was opened and the truck entered the yard inside was floodlit. The square on which the prisoners were ordered to jump down was surrounded by farmhouses. They had arrived at Gleina, and the Rapportführer of the camp, Unterscharführer Otto Möller, was waiting with a sheaf of papers in his hand to call the inevitable roll.

Once more Yeo-Thomas answered to the number and name of 81,642 Maurice Chouquet, and for a moment he had a feeling that the real 81,642 Maurice Chouquet was watching him do so: for around the square were ranged rows of spectral beings with large gleaming eyes who looked like the ghosts of the dead; the old prisoners had come to gaze upon the new.

The Kapo, a tall rugged Dutchman of about forty-five whom they were later to know as Hans Gentkow, then ordered them to file into one of the buildings. On his way in Tommy was stopped by a young good-looking man of about twenty-six.

'Etes-vous français?' the young man asked.

'*Oui,*' Tommy said.

'If you'll tell me your profession I'll try to see what I can do about putting you with other Frenchmen.'

The real Maurice Chouquet had been described on his identity papers as a carpenter, and Tommy's knowledge of carpentry was sketchy. He answered, therefore, that in civil life he had been the owner of a furniture business but that the SS had insisted on listing him as a carpenter. His new friend said that he would see what could be done to fit him in, and Tommy said nothing more. He wasn't really sure whether his new friend was his new friend or his new enemy; Buchenwald had taught him not to be surprised by the hatred of those with whom a shared misery ought to have bound him in love.

Carrying his pitiful bundle of luggage, he climbed a rickety staircase dripping with moisture to a landing on which there were three doors: the first was ajar, and through it could be both seen and smelt the long wooden trough which was the common urinal; the second opened into a square room filled with bunks and in which a double-check roll call was held. When Yeo-Thomas again answered to the name of Chouquet a young man wearing the red triangle of a German political prisoner stepped forward, had a word with the Kapo, and then introduced himself to Tommy as Hummelsheim. Tommy began to understand that the young Frenchman too was a friend when, after consultation with Hummelsheim and Gentkow, he offered to find him a bed for the night.

But even then it didn't seem that the bed was going to be a very comfortable one. Led by the Frenchman into a room behind the third door, Yeo-Thomas entered a dormitory crammed with bunks three tiers high with a central passage just broad enough for one man to pass. Although the room was only dimly lit by unshaded electric bulbs, what he saw of the occupants of the bunks horrified and frightened him. On each bunk was stretched a burning-eyed, emaciated man whose yellow skin glittered with feebleness and sweat. Most of these brittle bodies were covered with bandages stained with dirt, blood and pus. Stinking of urine, faeces, vomit and rot the frail men lay groaning, moaning, muttering and babbling appeals to God in which the rasp of a curse often mingled with the lonely yell of an unanswered *Eli, Eli, lama sabachthani?*

However, it was not among these storeys of the doomed that Yeo-Thomas was required to sleep. At the end of this long room was another smaller and more brightly lit room with twelve bunks in it, piled as usual in tiers of three. The rest of the furniture consisted of two long narrow benches made of planks and a couple of three-legged stools. Against the wall a makeshift stove constructed out of an old oven propped on bricks and coated with earth and cement gave out a restricted, weakly heat. After the spectacle which he had just witnessed these comforts seemed sybaritic.

It was soon clear that he had landed again in a hospital: his guide turned out to be a French Army doctor called Jean Dulac; of the three men lying in the bunks one was a Doctor Mendel: other Jewish doctors came in almost immediately, Doctor Holosz, Doctor Szekely, and Doctor Weiss, the father of the boy into whom Tommy had pumped pep in the truck. Among the few laymen were Paul Jacquin, a thickset man called Pierre Fauvage, a stripling of twenty called Foulquier and the registrar of the hospital, Pierre Kaan, a grey-haired man with spectacles. This last man looked puzzled when Yeo-Thomas introduced himself as 'Colonel Maurice Chouquet, de l'Armée de l'Air'. It was not without purpose that Tommy had decided not only to remain an officer but to promote himself: he wished to be in a position of authority if he was ever able to organize a mass escape, and he had already arranged with Kogon that he would be taken back to Buchenwald to lead an armed revolt there if an opportunity arose.

He was grateful when Dr. Dulac told him that he could have the last vacant bunk in the cubicle and that he would do his best to have him attached to the hospital staff as an orderly, instead of being sent to work with the others in Rehmsdorf. He handed over the food which the Kapo had given him, and from their ill-stocked larder Fauvage produced a special hot supper of potatoes and onions in honour of the newcomer's arrival. All through the meal Kaan kept looking at him queerly and the others looked at him queerly too when Hummelsheim dropped in and took him away to his room for a private conversation.

Hummelsheim's room was a cubicle partitioned off the store on the top floor. In spite of the rule forbidding the display of religious emblems, on the wall hung a crucifix, that hint of mercy which used to be understood throughout the Christian world, but whose universality progress has replaced by the cocktail shaker and Donald Duck. As the two men talked together an incense of Czechoslovakian tobacco arose to this chink of light in a terrible darkness and perhaps, because part of it was puffed from poor Hubble's pipe, the Lord received it for an odour of sweetness.

Hummelsheim, whom Kogon had not informed of Tommy's British nationality, told Yeo-Thomas that he would do all in his power to help him. Gleina, he said, was really only the Revier or hospital of the Jewish extermination camp, lying outside the main compound but strictly subject to the authority of the Commandant. This man, an SS Obersturmführer, was a sadist whose favourite pastime was flogging prisoners to death. Of the 320 SS guards only three were decent and their clemency was more than cancelled by the brutality of three prisoners in authority: the Polish cook at Gleina; Hans Wolff, the Lagerältester at Rehmsdorf; and a Czechoslovakian who was Kapo of the Revier. There were also feuds among the prisoners because the subterranean quarrel of the world, so very much more deadly than the open, divided the wretched as it was later to divide the victorious. Tommy returned to his quarters feeling that, apart from the removal of the threat of immediate death, he had done little more than exchange the frying-pan for the fire.

'*Aufstehen*' next morning in the fire was at the same time as it had been in Block 17 in the frying-pan: six o'clock. This time he made even the sick forget their agony for a little in their astonishment at the extensive ablutions which he performed with the Kapo's soap at the trough at the end of the ward. When he had dressed he found himself alone for a moment with Pierre Kaan.

'I know now who you are,' Kaan said. 'You're Shelley.'

Tommy was surprised, but not alarmed, because Frenchmen who knew Shelley were his friends.

'Shelley is dead; Chouquet is living,' he said sadly, because it wasn't only Shelley who had died with Shelley; with Shelley had perished also Thierry, Tirelli, Gaonach and Dodkin, each of whom had fought for the cause in his way. It was now his turn to look at Kaan closely, but if the Resistance world was small many brave men crowded it, and although Kaan's face seemed familiar he could not for the life of him remember where he had seen him before.

'You knew me before under the name of Biran, I think,' Kaan said, and then it all came back: it was Kaan who, on the already prehistoric 27th October, 1943, had been the Secretary at a meeting of the Comité Militaire at which Brossolette and he had attempted to resolve the differences between the Regional Military Officers and the Resistance Groups.

Yeo-Thomas told Kaan all that had happened to him since then. Kaan said that Tommy's conversation the night before with a privileged German prisoner like Hummelsheim had aroused the distrust of his colleagues, but that he would dispel all misunderstanding by telling them that Tommy had been a valuable member of French Resistance, without, however, disclosing his British nationality.

Their tête-à-tête was interrupted by Dulac, who informed Yeo-Thomas that he had obtained for him the double hospital appointment of *Totenträger* and *Pfleger*: he was to work with Fauvage and Foulquier, who would instruct him in his duties both towards the living and the dead.

His sinister task of carrying corpses from the hospital began at once, and during all the time he was at Gleina the routine never varied. First of all the SS Sanitäter, an Oberscharführer, came with a pair of pincers and yanked out any gold teeth there might be in the mouths of those who had died during the night. Then Yeo-Thomas and Foulquier carried the bodies to the small hut which was used as a morgue. There the often dysentery-fouled shirt and trousers were removed from each corpse, which was then piled on top of those already there, many of them already green with decay. Sometimes the morgue was so full that they had to stand on top of the old dead in order to slide in the new dead and under their weight the carcases would often eruct in ghoulish posthumous belches and farts. And yet in all their gruesome grocery they never became callous. They could not, Tommy says, 'administer the last rites', but when they had squeezed each new corpse into position on the common catafalque they bared their heads and stood for a few seconds in silence, honouring the mystery. Often while performing this reverence they were cursed and kicked by the supervising guards.

Nor was that the end of their duties to the dead: before they were removed from the morgue the bodies had to be placed in coffins, a clemency which amazed Yeo-Thomas until he learned the reason. Most of the prisoners at Rehmsdorf worked in the 'Brabag' factory at Zeitz, and one of the clauses in the contract of their servitude was that their employers should contribute sixty marks towards the burial expenses of those who died. The mistress of the Camp Commandant was an undertaker who also ran a subsidiary capable of producing thirteen coffins a day at a cost price of fifteen marks each. This meant that provided that there were thirteen deaths a day at Gleina—and there had to be thirteen deaths a day at Gleina—the Obersturmführer and his harlot shared a daily profit of 585 marks.

Tommy's duties towards the living were almost as heartrending. As an orderly he had to nurse the sick in their repulsive maladies. Because of malnutrition most of the patients suffered from carbuncles the size of small melons which, when lanced, spurted pus three feet across the ward, leaving a hole deep enough for him to plunge his fist in. Others had the bones of their arms and their legs laid bare by oedemas. On two occasions the living so closely resembled the dead that he and Foulquier carted them off to the morgue by mistake and, when they found that their hearts were still beating feebly, had to clothe them again in their soiled rags and carry them back to die among the others in whom life still flickered. The plight of the dying was made even more terrible by the fact that the Oberscharführer impounded the scanty medical supplies at their disposal and sold them to German civilians outside the camp.

Those of the patients who could still walk had to stagger through the snow on clogs or on bare feet to collect the scanty meals dished out by the Polish cook. It was part of Tommy's job to bring back the bread. On his first day he found that he could carry a sack of fifty loaves, but when he caught dysentery he quickly dropped to twenty: he took advantage of the extra trips which his disability involved to steal a few more SS rations for distribution among his patients. Between journeys he had to go to the latrine, where he sat on a tree trunk with his bottom bared to the biting winter wind, precariously perched above a trench containing six feet of faeces.

Every day the sick prisoners had to stand for two hours in blinding sleet or snow or in a temperature of 15° below zero centigrade while the Appell took place, in spite of the efforts of Rapportführer Otto Möller to shorten the process. Because of his intercession with authority on behalf of the prisoners Möller made himself unpopular with the Camp Commandant, who was merciless. Others who were humane enough to risk the Obersturmführer's displeasure were Rottenführer Kurt Hebestreit, N.C.O. in charge of the stores, who turned a blind eye to Tommy's larcenies, and Oberscharführer Saurbier, who prevented his colleagues from beating up prisoners while he was present. Both these men had been fighting soldiers before being compulsorily transferred to the SS, and when the Obersturmführer heard of Saurbier's allegiance to the old code he arrested him and sent him to gaol in Buchenwald.

There were no age limits in the call-up for suffering: among the prisoners were many Central European Jewish boys, little older than children. When they fell sick Dulac contrived to keep them in the Revier as long as possible, and some of them he saved from work in the factories by retaining them as orderlies. One of these latter was a boy of fourteen called Ivan, who helped Yeo-Thomas on his ghastly duties. His story was so typical that even those who befriended him did not regard it as especially tragic. The son of a Rabbi, he had been arrested in Budapesth while out for a walk with his grandmother, his mother and his little sister of eight. Without being allowed to bid farewell to their family, they were pushed into a cattle truck and taken to Auschwitz. There, as his grandmother was too old, his mother too ill and his sister too young to work, the three of them were thrown into the incinerator of the crematorium and burned alive. Ivan was sent to Buchenwald and thence to Rehmsdorf, to work in the Brabag factory, where he eventually fell ill. With this boy, whom he took under his protection, Yeo-Thomas formed a deep friendship.

It was natural that Tommy, who still wanted to be fighting with the Allied Armies on the day of victory, should think of escape. On one occasion he succeeded in being sent to Leipzig by Hummelsheim, who, as Schreiber of Gleina, had to keep in contact with the merchants who enriched themselves by selling tainted meat to the camp. There he could have escaped, but if he had done so Hummelsheim would have been executed. He was able, nevertheless, to send a message to Barbara through some British prisoners of war whom he saw carrying steel shutters across a factory yard. Although it had to be passed sentence by sentence to a succession of individual soldiers as they filed past him, the message reached England in its entirety, and Tommy is still grateful to the transmitters for their successful co-operation.

Thanks to Pierre Kaan, however, he had now regained the confidence of his new French friends, and with Dulac and others he had organized a small group of twenty who were on the watch for a suitable opportunity to escape. The physical weakness of the majority of the prisoners made the organization of a larger body impossible, and there was the added difficulty that the doctors regarded their work among the sick as an apostolate. As escape was for the moment out of the question they kept up their spirits by pranks and tomfoolery. For more serious relaxation Kaan, a Hungarian lawyer called Cazar, Yeo-Thomas and others played chess on Hubble's set, which was as sacred to Tommy as the tibia of a saint.

At the beginning of December the deaths jumped from round about a dozen a day to thirty or more, and in order to relieve the congestion in the morgue those who had so often shared a bunk had also to share a coffin. One day as Yeo-Thomas and Foulquier were carrying a casket to the truck the flimsily made bottom fell out and two bodies were precipitated on the snow under the eyes of the Obersturmführer, who was supervising the supervisors. The sight of these pitiable corpses lying on the cold earth moved the Camp Commandant neither to pity nor fear of the judgment: unmollified by Foulquier's explanation of the reasons of this duplication, he bellowed with rage at so evident an infringement of his profit, and ordered that the doctors should be beaten if they did not succeed in staggering the deaths of their patients so as not to exceed the statutory daily thirteen.

Although there was snow on the ground at Christmas their celebration was not the white indecency dreamed of in the sugary song. Perhaps happy men as well as rich men cannot hope to enter easily into the kingdom of heaven and perhaps it is only when men are bang up against terror and despair that they can appreciate the warmth once promised. Because of their poverty they were unable

229

to blaspheme hope with paper hats, hooters and gin. As their feast was a poor one it was also a holy one. The candles on their tree were made of margarine threaded with string. Their presents were loose cigarettes and pieces of bread wrapped in chalk-coloured paper. But there was nothing ersatz about their song, which reached back to an age in which faith was not obscured by mathematics:

> *Ergo qui natus*
> *Die hodierna,*
> *Jesus tibi sit gloria:*
> *Patris aeterni*
> *Verbo caro factum!*
> *Venite adoremus,*
> *Venite adoremus,*
> *Venite adoremus Dominum.*

And that night even Israel, weeping by the waters of its most terrible Babylon, believed and honoured the root which had come out of Jesse. With tears in their eyes Jews, Gentiles, and the dying of both dispensations sang hymns and canticles of gladness and, after praising the mercy which seemed so very far from them, they sang to Britain and France and America, whose undeliberately Christian armies had made the tenderness seem a little nearer. And even the floggers of the feeble and the usurers of their bodies a desire for holiness seemed to halo, for over the compound came the voices of the soldiers of the Schutzstaffeln [1] raised in plaintive choir:

> *Stille Nacht! Heilige Nacht!*
> *Alles schläft. Einsam wacht,*
> *Nur das traute, hochheilige Paar—*
> *Holder Knabe in lockigen Haar,*
> *Schlaf in himmlischer Ruh,*
> *Schlaf in himmlischer Ruh!*

'Merry Christmas', Kaan whispered under his breath to Yeo-Thomas, knowing that Tommy was hungry to hear an English word. And an SS guard called to wish them all '*Fröhliche Weihnacht*', weeping tears of emotion which did not seem to be entirely

[1] SS.

Schnaps. The very next day that same guard beat a prisoner to death; perhaps that is why even the best of Christmases is inevitably a let-down: the world always seems so very much more cruel on the 26th December.

And cruel for them all the world became in the New Year, when the Revier was transferred from Gleina to Rehmsdorf, within the barbed wire of the camp proper. They were now directly under the control of the Obersturmführer and his brutal lieutenant Lageraltester Hans Wolff. The hospital was crowded into two huts, each constructed to accommodate 150 and made to hold 600. The doctors had no longer a cubicle to themselves but had to sleep in bunks among the sick, two deep in tiers of four. Tommy, who occupied a middle bunk, had a foot and a half of space between his head and the boards of the bunk above: on those boards he pencilled the word BARBARA; it was the nearest he could get to a photograph.

For the 1,200 patients in the two huts there was one thermometer, and one bed-pan. Men dying of dysentery, tuberculosis and pneumonia had to go outside to the latrine until the orderlies installed oil drums behind wooden planking to mitigate their discomfort. Even then many of the patients were so weak that they fell into the drums and had to be pulled out and cleaned. Some collapsed and died on their way back to their bunks. Others fouled their bunks, and their ordures oozed through the boards and dripped on the faces of those underneath, who were generally too feeble themselves to protest. To add to this horror, the Obersturmführer, when he visited the wards, was in the habit of pulling patients out of their bunks by their feet and laughing when their skulls fractured on the stone floor.

Yeo-Thomas, Fauvage and Foulquier worked eighteen hours a day carting out the dead, feeling pulses and taking temperatures. Sometimes they took the temperatures of the dead as well as those of the living; for the patients, crammed three to a bunk, would, to obtain extra rations, slide the thermometer under the armpit of a deceased neighbour and, when Yeo-Thomas wasn't looking, rub the mercury up with their hands. As a result corpses were often stiff with the rigour of death when the orderlies removed them. But, stiff or still pliant, all corpses had to be laid out in a row at the entrance to the hut until the N.C.O. came to prise open their jaws with a piece of wood and extract their gold teeth for the SS regimental funds. This ritual was generally supererogatory because the SS guards, in their greed for this bullion, usually beat to death prisoners with gold teeth before they were ill enough to enter the Revier.

In a makeshift surgery railed off from the rest of the hut Mendel, Dulac and the other doctors punctured carbuncles and phlegmons and dressed oedemas, from which six to seven hundred of their patients were suffering. The few instruments could rarely be sterilized; the iodine was ersatz; there was one pair of scissors and no cotton-wool; and, as the small supply of chlorethyl had to be kept for major operations, there were for most no anaesthetics. Yeo-Thomas and the other orderlies held down the shrieking patients while the doctors lanced and the blood and pus spurted out like geysers.

And all the time that he was carrying out his grim duties Yeo-Thomas was feeling far from well himself. He suffered simultaneously from dysentery, boils on his back and a stone in his kidney which caused him agony until he succeeded in passing it out into his bladder. He dared not report sick for fear of being exterminated.

Yet bad as conditions were in the Revier they were worse in the main camp. It was bitterly cold, and the prisoners, who had no winter clothing, no socks and no gloves, had to work outside from morning till night under the threats and blows of the guards. They had almost no food. There was only one way to get extra rations and that was to be a first-class musician or a singer from the Viennese opera and entertain the SS guards while they sat swilling their potations. This privilege, however, carried its own special risks, for in Rehmsdorf even music had little power the savage breast to charm: if a drunken guard didn't like the way a violinist played *The Blue Danube* or a tenor's rendering of *La Donna è Mobile* the offender was likely to be dragged from the platform and beaten to death.

The Revier was the only real refuge from the brutality of the camp and sooner or later all those who weren't murdered qualified for it. Some, although they weren't technically enough near death to be validly excused from work, were admitted temporarily to the hospital by the doctors in order that they might regain their strength. Naturally their number was limited and their stay had to be short in order that as many as possible might benefit. Among them were a few malingerers, of whom one slept in the bunk under that of Cazar, the Hungarian lawyer.

Cazar suffered from an ailment of the bladder which made it necessary for him to pass water frequently. So as not to disturb his neighbours by frequent nocturnal visits to the oil drums he took to bed with him a tin which he used as a chamber-pot. One night he took by mistake the perforated tin used for watering the hut, and when he had micturated the urine trickled down on to the malingerer's head. Yeo-Thomas, Kaan and those in the vicinity were wakened by a banging on the bottom of Cazar's bunk and a violent protest:

'You swine! What are you doing?'

'What's the matter?' Cazar asked gently. 'Surely it's not *Auf-stehen* yet.'

'Stop pissing on my bed!'

'My dear friend, you must be mistaken. I am not pissing on your bed.'

'Yes, you are,' the malingerer roared. 'And what's more I'm soaked.'

'Impossible.'

'Damn you, more is trickling down this very minute. Can't you control yourself, you swine?'

'Really, you're crazy.'

'And you are a dirty pisser!'

'I am a pisser, I admit, but I am a clean pisser: I use my tin.'

'Well, you are not using it now, you lazy bastard.'

'Of course I am not using it now; I used it only a minute ago.'

'You clumsy idiot, you must have upset it.'

'No, I have not; my tin is still upright.'

'Well, you are still pissing. Stop it, you dirty pig.'

'Oh, dear,' said Cazar, after investigation. 'I am so sorry. You see, there is a hole.'

'Of course, there is a hole, you damned fool. I'm soaked.'

'But there is a hole.'

'Curse your hole.'

'Oh, dear, oh, dear, there is a hole. I am so very sorry that there is a hole.'

C. S. Lewis uses man's constant amusement at the incongruity of his physical functions with his dignity as an argument in favour of his immortality. Those who listened to this dialogue had suffered too much to need any such high considerations to make them laugh. Their laughter was deep and loud and from the belly and it cleansed them for a little from their misery.

And for what lay ahead of them as well as for what lay behind them they had need of laughter. In spite of the ever-increasing number of deaths the Revier was always full, and the SS, tired of feeding the unproductive, sent eastwards for extermination those they considered unlikely to recover. An SS officer would come clanking into the hut and order the sick to parade in front of him. Those unable to leave their bunks were sent on the next death convoy and the others, sticking out their bony chests as the merciless eyes passed along their ranks, were divided into those who would be murdered with them and those who would be reprieved for further work before they, in turn, were murdered or died of exhaustion. Many of those ordered to return to work were so weak that they collapsed as soon as they left the hut and were beaten to death by the guards. On two occasions the Revier was completely emptied by these inspections; but within three days both huts were full again.

Among those sent to be exterminated was the Jewish boy Ivan, who had contracted meningitis after leaving Gleina. The night before he was taken away he lay on a couple of boards in the camp washroom, and Yeo-Thomas squatted beside him, holding his hand. The boy was too ill to speak, but his eyes were eloquent with despair. Every time that Tommy moved, Ivan clutched his hand desperately. When the SS guards came for him in the morning they removed the blanket which covered his wasted limbs before carrying him out in a wood-fibre shirt into a temperature of 15° below zero centigrade. Tommy went with him to the gate of the camp, where the guards wrenched Ivan's hand from his and bore away the boy, groaning with despair, to die a brutal lonely death.

Seven thousand six hundred prisoners passed through Rehmsdorf while Yeo-Thomas was there, and such was their condition that he could find among them only forty with spirit enough left to co-operate in a plan for escape. Ten of these were Frenchmen, six Dutchmen and twenty-four Jews.

Their old quarters at Gleina had been turned into a P.O.W. camp for British Other Ranks, most of whom were commandos or paratroopers. With the complicity of Gentkow, now in charge of fatigue parties, Tommy entered into communication with the N.C.O. in charge of the camp, Corporal Stevenson of the Leicestershire Regiment, to whom he was able to prove his status through the happy accident of being able to mention the name of a captain in the regiment whom his cousin had married. Detailed by Gentkow for a potato and carrot-peeling fatigue at Gleina, he had an interview with the corporal in the cookhouse and, over a hot meal which Stevenson provided for him, arranged one of those desperate schemes whose merit is not only that they are courageous but that they sometimes come off. As the Allied troops advanced towards Leipzig, Stevenson and the British P.O.W.s would overpower their guards, seize their arms and march on Rehmsdorf, from which Yeo-Thomas and his forty men, armed with ten rifles, ten pistols and a few dozen hand grenades which they had managed to secure, would make a sortie to meet them. In earnest of this plan, which was never to come off, Tommy took back to Rehmsdorf a parcel of chocolate, biscuits, sugar and cigarettes to distribute among his patients.

And with the approach of spring Rehmsdorf became more than ever a place to escape from, for sadistic SS guards and blackmailing Kapos were no longer the only people they had to fear: their liberating friends came rushing through the skies dropping bombs with that approximation to accuracy that was so lauded by contemporary newsreel commentators in between their sneers at brave enemy generals and their sniggers at bathing beauties' breasts. A night-bomber raid on the Brabag factory, illuminated by R.A.F. Path-finders, was successful: 80 per cent. of the factory was destroyed and none of the prisoners was hurt, although the patients in the Revier clung to the doctors, screaming with fear. Two daylight raids in March on the same factory were, however, much less precise. In one of them, although a distance of four miles separated the camp from the Brabag, a five-hundred-pound bomb fell on a hut diagonally opposite the hospital, disintegrating it completely. Once again the patients blubbered with terror and smothered the doctors and orderlies, who had to throw them off roughly in order to run to the sundered hut.

Several more bombs landed in the camp while 'Monsieur Jean' and 'Monsieur Maurice' and the others began their work of necessarily rule-of-thumb mercy among rubble spattered with blood and brains. Legs and arms without bodies and bodies without legs and arms were strewn all around. On the top of a neighbouring hut lay the mangled trunk of a prisoner gushing blood from the raw hams of two stumps from which his legs had been blasted. Beneath the smoking ruins lay even greater miseries, and as they had no tools, the doctors and orderlies had to dig with their hands in order to pull out those buried underneath, many of whom were already dead.

In their makeshift surgery the doctors had no cotton-wool and even the ersatz iodine had run out. As the water supply had been cut they had to wash out wounds with substitute coffee diluted with disinfectant. Many died on the table before the paper bandages could be applied to their wounds. There were no proper surgical instruments. One man had his leg shattered below the knee and, after ineffectively doping him with two ampoules of chlorethyl, Yeo-Thomas held him down while Dulac proceeded to an amputation with a knife whose blade was one and a half inches long. As he had no clamps to clip on the arteries Dulac had to ligature them with cotton. At the end of an hour's hacking the shattered portion of the leg came away in Tommy's hand. The patient lived for several days before he expired, comforted no doubt by the thought that he had died for civilization, for television, for tired housewives, four-course dinners in airliners and *bidets* in all the best hotels.

One advantage, however, seemed to accrue to them from these air raids: the prisoners obtained permission to dig trenches in which to shelter, and Yeo-Thomas and Dulac took care to have them dug in strategic positions where, with their paltry armoury, they could make a last stand if their guards received the expected order to exterminate them.

For a new terror was now tearing at the bowels of the prisoners. As the Allied Armies advanced the Germans were evacuating the concentration camps and killing their inmates: some were locked into their huts and burned to death with flame-throwers; others were murdered as they marched along the road. Rehmsdorf, technically a Jewish extermination camp, could scarcely expect to escape the same fate. The sadists were taking precautions that none of their victims should remain alive to tell of the cruelties which had been practised upon them.

Morale in the camp sank lower and lower as rumour succeeded rumour. As food became scarcer the prisoners began to fight one another for their rations. Even patients so sick that they could not rise from their bunks tried to wrest bread from the grasp of those weaker than themselves. And even among those wrangling skeletons it took all Tommy's waning strength to restore order.

Their fears were justified, but the trenches were useless. On the night of 13th April the order came to evacuate the camp. The murder was to take place all right, but not on the spot. This knowledge gave Tommy hope; and, when he had collected his lighter, Hubble's pipe and chess set, he went to see Dulac.

'I am going to organize an attempt to escape during the evacuation,' he said. 'But you do not need to obey my orders if you don't wish to. You see, I'm not a French officer really. I am a Briton. I should like the others to know this too. Pierre Kaan will tell you who and what I am.'

But by now Dulac had learned to know his Tommy.

'I do not care who or what you are,' he said. 'I shall obey you just the same. And I know that the others will too.'

Then Tommy went and smashed the bedboard with 'BARBARA' written on it: he did not wish anybody else to gaze upon his sanctuary.

CHAPTER XVI

DEATH CONVOY

THE exodus was grim. Even the sick and the dying had to be loaded on to the train so that nobody might be left behind to tell tales. Those who were strong enough to walk had to carry the bedridden, and the doctors and the orderlies helped. Hundreds of moribunds, with pus oozing from festering sores and wounds, were packed into the open trucks. They were not allowed to take their blankets with them and wore only their shirts. There was an Appell, too, and the few who attempted to hide in the camp were rounded up and killed by the guards. The Obersturmführer was taking no chances: another murderer and torturer SS Oberschar- führer and not the benevolent SS Rapportführer Möller had been put in charge of the convoy. And the SS Oberscharführer wasn't making any mistakes either: in each truck there were three armed guards and at the front and the rear of the train there were covered wagons filled with other guards. While they were waiting to move off a few Allied fighters dived down to bomb and machine- gun the train, but, perhaps because they were aiming badly, nobody was hit.

The train moved off in the early morning of 14th April, but even then their journey was slow and punctuated with many stops. One of their halts was on a siding near a women's concentration camp whose inmates, herded by female SS in jackboots, waved to them from their enclosure. The gaolers lashed into the women at once with their long whips, and a couple of SS officers threw bricks at them. In a few minutes the women had all been shut up in their huts, and the prisoners in the train could hear them shouting insults at their guards, who were obviously unable to use their whips in the confined interiors of the huts.

Their journey was tortuous too, and within twenty-four hours they were back again in Rehmsdorf, but soon after were mov- ing eastwards and it became clear that they were heading for Czechoslovakia. Death accompanied them on their trip, and it came brutally as it had come in the camp, without sacraments or aspirations. As the men died of exposure or were murdered the SS guards slung their bodies, naked except for their paper bandages, from the train with words of committal whose unoriginal bestiality derived from the stupid Hitlerian grammar of abuse: 'Another pig dog of a Jew to fertilize the ground.' 'You mean to defile it with his filthy carcase.' 'Let's see how far we can swing this lousy Jewish bastard.' And jeering laughter followed each emaciated corpse as it went flying through the air, arms and legs flapping, eyes and mouth open and frozen fast in death, to land on rocks with a thud or hit a tree before it crashed to the ground and sagged as the miracle seemed to go out of it for the second time.

But 170 deaths in a single night were too much for even these brutal undertakers to handle; and on the morning of 16th April, after puffing up the long, rugged, woodlined slopes of the Bohemian foothills and passing through the small station of Marienburg-Gelobtland, the train stopped in a small clearing to permit of their burial in a common grave. Orders were given for the formation of two working parties: one to dig a deep hole slightly in front of and to the left of the engine; the other to throw the bodies out of the trucks on to the track, collect them, carry them to and throw them into the hole.

It was the opportunity for which Yeo-Thomas had been waiting. While on the right of the train the ground was rocky and difficult to negotiate, on the left it was smooth and merged into woods at about fifty yards from the site picked for the grave. He spoke with Dulac and Kaan and outlined his plan. Those who wanted to make an attempt to escape were to join the corpse-carrying working party. When, two to a body, they picked up a corpse to carry it to the grave they would remain bunched so as to deliver their loads in the hole simultaneously. They would then turn about as though to go and fetch another body, but, on a signal from Yeo-Thomas, would run as fast as they could towards the woods, which they must try to reach before the guards, strung out along the train and facing it, had time to swing round and fire on them. After that, he said, 'it would be a matter of luck'.

He tried, however, to leave as little as possible to luck. With 'Georges', a Belgian member of his group, acting as interpreter, he engineered, in a secluded spot some distance from their truck, a private conversation with Rapportführer Otto Möller, upon whom he tried a variant of the blackmail he had already practised successfully upon Sturmbannführer Ding-Schuler.

'Tell Möller,' he said to the astounded Georges, who had not been informed of Tommy's true nationality, 'tell him that I am a colonel in the British Intelligence Service. Tell him that I have been sent to Rehmsdorf specially in order to check up on the action of the SS. Tell him that I have already sent to the Allies a list of all officers and men in the SS and that this list is now in their hands.'

239

He watched the Rapportführer's face while Georges repeated what he had said in German. Was Möller going to denounce him or would he consent to bargain? The German's body stiffened slightly at the word 'Oberst', but otherwise his demeanour did not betray what he was thinking.

'Tell him that I am aware that he himself has never ill-treated any prisoner; on the contrary I know that he has been kind to them,' he went on. 'But the Allies won't know that unless somebody tells them. The mere fact that he is an SS will render him liable to be shot when he's captured. His only chance is to help us.'

'*Fragen Sie ihn, wie ich Ihnen helfen kann!*' [1] Möller asked. Although Yeo-Thomas knew little German, he knew what that meant: Möller was going to play; Möller was asking how he could help.

'Tell him that some of us are going to escape and that if he helps us I will see that no harm comes to him when he is caught.' Tommy then gave details of his plan. He said that he knew that Möller could not prevent the guards from shooting, but suggested that he might purposely misdirect their pursuit. Once they had escaped Möller could, if he liked, join them. They could then march along together as though he were taking them to a camp. When they approached the Allied lines he could put on civilian clothes and cross into custody under Tommy's protection.

His bluff succeeded. Möller accepted and told him of a small stream, some two miles inside the wood and running north-north-east, where they might meet after the chase had been called off.

The group was immediately alerted. There was no time to make elaborate preparations. They could not load themselves with food and in any case there was little food to take. In the pockets of Tommy's jacket there was room for only two pieces of bread: he took one piece of bread and Hubble's chess set.

They started to unload the dead from the trucks in which they sprawled in the pitiful congelation of their last sad perplexity. While they were laying them down beside the track one of the bearers, a poor miserable scarecrow who was almost dead himself, stooped to pick up a piece of potato peeling. For this dereliction of duty he was shot in the back of the skull by the Oberscharführer who happened to be passing.

[1] 'Ask him how I can help him.'

The grave was finished by the time all the bodies had been taken out of the trucks. In teams of two they picked up the corpses and slowly tramped towards the hole. Yeo-Thomas and Kaan led the way. Close behind them and keeping well together came the other eighteen members of the group who had agreed to make the attempt to escape. Approaching the grave, Tommy and Kaan threw in their burden and then stopped for a minute, pretending to rest. Dulac, Foulquier, Jacquin, Georges and the others did likewise. Then, when they were all collected together, they turned as though to go back for more bodies, but instead of going to the left went parallel to the train, thinning out on the way. Yeo-Thomas gave a quick glance round: none of the guards seemed to be looking in their direction. 'Go!' he shouted and he and his nineteen companions bounded towards the woods.

At once there were cries of '*Halt!*' and '*Zurück*', followed by the crack of Sten guns and the whizz of bullets as they sang through the air with piercing and very personal threat. Tommy ran on with his heart pounding and thudding inside him. The trees seemed much further off than when he had first seen them. As he tried to increase his speed bullets whistled past him in increasing number and with screeching velocity. He ducked his head down. The trees still seemed a long way off. He could see a few figures ahead of him, diving into the woods. His breath began to get shorter and the effort of running racked his weakened body. More bullets whined past him. 'How can the sods miss me?' he thought as his legs began to feel wobbly beneath him and to falter and flex. And as he stumbled on the sods did their best not to miss him. Suddenly, on the point of collapse, he felt brambles and other undergrowth clinging to his legs. He had reached the fringe of the wood. He pushed blindly on, through twigs and branches which scratched and lacerated his face. And still the bullets came after him, crashing into the trees and snipping off small branches. It seemed as though he was bound to be hit.

Breathless and puffing, his running degenerated into a faltering trot and the trot into a laboured walk. His chest felt as though it were about to burst. His breath came in gasps and sobs. He was exhausted. Behind him he heard voices shouting in German and heavy footsteps closing in on him. Through bloodshot and streaming eyes he saw a thick clump of trees and threw himself into bushes underneath. He landed on top of Foulquier. Foulquier was panting too, and Tommy began to be afraid that their pursuers would be guided to their hiding-place by the thumping of their hearts.

He buried his head in the ground to silence the gasps which were shaking him. He heard the heavy boots of guards crashing through the undergrowth. Looking up, he saw three pairs of jackboots within five yards of them and heard their wearers talking excitedly. Then, as Foulquier grasped his shoulder in fear, another pair of jackboots came up. Raising his head a little further he saw above them the face of Rapportführer Otto Möller.

'*Habt Ihr jemanden gesehen?*' [1] Möller asked.

'*Nein. Niemanden,*' [2] one of the other guards answered.

'*Da sind sie!*' [3] Möller shouted and, firing his pistol, charged off in the opposite direction, followed by the three guards, hallooing wildly. Other pursuers joined them, and soon the firing and the shouting died away into the distance. Otto Möller had kept his word.

Yeo-Thomas and Foulquier lay still. As their trembling limbs calmed they slowly regained their breath. When all noises had ceased for some time they made their way cautiously and as silently as they could in what they guessed to be the approximate direction of the stream. This they reached about an hour later. As its banks were bare they lay among the trees and waited for the others. Presently there was a crackling of branches and Dulac, Jacquin, Georges, a Frenchman called André and a Pole turned up. A few minutes later a Dutch boy they had known as Pete and two others arrived. Although they sent out a search party to look for the ten others they found no trace of them and were forced to conclude that they had failed in the attempt.

Among those who had failed was Pierre Kaan, of whose fate Tommy did not learn until the war was over. His glasses having brushed off his nose and lost as he entered the wood, he had been found wandering blindly about by Möller, who had smuggled him back into the train and saved him from the summary execution meted out to the others who had been caught. Suffering from a bad

---

[1] 'Have you seen anybody?'   [2] 'No. Nobody.'
[3] 'There they are!'

242

ulcer on one of his legs, he died a few weeks later in hospital after having been liberated by the Allies.

While waiting under cover for Möller to arrive, the ten successful fugitives discarded and buried their striped, badged and numbered uniforms under which they wore a motley of shoddy clothes which they had assembled in preparation for their flight. Tommy wore an old velvet jacket, a pair of frayed grey trousers and the boots which the Kapo had given him when he left Buchenwald and which he had concealed beneath rags wound round his feet. By avoiding contacts with the SS, which would have forced him to salute by removing his headgear, he had managed to grow a little hair, and he now discarded the beret which had hidden it. But it was Dulac who was the dandy of the party; using his privilege as a doctor, he had secured a pair of dark trousers and an overcoat with a red stripe down the middle of the back which he had rubbed out with petrol. The others wore an assortment of ill-matched and threadbare garments and in spite of Dulac's comparative elegance they all looked like a bevy of Wearie Willies and Tired Tims.

When after about three hours there was still no sign of Möller, Yeo-Thomas decided to wait no longer. As ten men moving about together would appear suspicious he divided the group up into three subsidiary teams: André and three others; Jacquin, Foulquier and Pete; and Dulac, Georges and himself. They were to leave at half-hour intervals and space out. As the Oberscharführer would have alerted the military, the Feldgendarmerie and the recently recruited Volkssturm, they were not immediately to take the short cut and go north, as their pursuers would naturally expect weak men like themselves to do; instead they were to walk for the rest of the day in the same direction as the train, turning first eastwards and then northwards after night had fallen. After that their action must be left to the discretion of the leader of each team.

The party of four left first; then Jacquin, Foulquier and Pete; and finally, in the middle of the afternoon, Dulac, Georges and Yeo-Thomas.

As they had no compasses, maps or watches, they set their course as best they could by the sun. They walked at a leisurely pace, both so as to avoid making unnecessary noise and to husband their strength. They moved in silence, keeping a sharp lookout and halting at the slightest suspicious sound. At dusk they stopped for a rest. When night came they were still in the woods. They could scarcely see the stars because of the trees. Fumbling through the darkness they eventually came to a clearing, and from the golden and far-away glory of the sky they plotted a rough bearing and plodded on into the blackness, swallowed up once more by the trees.

The night grew colder and colder. The wind rose and bit through their clothes and made them shiver. Although they would have liked to walk a little faster to keep warm they resisted the temptation and moved on slowly through the trees and through the wind. It was well after midnight when they stopped by a large tree and, flinging themselves down between two of its protruding roots, slept for about four hours under the blanket of Dulac's overcoat. It was still dark when they awoke, stiff and numbed with cold. When they had jumped about for a little to get their circulation going they turned northwards.

It was clear by now that they were in a large forest: they had seen nothing but trees since they started and still the trees went on and on. After a little, however, they came to a stream in which, stripping to the waist, they washed and from which they drank. When each had eaten a small portion of his bread they moved on again, into more trees. The milky sky of dawn melted into the pale blue sky of day but they were still in the forest, with trees all around them.

Towards midday they came to a clearing, stretching horizontally as far as the eye could see and vertically about five hundred yards. Ahead of them they heard the noise of axes being wielded by woodcutters and, keeping under cover of the trees, went westwards until they could no longer hear the axes. Then they made a dash for it; they had got about half-way across when they heard shouts of 'Halt', and, looking back over their shoulders, saw three men, one armed with an axe, running after them to cut them off. At once they turned left and ran with all their might as they had run the day before, diagonally towards the trees. The shouts of the men behind them helped them to effect a ruse: stopping running and moving laterally for a little, they crept cautiously back in the direction from which they had come and thus shook off their pursuers.

Exhausted, they rested for a little and ate some more bread before resuming their journey. When dusk came again they switched westwards, and when night fell, still kept walking on, steering their course as best they could by the inadequately glimpsed stars. Eventually they came to another clearing, and, crawling to the edge of it, saw a single railway line gleaming like silver in a cutting. Guessing that this was the track on which their train had run the previous day, they crossed it, frightened by the rattle of the ballast stones under their feet, and entered the wood on the other side, to plod on and on through more trees. Gradually the ground rose and walking became harder and, coming to a crest, they saw below them a wide river, dark and shining with night. Following the crest they stopped opposite a long bar of foam that stretched right across the river and looked as though it might be caused by rocks. However, as they climbed down, the steep face of the descent forced them to go at a slant, and when they reached the edge of the river they found themselves almost opposite a bridge whose stanchions spanned the water and threw another darkness upon it. But their luck was out, for reconnaissance soon showed that the bridge was guarded, so, skirting the mighty base of the ledge which reared above them, they walked back to the bar of the foam where after rolling up their trouser legs and removing their boots and hanging them round their necks, they stepped gingerly into the swirling water. The current was cold and strong and nearly swept them off their feet. Tommy, who was leading the closely packed group, slipped and plunged up to his waist into a hole, from which he was pulled by Dulac just in time to prevent him being carried away. Dulac then led the way and after a hazardous and unpleasant journey they reached the opposite bank, shivering with cold.

As there was no cover on the river bank they made across open ground for a clump of trees before drying their feet and putting on their boots. They crossed more open ground and came to another wood which was shallow and whose far side was bordered by a narrow stream, which they forded in the same manner as the river. Walking through more trees they found themselves in a factory yard with huts and buildings and girders all around them. Deciding that it might be more dangerous to retreat than to advance, they tiptoed through the yard and came to a large open gate which gave on to a street. They listened carefully and heard, as they had half-expected to hear, the measured tread of a sentry. Concealing themselves in the shadows, they saw his dark form pass the gate and, as the tramp of his feet diminished, peeped out and saw that the factory was the last building in the street and that beyond the house opposite, about twenty-five yards distant, were more trees; the sentry himself was standing some hundred yards to the left, looking to his right. Removing for the third time that night their boots and the rags that served for socks, they waited until the sentry had trudged past the gate again, and, when he was about fifty yards away with his back still turned, ran across the street to the trees. A couple of dogs barked mournfully, but that was all that happened.

They put on their socks and boots again and took their bearings. In front of their shelter of trees was a deeply furrowed field and beyond it more woods. As they were crossing the field they had to fling themselves flat on their faces in the furrows to avoid being caught in the stabbing white headlights of a car which came racing along the road. The car passed and diminished into a tiny glow moving towards the horizon and finally vanishing in darkness. They got up and, although very tired, pressed on to the trees and through them, desirous of leaving the village well behind them.

In the small hours of the morning they lay down to sleep, again with Dulac's overcoat on top of them. Yeo-Thomas did not sleep well because his dysentery, aggravated by the cold water which he had drunk, was troubling him again. When they woke it was quite light. Before starting out again they ate more of their bread; by now Tommy, who, because he had been unwilling to leave Hubble's chess set behind, had brought only about 1 lb. with him, had almost finished his.

The day was fine, with a bright sun from a blue sky sending shafts of light down into their cool cathedral of trees. They pressed on till they came to a clearing on one side of which was a plantation of young saplings. They ran across and gained the preserve. The saplings, although only six or seven feet high, were planted in orderly rows and afforded good cover. Within a few minutes however they had reached the edge of the plantation and came to a road, on the other side of which was another preserve. It was as well that they were wary, for presently they heard footsteps. Lying flat on their bellies they saw a patrol of about half a dozen Volkssturm soldiers armed with rifles and grenades approaching along the road. The patrol passed, walked a short distance, retraced its steps and passed again. When a couple of minutes later it came back again it was clear that it was on a very short beat indeed, and that a reconnaissance was necessary.

The results of their reconnaissance were not promising: walking parallel to the edge of the plantation, they found that it was almost as short as it was shallow and that the road ran straight on past its border. The only solution seemed to be speed from the most advantageous position at the most opportune moment: to wait at one end of the preserve until the patrol had gone a good distance down the road and then run and hope to reach the next batch of saplings before it turned to come back again. But while they were resting in order to gather strength for the attempt they heard a noise of people coming through the trees behind them. Fearing that they were now caught between two dangers, they lay as flat as they could and prepared for the worst. The danger from the rear, however, turned out to be only a compromising increase to their numbers; those who came walking through the saplings were Foulquier, Jacquin and Pete, who had blundered along much the same route as themselves.

Foulquier and his group, who had already had some narrow shaves, were not unduly alarmed when the situation was explained to them, and agreed with its proposed solution. The six of them went together to the fringe of the copse and waited for the best time to cross. They managed it in small batches of two, but because of the weakness of their undernourished bodies were exhausted by the effort and the excitement.

On the other side the two groups parted company again, Yeo-Thomas and his team moving on only after they had given the others a good start. Although the new plantation was much broader than the one they had left behind, it too ended in a clearing; but this time there was no road and no Volkssturm, and they ran across to the next preserve without danger or incident and repeated the process several times that morning.

Eventually they came to an expanse of open country at least a mile wide; the only shelter before reaching the woods on the other side was a small clump of trees in the middle. Another reconnaissance showed that there was no way round this hazard, and while they were resting before crossing it Yeo-Thomas finished his last piece of bread. His dysentery had by now become acute.

They crossed in what used to be called extended order, Yeo-Thomas on the left, Georges in the middle and Dulac on the right. The ground sloped upwards and the going was hard. When they were within about a hundred yards of the clump of trees they heard voices and saw men coming over the crest of the hill to meet them. Running obliquely to the left, Dulac and Georges outdistanced Yeo-Thomas, whose bowels were wrung with agony. Puffing and staggering, Tommy saw them disappear into the clump and, knowing that he could not reach it before the men saw him, threw himself down at the base of a solitary tree and pretended to be asleep. He lay huddled on his stomach, resting his head on his arms in such a way that he could keep a surreptitious watch out of one eye. The men almost missed him, but one of them saw him and called to him. The man and his companions came close and the man shouted at him again, but Yeo-Thomas did not answer and lay absolutely still. The men laughed together and Tommy gathered that they were upbraiding him for a lazy dog. He remained motionless, terrified that they would shake him and, when his lack of German had betrayed him, hand him over to the authorities. Fortunately after a few seconds they moved on, still laughing heartily.

He waited until they had passed out of sight and then he ran for the clump of trees. Dulac and Georges were nowhere to be seen and, as now only a downwards slope of about three hundred yards separated him from the wood, he gathered that they must have taken advantage of the Germans having passed over the ridge of the hill to run for more secure shelter. He himself was now too ill to run any more. He walked down and entered the wood. Once under cover he looked for Dulac and Georges. He failed to find them. He was alone.

His plight was desperate: he had no food; he was suffering agony in his entrails; and he had still a long journey in front of him. But now that he had come so far he was more determined than ever to succeed. He would go on west-north-west in the hope of striking

248

Chemnitz, whence he knew that he could easily find his way to safety.

So he started out on his lonely trek. Inside the wood the ground continued to slope downwards and he stumbled on until he came to a main road intersecting the trees. He scrambled down the embankment, crossed the road and plunged into the continuation of the forest.

Although the ground still sloped downwards, walking was not easy, for every now and then he had to stop while agonizing gripes twisted his bowels.

It began to rain: at first a drizzle which trickled gently down from the branches and soothed his brow and tempered his fever; then a downpour, which soaked through his corduroy jacket and made it feel as heavy as mail. He became very hungry and very cold. With aching feet, legs and belly, he went on until he came to the edge of the wood and saw that below him was another river. On the other side of the river more woods began at a distance of about three hundred yards from the bank.

Knowing that he could not hope to ford the river alone, he turned blindly to the right, and to his joy came upon a small and apparently unguarded wooden bridge. Then he saw that between the bridge and the wood was a small village, nestling by the side of the river. Circling round the village, he found that there was no way of avoiding it, and as darkness was now beginning to fall he took the risk of walking through it. His luck was in and he met nobody, and soon he was on the other side of the bridge, walking up towards the trees.

But the slope up towards the wood was steep, and the ground was mucky and slippery. The rain was now pouring down in torrents and he was drenched to the skin and cold. A more than usually violent pang of dysentery shook him, and, reeling with nausea, he had to sit on the stump of a felled tree to rest. Then he ploughed on up the hill, stumbling over roots, sliding in the mud, until he reached the trees.

In the wood the rain still fell heavily, pouring down his neck and back in icy streams. Stumbling upon a path he followed it in the hope that it might lead to a woodcutter's hut where he might pass the night. With his feet sloshing about in the slimy mud he slithered, slipped and slid along its winding, oozy track. Then he staggered and fell on something soft and, feeling about with his hands, discovered that he had tumbled into a deep pit of sapling branches; and there, when he had drawn the topmost ones over him as a quilt, he spent the night, sinking at once into a dreamless sleep.

When he awoke it was still raining, but the branches had protected him, and his body, although still damp, was warmer. He was hungry, but as he had no food he could only stagger on. All that day he went on through the trees and the rain, dragging his feet, which were terribly weighted down by the mud. That night he came to a potato field and scratched about all over it in hope, but he found no potatoes. It was still raining and he was wretchedly cold, but he walked on through the blackness until he reached a pile of logs at the foot of a tree, between which he flung himself down and slept.

It was still raining when he woke at dawn. He was racked with pain and hunger and his teeth were chattering with cold. Once again he went on, but his progress became more and more exhausting. Each step that he took sent shooting pains through his groins. Dysentery bent him double and his stomach was raw with hunger. Every bone in his body was sore and every muscle stiff, and his mind was as wrung as his bowels, with the cold biting slaps of despair. He began to talk to himself and to stumble and fall to the ground, and to blubber as he picked himself up, crying his hopelessness to the trees: 'I can't go on. I can't go on. I'll pack up and surrender at the nearest village.' But he thought of Barbara and of Britain, which meant so much more to him than to the loud dissemblers in the market place, and he plodded on, through the rain and through the trees.

That afternoon he came upon a road and, dazed with stupor, attempted to cross it without having looked to see if there was anybody on it. Men shouted at him and he saw a patrol about a hundred and fifty yards away advancing towards him. He turned and fled back into the woods, followed by the noise of running feet, rifle shots and whizzing bullets. Fear lent strength to his tired body and, with bursting lungs, he ran on until his legs crumpled up under him and he fell to the ground, shaking and heaving. He tried to rise, but could not stand because his legs were trembling too much to be able to bear his weight. His head was throbbing and he had stabbing pains behind his eyes. Violently sick, he tried to vomit, but there was nothing in his stomach to bring up; and while he had been running his bowels had emptied themselves, squirting their discharge down over his thighs. But there was neither sound nor sign of the patrol and he gathered that he had shaken it off.

He had to lie for about an hour before he could muster strength to go on again. From now onwards he had to stop frequently, as his legs seemed to be sinking away into his body. Each time that he fell down he thought that he would never be able to get up again, but each time he determined to have another try and succeeded. He was so cold and hungry that he began to be lightheaded and to have hallucinations: he saw rows and rows of steaming hot cups of tea, rows and rows of roast beef and Yorkshire pudding and rows and rows of pumpkin pies, stretching away into the distance and for ever evading his embrace as he tried to catch up with them. And after these phantoms he chased madly, sobbing each time that they eluded his grasp. The reality of the illusion was increased by the fact that he disliked pumpkin pies.

When night came again he still walked on, lost in a trance, falling, picking himself up again, banging his head and his face against trees. Suddenly the earth seemed to open under his feet and he fell through space, landing at the bottom of a pit twelve feet deep, filled with decaying leaves. He lay for a little looking up at the stars, and then tried to pull himself out, but the slope of the pit was steep and slippery and time after time he fell back. Panicking, he subsided and lay at the bottom, panting and sobbing, sure that he was going to die. Again he roused himself by thinking of Barbara and of the Britain he loved so simply, and once again his loyalties aided his endeavour. This time he pulled himself up slowly and carefully and, in spite of many a slither, eased himself up to the edge of the pit, where he lay until he had recovered enough strength to stand up. Too tired to walk any further, he huddled up against the trunk of a tree and slept.

Next morning when he woke the rain had thinned to a drizzle. He had a spasm of dysentery, and his hunger was intense. When he rose to his feet the forest spun round him like a merry-go-round and he crashed to the ground. He got up again and leaned against a tree until he had recovered his equilibrium. Then he went on, slowly and painfully. Every now and then his legs folded up under him, but always he picked himself up and always he went on.

The drizzle stopped and the sun began to shine and its rays refreshed and cheered him, and sent a short warmth through his body; and he stumbled on, with a new and stronger vision before him. But dysentery continued to weaken him and soon the world was swimming again in front of his eyes. When he came to a clearing it was with difficulty that he was able to make out a large copse on the other side. To this he staggered, and in it he found a large pit whose bottom was lined with Red Cross cartons. The cartons, however, were empty and indicated the nearness of purloining Germans rather than of friendly Allies, for with them were several dozen unopened letters addressed to British prisoners of war. Disappointed, he pushed on to the far edge of the copse. As he reached it his legs gave way under him and he lost consciousness.

When he came to he felt that somebody was pulling him up, and supposed that he must have been captured again, but was too weak to care. All that he could see was a blur and the blur moved with him as it raised him from the ground and sat him up against a tree. Then the blur became a man with a kindly, smiling face who spoke to him in a language which was not German. Unable to answer, Yeo-Thomas saw from the markings on his tattered uniform that he was a prisoner of war. Eventually he succeeded in saying a few words in French, and in the same language the man haltingly replied that he was a Yugoslav prisoner working nearby.

'I am a Frenchman trying to escape,' Tommy said when he could get the words out. He did not need to say that he was hungry and exhausted: the Yugoslav could see that for himself.

They smiled at each other with the friendliness born of a shared servitude. Yeo-Thomas tried to rise, but fell back to the ground at once. The Yugoslav shook his head, lifted him and carried him further back into the copse, where he propped him against another tree. '*Moi chercher manger, vous rester ici, pas bouger, reposer,*' [1] he said, and left Yeo-Thomas with the world all streaky in front of his eyes, floating away in wisps of misty trees and blotches of indeterminate sky.

A little later the Yugoslav came back and tapped the still half-

[1] 'I go get eat, you stay here, not move, rest.'

fainting Yeo-Thomas on the shoulder. From a haversack slung over his shoulders he produced a half-pound loaf of bread and a bottle of white wine. '*Manger*,' he said when he had cut off a piece of bread, but as soon as Tommy tried to eat it he vomited. The Yugoslav then let him drink a little wine, and the wine sent warmth back into his body and revived him. After that the Yugoslav cut the bread into small cubes, which he stuffed into Tommy's pockets, and from his haversack he took a small linen bag fitted with a sling, into which he put the bottle of wine. '*Pour vous*,' he said, '*Bonne chance!*'

Tommy was too moved and too weak to speak. He shook the man's hand, and the Yugoslav smiled at him. '*Méfier*,' the Yugoslav said. '*Dangereux. Ici beaucoup de soldats allemands.*'[1] In awkward, but understandable French he told Yeo-Thomas to wait until he signalled before starting to cross the field in front, as there were many Germans working nearby. And that was all he said before he left Tommy, but his smile said everything else and told Tommy not to worry about what he himself had been unable to say. An hour later he signalled that all was clear and, strengthened by the wine, Yeo-Thomas set out again. As he reached the trees on the far side of the field he turned to wave to the Yugoslav, who stood against the clouds and the sky and waved back at him. It had been the perfect evangelical encounter.

As he went on, he ate his bread a cube at a time; he had to munch each morsel very slowly before he was able to swallow it. The wine helped him more than the bread, but he resolved to ration himself to three sips a day. Even when the rain came on again and his dysentery dug daggers into his bowels he stuck to this resolution. He kept on walking and, because even a sip of wine maketh glad the heart of man, he was able to think of the simple, silly song about Felix who, in the early 1920s, had kept on walking too. But when night fell and it was still raining there was little courage left in him as he trudged heavily on through the sludgy, squelching mud. He kept on until his strength gave out. He lay down to sleep under a tree through whose leaves the rain continued to fall on his already drenched body.

Next morning he awoke cold and stiff. He was violently sick

[1] 'Be careful. Dangerous. Here many German soldiers.'

after eating two cubes of bread, but again the wine restored him. He got up and went on, thinking now of Barbara, now of Britain. His legs were badly swollen, his feet felt as though they had been flayed, his body was sore, his belly was on fire, but all that day he walked on, propelling himself by his loyalties. He was so soaked and cold and tired that, coming upon a temporarily driverless lorry standing in a small lane, he risked resting in the cab for a little and left a pool of water behind him when he got out again.

Gradually it became more difficult to find cover and, as houses increased, he realized that he was entering a thickly populated area. At dusk, after circumventing several villages, he came to a wood traversed by a small stream, in which, after stripping, he washed. But, although refreshed, he felt more frozen than before when he had put on his damp clothes again and, as he was too weak and sore to do any jumping about, he took a drink of wine and curled up to sleep under the shelter of a sapling.

When he awoke it was still dark, but it was no longer raining. He ate a few cubes of bread, drank a little wine and started off, taking his bearings from the waning stars. As dawn broke he descended a steep slope to find himself confronted by a broken wall which seemed to stretch for a long distance. Hearing no sounds, he clambered over and came to the ruins of a factory which had obviously been put out of action by bombing. But the wall on the other side of the factory was intact and, as the gates were locked, he had to climb over, tiring himself terribly and dropping on to a road with a jar which sent sharp pains stabbing through his legs. The road, which was straight and metalled, was obviously a main thoroughfare, and he walked along it in search of a signpost. The signpost, when he found it, read: CHEMNITZ 2 KM. He had aimed far more accurately than he had dared to hope. Now all that he had to do was to keep on going westwards.

Chemnitz was too big for him to lose time by making a detour and, encouraged by the excellence of his navigation, he set out towards it with a new will, determined to get through the town while the light was still dim. As soon as he reached the outskirts he saw that the town had been heavily bombed: everywhere there were ruins; roofless and gutted buildings threw their skeletons like escarpments against the pale, creamy early morning sky; and through the windowless grey streets drab men and women walked with buckets and containers, too set on their search for water to pay any attention to the appearance of a stranger whose outward signs of wretchedness made him one with themselves. He heard French spoken as he walked through those grim dilapidations and saw that among those whom he passed in the dismal streets were both French prisoners of war and French civilian workers, both of whom moved about freely in the sinister shadows.

This observation helped him when, safely through the town and marching boldly along the main road, he heard the clippety-clop and rub-a-dub-dub of a horse and cart coming up behind him. Driving the cart was a French prisoner of war, from whom he obtained a lift, saying that he was a French worker who had been bombed out of his employment and was trying to make his way homewards to France. The prisoner of war turned out to be a Parisian and, to avoid being asked where he had been working, Yeo-Thomas talked to him of the metropolis and of the streets which they both loved. In this way he covered twenty-five kilometres.

It was raining hard again when the prisoner of war set him down, but Tommy was now too elated to care. He ate his last cube of bread, drank almost his last drop of wine and pressed on on foot once more. Soon his legs were sore, his groin aching, his bowels burning, but on and on he went, through the day and far into the night. He slept briefly in a clump of trees.

Next morning it was still raining and he was soaked to the skin. He finished his wine, flung the bottle away, and went on. As he walked he began to get light-headed again and so to see more phantasmal processions of cups of hot tea, roasts of beef and Yorkshire pudding. Apart from these visions he does not remember much of what happened that day. Again he slept in a wood.

He awoke as usual to find that the rain had not stopped. But as he started off a blessed sound came to his ears: the muffled thump of cannon firing in the distance, and to him it was as sweet as the chanting of cherubim to a saint. By early afternoon the muffled thump had become a roar and, if he had any doubt that he was approaching where right and glory led, it was dispelled by the sight of a string of refugees, slopping wearily along the road, pushing their cheap possessions in carts, carrying canaries in cages and kittens in baskets: young girls with the rain plastering their flaxen hair against their cheeks, old men and old women with broken boots and blistered feet, babes in arms blinking at the nonsense of the world into which clergymen said that the love of God had dumped them, all the ragtag and bobtail of human misery called, in the cold classification of the chancelleries, displaced persons.

If his safety increased as he approached danger, his danger also increased as he approached safety: every step he took towards the Allied lines led him more deeply into the centre of the enemy formations, and as he debouched into the wood for concealment he almost ran bang into a Wehrmacht patrol. He lay flat on his belly and looked and listened: the woods were full of German troops combining and permuting in their private pattern of the bigger battle and from ahead came the crack of machine-guns and rifles. A peasant and a small girl came along a path carrying bundles of small branches and the soldiers let them pass. Picking up a few pieces of wood, Tommy tucked them under his arm and set off, head bent down, in the direction of the machine-gun and rifle fire.

But he was weaker than he had imagined and soon he had to throw away the branches. Every step was painful. He dropped to the ground and crawled through the undergrowth. As he came near to the edge of the wood he saw a German machine-gun emplacement. The quick rattle that the gun made when it fired did not sound unfriendly but the bullets that came whistling back in answer were definitely hostile. Yeo-Thomas ducked his head and lay down under cover.

When he had rested he crept nearer the edge of the wood. About two hundred yards to the right of the machine-gun nest there was a second, also firing. Sliding in between the two emplacements he saw, in the open ground beyond the fringe of the wood, a shallow path which crossed a field on the other side of which he guessed the Allied lines must be. Deciding to follow the path when night came, he lay down and waited impatiently for dusk, and passed the time in a lewd contemplation already popular with his compatriots: whoring in his heart after bacon and eggs.

At last dusk fell and then darkness. Because of his dysentery, bending double was now his natural position, and he moved for-

ward in the orthodox position, as though carrying a rifle at the trail.
When he reached the edge of the wood he looked left and right. He
could see nobody, but he could hear the rumble of armoured vehicles and the sound of gunfire. He waited until he heard only an
occasional rifle shot and then, realizing that he must beware of
friend as well as foe, moved out into no-man's-land. He had not
gone twenty-five yards when he heard a shout: '*Halt!*' He tried to
run. A couple of bullets hit the ground near his feet. He made
another effort and found that he could not even walk. Stars danced
before his eyes as he slumped to the ground. Footsteps came up
and he was turned over on his face by a kick in the side. He prepared to receive a shot or a bayonet thrust. But this time it was
fighting soldiers he was dealing with, and not the Gestapo: when
his captors saw that he could not stand up they dragged him back
into the woods. Once again he was a prisoner.

CHAPTER XVII

THE LAST LAP

AT first the N.C.O. in charge of the patrol which had captured him
thought that Yeo-Thomas was shamming weakness and cursed him
for encumbering the men with his weight. But when, in the cover
of the woods, he had inspected his prisoner's worn and filthy face,
his tone changed and he became compassionate, asking if he was
hungry and promising him food when he had been interrogated.

The interrogation took place in a heavily guarded hut about a
mile inside the wood and was conducted by a Hauptmann of the
Wehrmacht who, when the N.C.O. had told him the details of
Tommy's arrest, asked:

'*Name?*'

'*Maurice Thomas, adjutant-chef de l'Armée de l'Air Française,*'
Yeo-Thomas lied quickly, knowing that hesitation would be fatal,
since discovery that he had escaped from a concentration camp would

entail his being handed over to the SS for summary execution. He went on to say that he had been captured at Tours in 1940 and had escaped while his Stalag in Western Germany was being evacuated on account of the advance of the Allies. He had been trying to live on the country while making his way towards France and had got lost.

'Why did you try to escape?'

'Because it is the duty of every prisoner of war to escape if he can.'

This seemed to satisfy the officer. Yeo-Thomas was then taken to a shed where, under the incurious eyes of about a dozen German soldiers, he was given two pannikinsful of potato soup, which brought back his dysentery. After an escorted visit to the *Abort* he spent the rest of the night in the shed.

Next morning two soldiers marched him to a village some two miles on the other side of the wood. There the officer in charge, after telephoning the authorities for instructions, handed him over to a detachment of Hitler Jugend, who escorted him to a small town another ten miles behind the line. These boys between fifteen and seventeen had none of the chivalry of the combatants and, perceiving that their prisoner walked with difficulty, forced the pace and, when he stumbled, reviled him, kicked him, slapped him across the mouth, spat in his face, hit him with their rifle butts and prodded him with the points of their bayonets.

In the small town the local police took temporary charge of him and locked him in a darkened cell in which he punched a common law offender on the nose for attempting to steal Hubble's chess set. After further interrogation he was put in a truck and driven back to Chemnitz, where he spent the night in the guardroom of the barracks and told the N.C.O. in charge to go to hell when he ordered him to sweep the floor. His strength was returning.

And, in spite of the fact that he was still suffering from dysentery and that his feet were so sore and badly swollen that he could not remove his boots, his mind was as alert as ever. Next morning, when interrogated by a French-speaking colonel at Wehrmacht H.Q., he added to the story of his being Adjutant-Chef Maurice Thomas of the French Air Force, captured in 1940, the information that he had belonged to the 34th Bataillon de l'Armée de l'Air, stationed at Le Bourget until its retreat to Tours. In this way, because he himself had served alongside this unit, he was able, when the Colonel asked him for the name, to say that his commanding officer had been Colonel Rubis. After corroborating this statement from a French Air Force List on his desk, the Colonel dismissed him with a homily on the folly of attempting to escape.

The following afternoon, after seeing a Canadian P.O.W. beaten up by the guardroom N.C.O., he was, in company with an assortment of other French and British prisoners, marched to a dilapidated transit camp on the outskirts of the town, where they spent the night. Here no rations were issued to them, and next day, still unfed, they were put on the road again. On their way they met a Russian P.O.W., who gave them a few slices of beetroot flavoured with petrol, but when they reached a French Stalag late that afternoon they were still so hungry that they had to make themselves soup by boiling nettles.

At dawn they were marched on again, and in the middle of the day were split into two parties, one British and the other French, each of which took a different direction. Yeo-Thomas naturally remained with the French, who in turn were whittled down by various splits, until he was left alone with his escort. Towards evening he was delivered to the Stalag for French N.C.O.s at Grunhainigen, which was to be his new abode.

Naturally the French N.C.O.s started asking him questions, and at first all went well: he was able to say where he had lived in France, how he had earned his livelihood before the war and to give particulars of the unit with which he had served. But when he said that he had escaped from Stalag IVB, he saw one of the N.C.O.s look at him suspiciously and then rise and beckon the Senior of the camp to follow him. A few minutes later the N.C.O. came back again and sat down opposite Yeo-Thomas, who was sitting alone at a table, resting his head in his hands.

'There's something about your story that I don't like,' he said. 'I was at Stalag IVB but I never saw you there. How was that?'

Tommy knew that he must tell the truth if he wanted to avoid the risk of being regarded as a stool pigeon.

'Because I was never there,' he said. 'I am sorry I had to lie to you, but if you will be kind enough to go and get the Senior N.C.O.

I think that I shall be able to make you understand why. Only I must ask you to keep this information to yourselves because the slightest indiscretion might easily cost me my life.'

'I think perhaps you'd better talk first and we can promise afterwards,' the N.C.O. said as he rose to fetch the Senior man.

The two Frenchmen listened carefully while Yeo-Thomas recounted his story. He told them that he was a British officer who had been captured by the Gestapo while working with the French Resistance. He described the prison at Fresnes and the camps at Compiègne, Saarbrücken, Buchenwald, Gleina and Rehmsdorf. When he had finished the Senior N.C.O. said:

'It's all possible, of course, but what proof have we that you are not working for the Germans?'

It was a natural enough suspicion in a war in which the Queensberry rules had been thrown overboard, the kick in the testicles called strategy and the greater lie used to outwit the lesser. Tommy had no answer to this question because he had no papers. Then he remembered the relic of his saint, and the relic of his saint came to his rescue. He told them about Hubble, showed them the British trade mark on his chess set and after that they believed him.

And they believed him practically. They helped him to cut the uppers off his boots so that he could remove them and tend his swollen feet. They gave him hot water and salt to wash out the festering blisters, and cloth and sulphonamide powder with which to bandage them. That night, for the first time for three weeks, he slept with a blanket over him. Next morning a third N.C.O. called Albaret, who had been let into his secret, provided him with a false P.O.W. identity plaque.

Soon it was no longer a question of believing Yeo-Thomas; it was a matter of following his lead. When he told them that he intended to make another attempt to escape and called for volunteers they at first demurred, saying that it would be foolish to risk their lives unnecessarily when liberation was so near. To this Tommy replied that, as far as he was concerned, the necessity was imperative: he had been silly enough to get captured, therefore it was his duty to escape; and he soon had eleven of the others accepting this not unassailable syllogism. The Senior N.C.O., however, declined to be of the party, as he thought that he could be of more use if he stayed behind to impede the search which would be made when their flight had been discovered.

But a P.O.W.s scanty ration of potatoes did little to restore Tommy's strength, exhausted by exposure and an average of twenty evacuations a day, and so he decided that they would have to escape by train. Circumstances were in his favour. Not only were there trains from Grunhainigen to Chemnitz, but there were also night trains. A P.O.W. obtained official-looking papers from a girl in the village. Another, who worked in the local Town Hall, stole a rubber stamp, and within forty-eight hours they had forged documents and Ausweise describing themselves as foreign labourers, dismissed by a factory in Grunhainigen and free to take up employment elsewhere.

During Tommy's third afternoon in the camp the wire stretched across one of the windows was unfastened, and that same night the eleven set out across the fields for the station, walking warily behind hedges. Although the station was blacked out they had to be careful in case any of the local inhabitants recognized them, and so Yeo-Thomas, who was completely unknown in the district, bought tickets for a number of them, while two of the others bought the rest. Then, separating, they waited in the shadows until the train came in, when Yeo-Thomas and Albaret got into a compartment together and the rest into different compartments in the same carriage. It was as simple as all that.

The train was a local which stopped at every station and it was soon crowded. Yeo-Thomas made the mistake of speaking English when he rose to offer his seat to a woman, but the lady was too surprised by the gesture to notice the language, and the other passengers were too busy talking. They reached Chemnitz in the early hours of the morning.

Two by two and keeping a distance between each couple, they walked westwards and by dawn had left the suburbs behind them. By now the battle had moved much nearer and they soon heard gunfire. To avoid being seen by troops or patrols they left the road and walked under cover. This meant much harder going for Yeo-Thomas, who had presumed too much on his strength and was quickly in difficulties. All his old pains came back: his feet felt like open stumps; his stiff legs sank like pistons into his pelvis; and his bowels were aflame with diarrhoea. Only the desire not to embarrass his companions and the fear, for now they all knew his story, of disgracing his country in their eyes kept him going. Seeing the sweat pouring down his face, Albaret gave him some chocolate and made him rest. But neither helped much and when they moved on again he had to lean on Albaret's arm. And all the time the evidences of conflict kept increasing: the firing became louder and louder, and soon they could hear the clack and the click of automatic arms. While making a detour to avoid some camouflaged tanks Tommy collapsed. Albaret helped him up and he fell down again. The others stopped and grouped themselves around him.

'It's no use,' Yeo-Thomas said. 'I'm done for. You'll just have to go on without me. Leave me a bit of bread though and I'll see what I can do when I've had a rest.'

They all refused, and from their hearts as well as from their lips. They had no need to stretch their mouths in a lying smile or squeeze a glow they didn't feel into their eyes. They meant what they said. They might have known Yeo-Thomas only for four days but already they had come to love him.

'It's an order,' Tommy said. 'Albaret, I order you and the others to go on and leave me here.'

'You don't seem to know much about the French after all,' Albaret said. 'We Frenchmen aren't always awfully good at obeying our own officers, so I'm damned if we're going to obey a British officer.'

'Once and for all, Albaret, I won't have the rest of you risking your lives for me.'

But with the genius for disobedience of all Gaul they declined to listen to him. Hoisting his arms around their shoulders and linking their hands behind his back, two of them carried him. For hour after hour they progressed like this, the men relaying one another as bearers.

In the late afternoon they came to a wood. Although there were both sniping and shelling they could see no troops and the greater part of the firing seemed to come from their flanks. They passed through the wood and lay down in the fringe. In front of them stretched an open field: Yeo-Thomas was back on the edge of no-man's-land again.

Most of them wanted to wait for nightfall before attempting to cross, but Yeo-Thomas remembered his previous failure. If they crossed in darkness there was the additional risk of falling into an Allied ambush and being shot at as Germans, whereas if they crossed in daylight their friends would be able to see that they were unarmed and that they were not wearing enemy uniform. The absence of troops in their part of the wood and the fact that the firing came from either side of them seemed to prove that the sector in which they were was not strongly held. With luck they could get more than half-way across before the Germans saw them and such fire as they attracted would be diagonal. He made his decision, and this time even the piddlers against DEFENSE D'URINER notices had to obey: they would cross by daylight, as soon as an opportunity offered.

As everything in the vicinity was quiet they made the attempt at once. Yeo-Thomas left cover first, with Albaret and another man on either side of him, assisting him; the others followed behind, in single file. Because of Tommy's weakness it cannot have been a very speedy dash for it and in any case it was also a short one: they had only got about a quarter of the way across when they saw two G.I.s in American battle bowlers emerge from the wood opposite and point sub-machine-guns at them.

Yeo-Thomas mustered all his strength and shouted:

'DON'T SHOOT. ESCAPING PRISONERS OF WAR. PRISONERS OF WAR. DON'T SHOOT.'

It was the turn of the transatlantic disobeyers to obey, and fortunately they did so. They shouted something back which Yeo-Thomas could not catch, and he and his companions went on until they reached the wood. There they were surrounded by more American soldiers, all covering them with Tommy guns.

'Who the hell are you?' their leader asked.

It was a little difficult to be coherent in such circumstances but Yeo-Thomas managed to get across the gist of their innocence:

'I am a British Air Force officer, escaped from a concentration camp. The others are French P.O.W.'

'Well, you guys are goddam lucky; you've just crossed a mine-field.'

But Yeo-Thomas was too overpowered by happiness at the

knowledge that he was at long last back among friends to be surprised by this last stroke of good fortune or to feel grateful for it.

Escorted back to a village called Hondorf, Yeo-Thomas had to tell their story all over again to a young American lieutenant:

'I am a British Air Force officer captured on secret service in German-occupied territory. I escaped from a concentration camp. I was captured again and landed in a French Stalag. I escaped from the French Stalag and these French soldiers came with me.'

But there lived more doubt in honest faith than faith in honest doubt.

'How do I know that you are telling the truth? What papers have you got?'

'How can I have any papers after having been in a concentration camp?' Tommy was reminded of the Air Commodore who had expected him to read Air Ministry Orders while dodging the Gestapo in Paris, but he was patient with the Lieutenant because he knew that scepticism was part of his duty, and because he was not puffed up. 'Listen. I worked with your O.S.S.[1] in London. Take me to your Commanding Officer and I'll tell him how to prove my identity.'

'What about those other guys?'

'They have P.O.W. plaques and French identity discs. You can easily check on them.'

The Lieutenant began to be convinced that Yeo-Thomas was telling the truth and that, in spite of his scruffy appearance, he really was a British officer.

'O.K.' The Lieutenant turned to a top sergeant. 'Check on the Frogs and have them looked after and sent back. In the meantime I'll have a talk with this Englishman.'

But before Tommy could either listen or explain he had to be refreshed. He declined a carton of American rations as being too substantial and chose instead two oranges and a cup of coffee, which did the trick. When he had told the Lieutenant his story he was taken to a Major, who consented to see him only under protest. Standing to attention in his rags before the Major, Yeo-Thomas told his name, rank, number and story, said that he had valuable information for G.H.Q. and prepared to be doubted again.

[1] Office of Strategic Services.

264

And he was doubted, precisely, coldly, officially:

'Very interesting. But what means have I of verifying your *bona fides?*'

He had Hubble's chess set in his pocket, but this time he thought that more substantial proof was needed.

'If you will wireless to Major-General C. McV. Gubbins of S.O.E. in London you will get immediate confirmation.'

But because of the smallness of the Resistance world the message never required to be sent. As the Major was explaining the difficulty of communicating with London from so advanced a position Lieutenant Javal, whom Yeo-Thomas had known in London, but whom he did not immediately recognize and who certainly did not recognize Tommy, walked into the Major's office.

'For crying out loud!' the Major said. 'You're the very fellow we want. This guy says he's a Britisher who worked with French Resistance. Says he speaks the lingo like a native. Check up on him, will you?'

Javal turned to Yeo-Thomas.

'*Vous parlez français, paraît-il?*'

'*Mais oui, Lieutenant, je parle français.*'

Javal looked at him closely.

'Your voice is familiar. I seem to know you, but I'm not sure. What's your name?'

Tired and weary, Tommy drew himself up as he stated his brief but tremendous title to trust:

'Yeo-Thomas, better known to the Resistance as Shelley.'

Javal was wild with emotion and delight.

'*Mais naturellement je vous connais.* We've all been moving heaven and earth to find you. You know me too. I'm Javal.'

They did not immediately kill the fatted calf. First the Major got out his maps and Yeo-Thomas showed him the route which he and the others had followed, and pointed out the enemy troop and battery locations. The Major decided to do a cleaning-up action that night, using light tanks and infantry. Yeo-Thomas, to his regret, was refused permission to take part in it.

Instead he was given a bath, clean linen and the first pair of socks which he had worn on his sore feet since Buchenwald. Then, lost in an outsize black suit which had belonged to the Bürgermeister of

Hondorf, he had a light meal with the Major and drank three-quarters of a bottle of Napoleon brandy while news of the operation which his information had initiated was coming in.

Next morning he was driven back in a jeep to Divisional Headquarters. They had to keep him there for three days because he was so weak. Then he was taken to Weimar and, while trying to find the British Liaison Officer, fell in with another old Resistance friend, Colonel Fourcauld and his F.A.N.Y. wife, who, startled by his appearance, insisted on driving him back to Paris. There, after being fired on on the way by a pocket of resisting Germans, he arrived very appropriately on 8th May and celebrated V.E. day by dining with Major Thackthwaite and José Dupuis in the British Officers' Club in the rue du Faubourg St. Honoré.

His father said little next morning when Tommy called to see him. That brave old man kept his shock for those who were able to bear it: 'My son has returned, but he looks like an old man of seventy.'

But it was with a light heart that, later that same day, the old man of seventy, still wearing the Bürgermeister's baggy suit, climbed into the plane for London. This time there was no flak over the French coast and the aircraft sailed calmly over the hyphen of sea towards the gentle green fields. The plane landed at Croydon, and carried an undefeated man into an undefeated city.

Colonel Dismore was waiting on the airstrip, and behind him stood Barbara, wearing a very wobbly smile. The White Rabbit had returned to his hutch again, but instead of the now archaic iodoform the Third Supplement to the *London Gazette* of 12th February, 1946, carried these words:

'The King has been graciously pleased to award the GEORGE CROSS to Acting Wing Commander Forest Frederick Yeo-Thomas, M.C. (89215), Royal Air Force Volunteer Reserve.'

03-01

B
Yeo-Thomas
Marshall
The White Rabbit